Perceptions

Perceptions

Challenging Religious Concepts

Sam Mansourou

Cover art by:

Sam Mansourou   Adam Radick   Athena Garcia.

For Ann-Margret Yonan

Contents

Introduction

The social impact of perceived religion -whether it is a personal relationship with a claimed deity, or the actions of those directly and indirectly affected by religious notions- without doubt has a large influence over most of modern civilization (According to the *World Book Encyclopedia,* all societies have religion. Charles Haynes wrote about the power religion has in *Faces* when he noted: "few factors have influenced the history of the world more than religion... from the spread of language to the clothes people wear."[1] Bernard Lewis also voiced this in *Atlantic Monthly in the sense* that Christianity and Islam are civilization defining.[2]) It does not matter if we don't believe, no longer believe, or do not practice religious faith. The boundaries of these religious-based views have been set for us in our daily lives, and in various ways shape our reality in society.

The amount of strength these views have on our perception of life within this perceived reality is impressive: regardless of the view of the non-believer, his/her life is no doubt directly affected in the generational cultural influence. These influences, however, are limiting and ignore the fundamentally basic of many subjects regarding explanation of reality and how to cope with daily life. The locality and vacancy of many religious concepts is obvious even in today's modern theological arguments and will be looked at in this book. In many ways, the referencing of religion in this book is different than that of other modern works. Rather than calling accountability to extremist behavior or criticizing theism using generalizations and comparisons of what is within reason, this book will look at what is not always described among religious critics.

Not to mention its violent, childish and oppressive nature, the very setting of life and reality portrayed in religious documents such as the Bible, along with religious influence is questionable at best. Challenging religious concepts and their influence, the premise for this book -as well as its continuous theme throughout- is the notion that religion is not only vacant, but that vacancy provides a reality that cannot be maintained realistically in today's world, and their undertones are just as local and vacant, even when "interpreted" by modern theology. Heaven's gold street described in Revelations is one example of such a subtextual undertone. What materialist and shallow concept utterly void of a spiritual or intellectual path is the gold street supposed to represent? The similarly inept and vacant interpretation that modern theologians assert regarding such verses may include words like "faith" or "belief", but still mean nothing beyond the shallow and meaningless in today's society that demands more from our institutions than control over the masses.

Psychology professor Jefferson Fish noted a distinctive view of religion when he asserted regarding the faith/science debate, "by implicitly treating the debate as essentially a philosophical one, it often overlooks important cultural information."[3] It is in this sense that religious proponents accuse anti-theist authors of referencing a limited perceptive view of religion. For example, religious proponents Alister McGrath and Joanna McGrath accuse Richard Dawkins of such a general view in their book, The *Dawkins Delusion?* (as well as Daniel Dennett) when their indictment included his referencing religion "almost exclusively in terms of 'belief in God'." They added with regard to religion in a broader sense, "yet this certainly is not the sole aspect of religion, nor is it necessarily the most fundamental. A more reliable description of religion would make reference to its many aspects, including knowledge, beliefs, experience, ritual practices, social affiliation, motivation and behavioral consequences".[4] Those authors don't have to worry about that with this book because we will explore those subjects here.

This book will argue against the concepts of religion and its limiting influence, not its general and easily arguable notions. It will look at what makes religion tick through its inner concepts, what its actual lessons are underneath the already-known themes as well as what the repercussions might be personally and in society. In Rosemary Joyce's words, "not what religion *is* but what it *does*" (emphasis in the original).[5] The book will also attempt to show that religious notions make escape from this limited paradigm world-view impossible and create a prison for the practitioner due to such an oppressive obedience to its rules.

The lack of explanation in religious authorship throughout the centuries for things like society or what is needed to maintain a healthy one as well as the misguided instruction given to followers based on uncivilized and ignorant view-points are still blindingly obvious despite claims from today's religious proponents of fantastic modernity. Theo Hobson can claim in *Christian Century* that the Bible "detaches God from any form of state power, and it rejects theocracy",[6] but as we will see, the word "rejects" actually means "not aware of", and "detaches" means "is ignorant of".

There is no depth beyond the lowest common denominator in religious scripture and modern notions it inspires, and we will see this theme throughout the book time and again. As a result, the effects of this encouragement from religion is self-evident in society today. This book will continually stress that ignorance of not only Biblical authorship, but theology in reference to any significant individual or collective progression of those lessons. It will attempt to show how religious scripture and centuries of teaching do not reach beyond the local, the immediate. Judaism and Islam will not be so much discussed here as Christianity, but the main theme of the argument encompasses all mainstream religion.

General argumentative counters from religious proponents, like the notion that the world is safer and more civilized because of religion will be challenged in this book, as well as the counter that their respective religion concerns what is not physical and belongs to the more personal perceptive analysis. But ultimately this book discusses religious concepts and the perceptions they evolve into, how its limitation, lack of depth concerning the metaphysical, vacancy and locality encourages behavior to the point which in modern times is considered uncivilized, unhealthy and unacceptable by many.

This is not to say that religion cannot be positive in multiple areas. Does religion promote positivity? Of course. Any half positive-based cooperative of notions can, but the illiteracy of what is positive and healthy in the traditional lessons and even the modern scripture-based notions, the uncivilized paradigm that encompasses religious worldview are exemplified in modern society, contradicting of claims that religious-based notions are superior to scientific inquiry. We will see what those notions have to offer. Because so far religion has yet to promote anything above a few comforting notions in a world where we need way, way more than comfort and the promise of being watched over by an unknown, unproved, easily threatened child of a creator when viewing the looming modern human dilemmas that we face as a society.

After an introductory chapter, the chapter titled Primates explores religious claims of exceptionalism such as morality and evil, and challenges religious concepts relating to human existence. Challenging religious concepts relating to the metaphysical, the chapter titled The Unseen looks at religious claims of the metaphysical such as the holy spirit, heaven, hell, and other notions involving what we cannot perceive. These include claims of the personal, such as belief. The Limitations chapter looks at how religious influence, including scriptures fail time and again to provide any real explanation for reality, basic psychology, or even common knowledge of the all-important socioeconomics which populations depend on. The chapter will also challenge vacant themes in religious scripture.

82% looks at a religious influence that does not show an understanding of economics or ethical business practice. It looks at what scripture fails to address, such as hedonism, war, and predatory economics. The chapter Twists will show the study and individuals of modern theology well as the arguments they present. It explores theological claims of religious relevance and credibility, as well as influential religious-leaning figures in science and education.

'Happiness' looks at alternatives in mental health, man-made systems which do not subscribe to a deity and work more than the themes of mainstream religion. Contrary to popular belief, religion is not the same thing as spirituality, and spiritual themes are explored in the chapter to counter the religious claim of dominance in such fields. Systems which are more effective than mainstream religious concepts, man-made, and centuries older than the teachings of Jesus will be briefly discussed. The chapter Service takes a look at religious influence on perceptive worldviews regarding socioeconomics and their consequences, as well as what our role in a possible future of humanity might be. Armed with the ignorance that is scriptural advice on modernity in terms of such economics, we look at catalysts of what just might be humanity-altering events.

The vacancy in religion claimed in this book is nothing new. With criticism stemming as far back as the atomists in the 5th Century, up to Albert Einstein's famous letter to Eric Gutkind claiming that the Bible was primitive and childish ("The word god is for me nothing more than the expression and product of human weaknesses, the Bible a collection of honourable, but still primitive legends which are nevertheless pretty childish. No interpretation no matter how subtle can (for me) change this."[7]) and up to the best-selling anti-theist books of the modern era, the indictments have been many. This book is another indictment. Even with the Golden Age of Christianity, the claim that religion provides explanation and exultation has been repeatedly challenged. The defense from religious proponents has been consistently weak, with just as much flaws as ones from centuries before.

Even if mere inspiration, sense of the communal and comfort are life-changing to those who convert, then should we as a society see that as sufficient regarding the effectiveness of religion? Should we mind our business and leave religion alone? Or should society hold those people accountable for what religion holds societies to? The education system promoting false information of religious teaching in schoolbooks and other direct attempts at validating the increasingly irrelevant scriptures do not hide the fact that religion discourages critical thought, and strictly forbids concepts outside of its own limited domain. That limited perceived reality is directly from the boundaries set by their religions and is dangerous when confronted with modern human and society dilemmas. So, that answer is no. We should not leave such notions alone because they deserve to be kicked out of the human psyche in modern times when dealing with modern adversity, just like any system that is not working and claims to.

This book will not be kind to religion, the words 'ignorance' and 'plagiarism' will be used.

Chapter One

Primates

The following excerpt is from *The Encyclopedia of Philosophy* regarding Christian belief:

"Perhaps the first thing that should be said about Christian belief is that it does not constitute a philosophy. That is to say, it is not a metaphysical system comparable, for example to Platonism or the systems of Aristotle and Spinoza. Although the body of Christian doctrine does consist largely of metaphysical beliefs, in the sense that they are beliefs whose scope transcends the empirical world, it differs from what are usually identified as philosophical systems by its essential relation to and dependence on popular historical events and experiences. Such systems as Platonism begin with philosophical concepts and principles and seek by means of these to construct a comprehensive mental picture of the universe. Christianity, on the other hand, begins with particular, non-recurrent historical events that are regarded as revelatory and on the basis of which Christian faith makes certain limited statements about the ultimate nature and structure of reality."[1]

The relationship with historical events and experiences which Christian thought and analysis rely upon is no doubt an important aspect in gauging the Christian philosophy, but the events of the Bible mentioned above, the premise for the Christian belief, simply do not provide religious scholars with what is needed for the foundation of an adequate social system. What is left is something vacant and to be looked at rather than looked upon for guidance in the world. What significant theory on direct religious influence in explaining reality arose from non-recurrent Biblical events? Society can afford to look at Biblical verses more critically through the scope of modernity. We can scrutinize a little more and a little differently.

The vacancy of Biblical events explained above is the premise for a foundation of the three connecting mainstream religions. The arrogance shown by many concerning man and his role on earth exemplify the ignorance displayed with something event-filled as the Bible, along with a great vacancy in many other aspects. This emptiness leaves the practitioner stranded, and with the exact traits one is to expect with such a following: arrogance. The amount of arrogance shown in the Bible no doubt encourages a tone of classism among the religious. We hear the remnants of that type of thinking in the Bible every day in churches and among the lay. Any attempt to deny this by religious proponents is to also deny the countless Bible verses encouraging to do just that as well as the countless sermons since Biblical authorship encouraging the exact same viewpoints. So, if we can be honest with ourselves about this arrogance displayed by many mainstream religious followers regarding man and our place in the world, we can have a discussion on it.

This arrogance is from an overall lack of spirituality coming from religion and is directly from the lack of any real explanation of life or humans. It can also be seen in the lay and in the sermons to them. Simple traits like lack of self-awareness, pride and vanity are abundant in the religious masses, the religious notions of centuries ago lacking any effective instruction on how to deal with such traits. This even when the works like the Bible address those traits specifically. There is no more proof needed for such a claim other than the behavior of the majority of the modern religious. Even if they have a need to change from such a paradigm of thought, their religion's strict instructions forbid it because the change will involve notions outside the religion.

The vacancy that envelops lessons and practices is blinding and involves real -if unseen- consequences in today's society. The vacancy in religion is why economy lecturer Simon Bromley called religious thought "a scholastic form that lacks an identity as well as a common theme", and in his words, "one that lacks any widely-shared understanding of its central topic, or of the methods appropriate to the study of this topic."[2] It is also why Professor Richard Dawkins publicly asked several times what the actual study of theology is, and how one receives a PhD in theology. It is this vacancy that is noteworthy, and why it will be a continuous theme throughout the chapters. Religious thought may have the guise of the complex, the misunderstood or misinterpreted, but as we will see later, it is a thin veil.

This chapter will argue that, although the religious influence is impressive in the number of practitioners around the globe, this influence creates certain viewpoints which limit personal growth and wisdom. The chapter also asserts that such a perception of a vacant structure in a religious system encourages a limited mindset, and unfortunately the modern world of today is a very good example. That arrogance in notions asserted by the religious is what we will focus on in this chapter. The view of humanity in many among the religious community is that humans belong to an exceptional class -the rest of the world not viewed as inherently special humans by them according to their respective religious scriptures. But clearly there is a difference between religious explanation of what we are and what science tells us we are. Even though religion was disproved by science hundreds of years ago, we can see this arrogance that traditional religious teaching encourages with notions concerning human morality, divine intervention, evil and human suffering held by religious proponents. Those subjects will be looked at in this chapter in relation to religious-inspired notions and their vacancy resulting in an arrogant, ignorant worldview.

Not that there is even an agreement as to the form or nature of a benevolent deity with regard to such notions among the religious. Even if by some chance there were, why would this agreement include a god that needs idolatry and total submission? Why would he be a jealous mass murderer? Shouldn't his actions represent that of someone different from the Bronze Age or Iron Age thinking? The primitive social by-products alone created by this religious influence have had horrendous effects throughout history as a result. Even views towards women, animals and alcohol in the Bible are all examples of a lingering ignorance that seems to permeate the masses in a never-ending collective of false explanation and vacant themes for the generations to consume. The above-mentioned religious claims of human morality and divine intervention are testaments to this, along with religious arguments as to the nature of human inner suffering and those concerning perceived evil. Although it appears aggressive to attack these notions, they were chosen for this chapter to look at religious notions regarding explanation of reality. They also look at religious exceptionalism.

Regarding the morality argument, religious proponents often claim human morality and ethics, but since Christ is widely thought of as having preached morals, they should be able to stand criticism regarding the claim. Divine intervention is claimed by so many (one has to perform two miracles post mortem to be considered for sainthood in Catholicism) that it would seem like a good idea to discuss it here too, seeing as it is such a popular and deeply-held notion among the religious masses. Claims based on religious notions of these subjects can be looked at as an inadequate source of a premise for such an exceptional tone in religious-inspired worldview. If we are to believe anything, let it be from the truth, not a view of what the truth might be. While all the subjects discussed in this chapter may not be the ordinary themes explored in religious criticism to some, they are subjects which reveal a deeper sense of religious influence that is stifling in many ways.

The following was taken from a *U.S. News* and *Belief Net* survey that asked those who prayed for examples of prayer being answered in their lives. Respondents revealed the following:

> "Prayers of protection were answered when something told me to look up from a dead stop behind another vehicle turning to see a car behind me unable to stop. I pulled over to the shoulder at the last minute (something I normally would have not thought to do...) to witness a five-car crash, which would have been seven and an eighteen-wheeler, had not a pregnant woman behind me followed my lead so the truck behind her had room to stop."

> "Peace flows into my heart every time I offer prayer and praises to Allah."

> "Prayed for care for my daughter who had a great need but not a lot of money. Asked the Lord to send her a reliable car that she could afford. The next day in talking to coworker she mentioned that she was selling her second car. Price was right, and the deal happened."

"For me prayer is being in harmony with the universe. When I am in harmony with it my prayers are answered."

"God healed me of a heart condition and cancer. "

"When I was looking for a new job, when God has protected me from harm, when God has healed or improved the health of a loved one, and once in a while--when I really need a parking space."[3]

The lay are not alone in their views of divine intervention, religious scholars affirm the belief in intervening on behalf of humans by a claimed other world. Theologian Alvin Plantinga, for example, once claimed, "God constantly responds to events in this world." According to evangelical author Eric Metaxas, most "miracles" are because of prayer.[4] These assertions and testimonials from personal experiences present a portrait of a merciful supreme being, a caring father who interferes in human affairs. The claims from modern theological voices sound like they are certain of this notion. However, with Sub Saharan Africa alone being home to the highest population of Christians in any global region, also home to 69% of global HIV victims according to UNICEF and 40% of the world's child deaths, assertions of divine action are difficult to make. Stats like this present sobering thoughts, and one that should be taken into consideration when perceiving notions like divine action or divine intervention.

An arrogant tone by religious proponents is evident in the influence of many notions concerning divine action, and a notion accompanied by considerable favor in the religious community exemplifies this tone taken. Their hearts in the right place, the individual experience interpreted by each person above represents for them their viewpoint on what occurred in those experiences. Their views, however, became religiously based, and they were influenced by something that has had a history of being discredited by scientists for ages. If the very premise of the notion is false, what expectations can be made for offshoot notions?

Is there something wrong with the faith in Christ held by Sub Saharan African Christians? Is there something different that they are doing in that region's Christianity that will not allow for a deity to help their plight? The problem with claims of divine action is that they have to somehow be accompanied with some type of credibility. What is the measure of divine action? How does one know if it is divine? If there is a sympathetic god who intervenes, why are Sub Saharan African Christians suffering such disease and famine? It is notions like divine action that create a false reality for the practitioner.

The product of many generations, an agreed upon notion of divine action has gone through many changes throughout the ages regardless of its vague and confusing definition, and religious scholarship claims of divine action vary. For example, in the periodical *Commonweal*, religious proponent Brian Davies contemplates a possible emotional foundation for human intervention by a deity. "One might think that if God isn't capable of suffering (as you and I are), then God cannot be involved with us. Or one might think that God should be with us in our suffering as one who sympathizes in the way that I can sympathize with you. Yet thoughts like these seem not to be taking seriously what it means to speak of God as the Creator. If God the Creator can suffer, then it would seem that he is passive to the action of something he creates."[5] This emotional reference or humanity inspired notion linking God to a friendly observer is popular in the religious community. Others contend that divine action is evident in the actual creation of the universe such as Alvin Plantinga and David Wolpe, and religious scholar Franz Jozef van Beeck asserts that self-communication was divine intervention.[6] Either way, the view towards divine action among religious scholarship seems to point toward a deity who can and does interfere with human life to their seemingly immediate benefit, a kind of helper along the way.

Unfortunately, the works of religious scholars are as good as it gets when it comes to perception of divine intervention and global events. The average lay who are told in church every weekend about the divine have a less complex concept of the claim. For instance, it is doubtful that the average religious person does not disagree with the blanketed phrase, "God will set the chaotic world events correct by Divine judgment".[7] Despite lack of merit or logic, the notion of divine action or divine intervention is claimed among both the masses and religious scholarship and is believed by many in the religious public. Although attempts by religious proponents to properly define the notion of divine intervention have been unsuccessful, the topic is still strong among believers, promoting comfort.

But if divine intervention occurs, how do we know? Are there no parameters or variables to measure such actions yet from thousands of years of study? Just physics alone has accounted for such metaphysical variables and properties for some time now, and has been doing so since Isaac Newton, yet we don't have one defined theme of divine action, no patterns to compare with others -if they even existed before. Aren't religious claims of metaphysical properties of the same unproveable notions as attempts of physical explanation from religious scriptures? If the major claims of the Bible in the physical realm have been proved wrong, what qualifies their metaphysical explanation as any indicator of truth?

An architect can prove his math on a design, a physics professor can explain quantum physics to us in a scholarly way. On what basis do religious proponents make claims about something that never occurs on some measurable level? On what basis can some make the claim that self-communication is divine intervention? The fact is that billions of practitioners have not yet been able to provide evidence of divine accordance and divine action including claims of God healing the sick or the wheelchair stricken.[8] Despite what is claimed or "believed", there has yet to be one single solitary piece of evidence to prove these claims. This is why it is well known now that those claimed to be healed through religious practice were injuries that can heal on their own, and that it is never healed teeth because teeth don't heal, it is never something impossible for modern medicine.

Even though these complex and metaphysical based thoughts on divine intervention by theologians appear impressive, they cannot hide how basic most religious proponents perceive this concept, as the notion of God providing all that is needed is prevalent among the three main religions of monotheism. Perhaps this is because these concepts have been enveloped in world views and infused into religious societies with a tone that sends a never-ending stream of blindly encouraging messages to be followed. Catholic saint researcher Patricia Treece provides an example of this generalized viewpoint of the religious masses concerning divine intervention in a piece published in *Catholic Digest* regarding the ability to receive what she calls the gifts of God for individuals who become saints. Notice the freedom taken in logical boundaries and generalities used. "Almost all saints begin as 'ordinary people'. So sure, any of us can position ourselves to develop unusual abilities by putting Christ at the absolute center of our life and loving our neighbors — enemies too — heroically. Obviously, you'll need God's help. Prayer will open you more and more to receive it. To sum up, let God make you holy and who knows what gifts God — who gives as God wills — may give you."[9]

Here we have an example of allowing a god to provide all that is needed. This is heartfelt, but wishful thinking -not to mention the assault on our intelligence with the philosophy involved in such a statement. What is the holy? What are the gifts of God? It would be interesting for the religious to provide at least an agreed upon definition of either. Likewise, theologian Craig Keener has written about divine action, releasing multiple books about miracles, but what is the make-up, the variables of anything outside of theology and the support of religious-leaning scientists (which account for less than a tenth of the scientific community)?

The notion of divine intervention has even spilled in to social and economic assertions for some. This can be seen in modern theological essays which reflect such thought. Religious proponents take liberties that are quite impressive in their attempts to link divine intervention socially in their works. Luis Lugo gives us a good example in *Society* when he infuses divine action with world affairs. "Given the widespread notion that the USA enjoys divine protection and plays a special role in world affairs, it is perhaps not surprising that many Americans support an internationalist approach to American foreign policy."[10]

This explanation of economics in a religious sense is not even accurate, as only the narrow would not realize the empire-like role that the United States plays with its military power alone. Also, if anyone reading that piece in *Society* knows anything about U.S. foreign policy, they would not dare mention it even in the same paragraph as the word "divine", unless discussing the massacres of the Old Testament (OT). Aside from this, even if the assertion of a divine protector of the U.S. was correct, what exactly about the divine is responsible for the father-figure role the United States is claimed to play in the preceding quote? Once again, what are the measurable variables other than the claimed general "love" of a deity?

Arguments defending divine action include the argument that criticizing divine intervention is needless, as our human understanding is not capable of such comprehension, or that it does not matter whether or not humans understand the divine, as the world is "in God's hands". Religious authors Francis Chan and Preston Sprinkle, for instance, write in their book, *Erasing Hell* regarding such a notion, "Scripture is filled with divine actions that don't fit our human standards of logic or morality. But they don't need to, because we are the clay and he is the potter."[11] This is difficult to accept considering even interpretation of possible divine intervention in scriptures is confusing and vague. Consider Jesus performing miracles in the four Gospels. His miracles are based on one hand the faith held by his listeners in Matthew, Mark and Luke, and then performs the miracles in order to gain the faith of his listeners in John's gospel.[12] What is the interpretation explaining the reason for the miracles?

Also, why does Mark's gospel begin by portraying Jesus as different than the harmless lamb seen on church windows, including being an intimidating authority figure who fought dessert battles with Satan? It is as if basic lessons which could be used for survival unknown at the time among the public were deemed not as important as countless trivial tales and even songs which make the Bible's final cut(s). Is it that a deity does not feel obliged to allow for the understanding of his vastly complex workings and left dribble for an audience he severely underestimated intellectually, or is it that the authors as well as religious scholarship and hierarchy are unaware the entire time of just what they are talking about?

To illustrate a contrast between the two different narratives of scientific inquiry and religious notions like divine action, in evolution we have multiple reports from biologists of an indifferent, blind process, rather than a caring, paternal guide. Physicist Stefan Klein in his book, *The Science of Happiness*, provides us with an interesting look at the stoic, but active course evolution takes, a stark contrast from the blunt and vague concepts of the claimed divine:

"In the course of evolution brains and emotions developed in synchrony. The more brains developed the bigger and more complex they grew the richer and more differentiated emotions became. As humans adapted to more complex surroundings they required greater awareness, great use of resources in order to survive." Of the reasoning for certain functions or a certain 'favoritism' why did nature spend so much energy in creating ever more capable brains? To equip a jelly fish that moves through ocean and filters microorganisms through water with intuition and ingenious mind would have been a waste".[13]

This logic of a designer without favoritism or sympathetic viewpoint towards the plight of one species or another suggests a designer that merely creates. The indifferent design is one that counters the concept of a concerned deity at its core.

University of California Berkeley psychology professor Shlomo Breznitz and Collins Hemingway provide another example of an indifferent method used by evolution in their book, *Maximum Brainpower* when they describe human behavior and interactions with one another. Discussing reactions to stressful circumstances, they contend the following:

"As a species our biology has evolved to deal with immediate stress of life-threatening dangers. Whether we are dodging a lion or engaging in a fist fight, we are wired to deal with short, dramatic events. We mobilize, we run or do battle, we come down. We do not care about the long-term down side of stress if it saves our lives today. Truth be told, until the last hundred years very few people lived long enough for chronic stress to contribute to their deaths."[14]

Notice the difference when describing the study of evolution verses notions religious proponents push forward? What is divinely gifted about being wired in such short-termed and limited ways? Why do humans even need to fight? Why has there pretty much always been war between humans? What comedy of errors is that design? Discoveries like these are why The National Association of Biology Teachers calls evolution "an unsupervised, impersonal, unpredictable and unnatural process." Even if there was an intelligent mind guiding life with a certain agenda, the assurance of survival of human beings is not evident, as the destruction of even society as we know it is a very real possibility, and its end results have been predicted to contrast with those from which religious works like Revelation describe. If God was a loving creator who intervenes in human affairs occasionally, why have almost all species gone extinct? The religious can claim exceptionalism, but it remains an arrogant viewpoint.

Another contention from religious proponents in a reflection of exceptionalism and a detached worldview is the claim of human morality. Theologians and others sympathetic to religion assert morality frequently in arguments and are often defending the validity of it as proof that a god exists. Assertions of morality are many and vary from religious proponents depending on each belief system. From the declaration of inherent moral imperatives to science being unable to account for the nature of morality, these arguments attempt to present an understanding of ethics as well as present a divine-guided presence in notions asserted. However, like most arguments from the religious, they become problematic when considering reason and logic.

Although there exists a mountain of scientific studies and literature on perceived human morality, there are still many questions on the subject.[15] Mostly considered broad, morality's description differs around the world.[16] Darwin suggests in his *Descent of Man* that evolution and man's own critical thought is human morality.[17] Evolution tells us that there is no morality, but simply the urge to survive. Some social theorists contend that values are the result of social and cultural construction, what sociologist Philip Gorski calls "a contingent result of history and power, lacking any objective or rational foundation."[18] There are scientists who disagree as to the general description of morality[19,20], but most would agree that a comprehensive understanding of human morality is not an unreasonable common goal and it will only be a matter of time before the scientific community discovers what it is.

Nevertheless, a philosophical view of morality differs from religious concepts on the subject. Compare the moral lessons of the Bible with what Thalia Wheatley and Walter Armstrong assert for even a possible framework for identifying morality. "When philosophical moral theories depend on empirical presuppositions and premises, psychology and neuroscience can test those assumptions."[21] Specifically relating to science, consider what Joseph Davis suggests in *Society* regarding values: "Our values are not just intuitions or emotions, but convictions informed by understandings of human nature and the human condition. We must be attentive, therefore, to both the relation of values to science and the relation of science to values. Social science alerts us to context, and in a context of liberal individualism there is a powerful incentive to privilege conceptions of the good by giving them scientific warrant."[22] This type of understanding is not found in the mainstream religious scriptures at all. This is odd, considering the arrogance displayed for hundreds of years by the religious when it came to explanation of reality.

In fact, misunderstanding of women alone in the Bible - while not surprising considering the locality of the time- is an example, a reflection of the unfairness promoted by such ignorance to human morality in religion. Such blatant and irresponsible thinking translates centuries later to the behavior of the average believer who has to this day mistreated and misunderstood others, indicating basic mental health clearly not addressed in religion. The religious scriptures and teachings are simply outmatched, incapable of illustrating these basic necessities that create a moral mindset, much less explain it, and to this day many religious display the ignorance that would coincide with such lessons because the vacancy of religion does not allow for any deep moral discussions.

If apologists submit that errors in Biblical morality was just a misunderstanding (Paul's chauvinistic recommendations regarding women in church are claimed to be misunderstood and for the benefit of women) the following from 5th Century theologian Augustine on women should be crystal clear in its assumptions. "Women should not be enlightened or educated in any way. They should, in fact be segregated..." Also, shrouded in absolute clarity is the morning prayer of Orthodox Jewish men thanking God for not making them women. This is not some metaphorical complexity beyond understanding, but plain blindness typical of a traditional worldview of the ignorant.

A staff editorial in *Christian Science Monitor* regarding the escape of religious oppression for females should tell one all they need to know regarding morality in Christianity:

> "The best way out of such dilemmas is for women held in mental or even physical bondage by a religious group to be their own agents of change. Many Christian and Jewish women broke the norms of their faiths in the 19th and 20th centuries. Today, it is Muslim women in the Arab Spring who are setting the pace for their own liberation from inhibiting norms. Many Arab female scholars, for example, are challenging male Islamic leaders about interpretations of the Quran and women's role in marriage and

society, just as Bible scholars have recently challenged presumptions of women's role in Christian churches."[23]

It is easy to see why females would want to be free of such an ignorant frame of mindset, as any sensible person would be who is vaguely familiar with the historical role females play in Christianity.

Homosexuals can also be added to the list of the mistreated and misunderstood in a perceptive viewpoint ignorant to true moral behavior by the religious. This was how a *PBS Frontline* story appeared on the findings of geneticist Dean Hamer's discovery of homosexuality in genes. "[T]he underlying idea seemed to carry enormous implications: Homosexuality was not a choice -'the wrong choice', as many religious and political leaders have demagogued on the issue. Instead, homosexuality was as much a biological fact as eye color".[24] With the "gay gene" identified, and more studies on the subject ongoing, there is no longer a superstitious notion to be held on to regarding homosexuality and the treatment of gays.

What in the Christian morality accounts for the intolerance of gays and lesbians? Because that is what Romans 1:26-27, 1 Timothy 1:9-10 and 1 Corinthians 6:9 recommend. It does not matter which interpretation is the claimed "correct" one, as they all represent an ignorant, intolerant viewpoint that is currently deemed uncivilized. Do the three main religions not promote such narrow-minded viewpoints which last to this day regarding homosexuality? Of course they do. To deny this is just to continue an unhealthy viewpoint and promote an intolerance, rather than reaching for an understanding and more awareness.

Is the direct religious influence of animal abuse included in the claim of morality as well? According to the Humane Society countless animal abuse cases occur on a daily basis in the United States alone – a highly Christian nation, and, according to University of California Berkley biologist Anthony Barnosky, humans have killed half of the vertebrate globally in four decades and nine tenths of the world's fish.[25] Currently 55 billion animals are killed per year by humans for consumption. In what way can it be denied that scriptures directly influence this type of mindset with the number of animal sacrifices and animal mistreatment in the Bible?

In Matthew 6:26 we see some roots of this influence regarding animals, as the verse is accompanied by the usual bluntness of Biblical authorship. "Look at the birds of the air: they neither sow nor reap nor gather into barns, and yet your heavenly Father feeds them. Are you not of more value than they?" To think that this would not have a psychological impact on the uneducated is to be naïve. Another example of this direct influence regarding animals comes from Genesis 1. "And let them have dominion over the fish of the sea and over the birds of the heavens and over the livestock and over all the earth and over every creeping thing that creeps on the earth." Despite the verse sounding like it is from a Tim Burton film, the message is clear regarding the arrogant attitude to be taken by practitioners towards animals. The Koran takes roughly the same tone.

The previous examples do not reflect the genocides, slavery and war found in the Bible -which are the points of several attacks on religion- but reflect more the awareness of the practitioner today due to Biblical references and stifling teaching throughout the centuries. Detachment (most) practitioners have made from these extreme notions point out the positive impact of letting go of that paradigm which holds back individuals and society. The behavior of humans including vanity, sex or fraud scandals involving religious leaders globally along with racism, corruption and greed in all levels of government worldwide today are all constant reminders of how remedial the moral claim is by the religious. How moral are the two thousand clergymen that Pope Francis publicly admitted were pedophiles when they earn the trust of children for immoral reasons?

The slow progression of scientific study concerning morality and subjects like life sciences will continue, telling previously unimaginable facts about the human psyche and perceived morals. It is clear now that religion will not have anything to do with these discoveries, as they never had anything to do with them. Even the Socratic method discussing the depths of virtues predates Christ by 400 years along with Eastern philosophy maintaining similar foundations near the same time span. Concerning philosophical notions on morality presented since Biblical times, if religion could not match with philosophy and the sciences that formed due to its simple foundations, what is to be expected of religious scholarship, an institution that must adhere to the basic principles of the Bible? For instance, where is there anything like the following quote by Wake Forest University philosopher Adam Kadlac in the scriptures?

"We may be embroiled in vigorous debates regarding the appropriate moral principles to adopt or how to order the values that should govern our lives—debates that are fraught with difficulties of their own. But because there is often tantalizingly broad agreement about some of these matters, it seems that if progress can be made on questions where opinions are more divided, then empirical investigation will complete the process and tell us what moral conclusions should be drawn."[26]

There is not anything this advanced in the scriptures that religious scholarship can then analyze. Instead, the vacancy of the scriptures is evident in the endless tales and psalms that include celebrating the destruction of enemies.

Although science does not know a great deal of morality yet, scientific studies conducted on morality include compelling information about the human mind and human behavior, information which suggests a different explanation from the simple religious-based notions of long ago. This data suggests something far more complex regarding morality than the ones described throughout the centuries. One such study out of Harvard conducted a survey on morality, asking individuals if they would knowingly take the lives of three people in order to save dozens in the process. The respondents reportedly chose roughly even, and the brain scans taken while the respondents considered the dilemma revealed increased brain power of those who decided to save more people than those who chose otherwise. Kristin Ohlson reported in *Discover*," But these powerful instincts are not commands from a higher power, they are just emotions hardwired into the brain. Our first reaction under pressure --

the default response -- is to go with our gut. It takes more time and far more brain power to reason the situation out."

Ohlson quotes study team member and director of Harvard's Moral Psychology Research Lab Fiery Cushman as saying, "The reason we feel caught in moral dilemmas is that truly, our brain has two different solutions to the problem... Those processes can conflict because the brain is at war with itself."[27] Findings have been presented regarding moral inclinations in children as well, as Bruce Bower noted in *Science News*, "Findings support the idea that universal concerns among children -- such as a need to feel in control of one's behavior and disapproval of harming others -- shape moral development far more than cultural values do."[28] The impact of such decisions in a child is noteworthy. This essentially points towards the possibility of natural tendencies appearing overwhelming even in cultural influence settings such as religion regardless of a religious "inherency" claimed. These and other examples can be found anywhere in the advancing life sciences today. In contrast, the lack of awareness of morality in the three major religions in every sense can be attributed by an overall blanket of generalities that has not advanced in depth of meaning since the time of the scriptures. Again, this is odd, considering Lucretius was studying the nature of the mind about a hundred years before the Christ and Plato was asserting nis notions on moral philosophy in his *Ethics* about three hundred and fifty years before the Christ.

Religious proponents may claim that New Testament (NT) values take precedence over the harsher tone of OT values and an approach from the heart in the NT is what in a sense overrules the tone of the OT, yet the NT teachings on values are in many ways just as local as those in the OT. How is it that the NT ignores what is natural and prevalent in humanity? How can it utterly fail to provide anything that addresses basic human instinct, or even correctly identify it? The behavior of the religious masses consequently is obvious.

Even religious proponent claims of tithing as a moral contrast between the religious and non-religious are muddled, as the religious are actually less motivated by compassion than non-believers when it comes to donating and more motivated by society stature.[29] In fact, human kindness is not even exceptional when compared to other planetary species. Don't most large species display varying forms of kindness? Even the 60,000-year-old Neanderthal male discovered inside The Zagros Mountains was discovered with flowers and inside a hole 132-feet deep. Animals constantly take on the helpless offspring of other animals and nurture them. How is humanity exceptional in such a regard?

A curious thing about religious notions is that they become sillier as time continues and science progresses. Their effect on the world remains just as vacant to the senses. The inclination or predisposition to become religious is only natural: before the popularity of monotheism, notions of polytheism of nature forces were ubiquitous.[30] But it is also important to note the limited voice this school of thought presents. Based on faith and dogma according to biology professor Jerry Coyne, religion promotes what is impossible to discover given its borders and ridiculous rules.

Psychology professor Jefferson Fish sums up this section when he echoes Spinoza's call for enlightenment regarding morals, not religious instructions: "Knowledge of what the world is actually like better equips one to make moral judgments than do faith and dogma."[31] The ignorance to the real world that is accompanied with each and every Bible and Koran is a testament to this statement. Not only are moral claims from the religious unreasonable, but it also appears that religious scholarship cannot define what it is they're discussing in the first place.

Not just claims of morality and divine action permeate arrogant religious notions, religious proponent attempts at explaining immorality are subjected to similar philosophical problems. Noted often by critics of religion, the 'problem of evil' is a well-known stumbling block of religious-backed arguments. Proponents often assert notions explaining away evil, but there are several weaknesses in these arguments. The problems regard logic. We have David Albert Jones, for example, who writes of immorality among "demons" in his book, *Angels*. Notice the obvious freedom taken regarding notions claimed, as is often the case with religious philosophy. Jones writes, "The idea that demons are fallen angels neatly takes care of the question as to what demons are and where they come from. It also avoids holding God responsible for creating such malicious beings. When God created them, they were good."[32] That was definitely ridiculous. This make-it-up-as-we-go-along theme regarding religious-based notions will be a recurring one throughout the book. Jones couldn't possibly know any of what he is talking about. If he did, he would not have to take such liberties.

Similarly, Ian Markham's thoughts on immorality in *Modern Theology* bares the same tone: "One might object, perhaps on theological grounds, to the distinction between types of sin. All sin before God is ugly and repugnant. Therefore, a universe with moderately bad people is just as bad as a universe with exceptionally bad people. It is true that the entire argument depends upon this distinction between moderate evil and extreme evil. Granted, deciding what precisely falls either side of this line is extremely difficult."[33] All of it is difficult, as it all involves a broad spectrum that theology is not suited for. The amount of liberties taken on subjects he discussed is alarming and belongs where modern religious notions are currently, outcast from serious philosophical discussion. How does this man know about the boundaries of immorality? Where is the proven path laced with evidence from which he can then base claims?

Jones and Markham make clear that the religious literature on immorality is no more improved than religious proponent explanations of morality. The notions asserted by each author are not even logical. Their solutions to basic logical dilemmas in their arguments are to basically pretend they don't exist. They serve no purpose other than in the realm of religious philosophy only, a realm where we suspend disbelief and where the theologian begs the reader's pardon when it comes to a logical explanation. Such an arrogance might be forgiven, applauded in religious proponent circles, but holds no weight in any discussion outside of those relating to theism. It is due to this desperation and lack of reasoning in their arguments that religious proponents cannot be taken seriously beyond the choir they preach to.

The masses do not subscribe to a different philosophy when it comes to immorality than theologians and religious-leaning scientists. This includes famous Christian sayings when it comes to morals in everyday life. Jay Wenger and Amy Daniels write of one saying and describe how many of the religious view acts of immorality among Christians in

Journal of Social Psychology when they write of a popular Christian one-liner: "'Love the sinner—hate the sin' is an expression that people in religious domains often use to refer to the distinction necessary for loving a person who is engaged in an activity that they consider unacceptable."[34] Vague instructions such as this is what spreads from one generation to the next. No psychological lessons or step-by-step paths to awareness but notions of sin and vacant one-liners from the local. What is the sin? What is it comprised of? What exactly do we use to counter the sin that we are supposed to hate? As with other religious notions, the more we hold religion accountable for explanation of the real, the more those notions appear weak.

As is the case with religious claims of morality, scientific analysis presents a more complicated explanation of immorality than religious-based explanations. One that comes from data analysis and scientific conclusion which has been reviewed. It is a different explanation than the generalizing of an ominous evil that the religious assert. Not that this is needed, even the acknowledgement of what is immoral is different to different customs. While seen by many to be immoral, stoning a woman to death for showing skin on a body part in a staunchly Islamic nation is not only encouraged but is taken as a form of a holy directive.

It turns out that studies show we are born with aggression, and do not actually succumb to a mysterious force that can be passed off as other worldly. According to one study, authors Luciano Gasser and Tina Malti tell us in *Journal of Genetic Psychology* that aggression is not only natural, but rampant. Of childhood aggression specifically, "Comparing aggressive and non-aggressive children's moral judgments and emotions during unprovoked and provoked aggression, the nonaggressive children were found to judge retaliation more serious than the aggressive, as well as the consequences involved with the retaliation."[35] This explanation can clarify why each day 160,000 children miss school to avoid being bullied by aggressive children. Aggression in children is rampant. What is the religious notion of sin to answer for that? It is important to note that this trait is not an unexplained force or Satan at work, but instead a biological human tendency. This is inherent among humans regardless of what cultural aspects are claimed, religion included.

There are theists who defend their position when it comes to the theological problem of evil, but as with other religious arguments, those defenses are weak. In his criticism of scientific inquiry and its inability to explain immorality, for example, Dinesh D'Souza once claimed in a debate:

> "Evolution cannot explain the depth of human evil… Evolution presumes cruelty, evolution presumes harshness, but it is a harshness tempered by necessity. Think of a lion. It wants to eat the antelope because it's hungry, but have you ever heard of a lion that wants to wipe every antelope off the face of the earth? No. So, how do you explain this human evil that far outruns necessity, and reaches depths that seem almost unfathomable?"

Although he is right that evolution does not have an opinion on immorality, perhaps D'Souza is not aware of the fact that, not only do lions in the wild kill when not hungry, but want every infant of competing males wiped off the face of the Earth and personally ensure this to the greatest of their ability and senses regardless of what the females they are trying to court think and regardless of what is best for the pride as a whole. This is seen as unfathomable among most societies even with child sacrifice to appease gods prevalent among humans ages ago. How do sharks in uteri that eat their sibling embryos account for D'Souza's argument? What exactly is God's design for the cheetah to reproduce involving mostly multiple males, usually brothers, forcing themselves on a single female?

Another example of defending a theist stance on immorality is professor of religion John Teehan's piece in *The Monist* regarding the theological problem of evil:

> "Why is there even a problem of evil at all? This is not a philosophical or theological question, but rather one of religious psychology- why is it that people come to view their gods in morally relevant ways? We can only have a problem of evil if we first have a conception that God cares about human welfare and acts in a way that we can somehow recognize as just, or at least justifiable, and this appears to be a cross-culturally recurrent feature of beliefs about supernatural agents; but why should we conceive of gods in this way?"[36]

Not that there is any such thing as a credible and recognized field of religious psychology, but Teehan attempts to narrow the subject to something that can be defined only on religious-based terms, all one has to do is not "conceive" of gods in a way that dismisses their ideas being wrong. Also, notice how the author attempts to narrow the possibility of evil existing to something rooted in nothing more than mythology as a premise. The suggestion of a subject outside the senses as a premise for the argument made is convenient for the author, but not realistic in any analysis to be respected.

Another reflection of an exceptional tone taken by the religious is seen in their view of human emotional suffering. Such an impact on human emotions, suffering was once described by history scholar Joseph Amato in *International Social Science Review* as pervading all life.[37] Something with the power to be largely influential on human affairs, emotional suffering is something that has been written about for centuries, and is so entrenched in humanity that many find it difficult to escape its grasp. Emotional suffering also can be so overwhelming sometimes that suicides are drawn from it along with a host of other unfortunate circumstances. Even rituals concerning inner suffering have been a theme throughout the ages in attempts to lessen the emotional burden of overwhelming emotional turmoil.

The search to end this inner suffering has been pervasive. While the question of the existence of personal suffering has remained beyond the grasp of human intelligence for millennia, there exist many notions and theories regarding its nature and beginnings. Biologists tell us that suffering is a result of free time that modernity has provided, although science is largely still unclear on how to control fully the endless waves of emotions our biology designs us to perceive. Even though scientific inquiry is so far limited in its analysis, the current scientific understanding is -not surprisingly- different than the theistic or religious understanding of it.

Proposed explanations from religious scholarship concerning suffering reads what would be written if the basis of the premise of notions are from Bronze Age philosophy and given other worldly figures and realms thought of in times even more ignorant. Theologians admittedly are not even aware of God's suffering, or whether he does or not. This is why theologian John Haught asserts, "Of course, what it means to say that God suffers has always been a matter of dispute in theology, and the issue remains unsettled."[38] Regardless, even if there was a benevolent creator who was concerned with out emotional well-being, he/she appears strangely indifferent to human plight. This entity either possesses the personality of a child, or one that is directly in line with the authorship of the times. One doesn't need even a basic understanding of inner suffering to be able to perceive something as obvious and crude as an ancient deity.

The author of Revelations does tell us that God will end suffering, and many religious inspired sayings regarding suffering have become almost proverb. One of the most repeated variations of a comforting phrase among Christians is found in evangelist Mary Kay Baxter's quote, "Some challenges come from God to test our faith and perfect our character."[39] John Martens gives another when he writes in the Christian leaning periodical *America* that even though humans all suffer, "it is important to know that the Good Shepherd knows our suffering."[40] These and other generalizations provide little explanation as to the reality of our plight and of suffering. Also, this claimed relationship humans have with a deity is troubling considering what used to be believed regarding child sacrifice throughout human history. As religious author John Teehan admits in the *Monist*, "Why did the rumbling of the earth or the thundering of the sky drive our ancestors to devise rituals of appeasement? Why did Agamemnon believe that only his daughter's death could sate Artemis's anger? And why would Abraham so readily accept that any god could demand a child as a burnt offering?"[41] Also, how do Baxter and Martens know what they are talking about? Is there at least a language, some type of quantifiable form of analyzing this, something that isn't a conveniently placed inarguable theory by theologians? Does this argument of being elusive to scientific analyses make up the only premise explaining such processes? Is there no other way to define the divine in any specific language which could then be verified? The liberty taken by religious proponents to give credit to such theist notions is impressive.

Other popular generalizations concerning suffering from religious proponents include age-old notions of claimed sin relating to human suffering. Stephen Prothero, for instance wrote in his book. *Religious Literacy*, "Christians see sin as the core human problem and describe liberation from sin as salvation". Marcus Borg calls systemic evil as "perhaps the single greatest cause" of human suffering.[42] However, this notion of a force beyond our control is problematic. Rather than taking accountability for behavior, the burden lies in an unknown "sin", a force which we have no control over. We can only try to control what that force makes us do. What exactly does evil consist of? What exactly is the salvation that Stephen Prothero mentions?

According to these notions, adhering to religious instruction is pretty much all we need to become protected from suffering rather than engaging a mentally healthy regimen or seeking help or education to take control of our emotions. This isn't including other frail notions of command and comfort based on Biblical teaching that make up the prescription for the effect human suffering has. There is no real account for suffering in scripture,[43] and as Bertrand Russell once noted, the four Gospels never elude to intelligence. Why? This is important when taking into consideration that many have accused religion of being created for control.

Oversimplified answers which are rampant in today's religious vernacular not only offer vague descriptions of suffering, but also fail in their attempts to encourage ways to offset or even bear the brunt of personal suffering. There is no proven way to overcome suffering's dominance in certain weak moments, but unfortunately the scriptural one-liners and commands from Jesus didn't cover such complex topics. The false teachings are evident in the work of modern religious experts, as their writings are examples of this limited knowledge. Baxter, who received her doctorate in ministry, gives advice in the book. *Divine Revelation of Deliverance* on how to overcome suffering from demons (yes, demons). "Territorial demons may have the 'right' to bind you in certain areas due to the generational curses that have been allowed to fester in the family throughout the years- unless you overcome them through the name and blood of Christ who took the punishment on the cross to set you free."[44]

What on Earth is this woman talking about? How does she know what occurs in such a realm? If these notions exist in the personal, and are not to be measured by science, then are there no foundations for personal notions one can analyze from religious philosophy? Equally vague is Henry Fehren's explanation of suffering and advice for when we do suffer in his article for *U.S. Catholic.* "If suffering were pointless,

Jesus would not have accepted it. Yet if suffering causes us to lose our faith, that is where the real despair comes in. Only great faith can make us able to accept severe suffering."[45] Again, how does this man know that only great faith causes resilience of suffering? Where is his math or any work done to prove this? Where is the line drawn when measuring faith or measuring suffering in any type of metric? Such claims are again without merit, much less identification of just how much faith causes what.

As far as the advice given by theologians on how to actually deal with the claimed sin which is supposed to cause our suffering, Christians are taught to control themselves and their desires when it comes to "sin". But how? What are the proven ways? If not intelligence, does the Bible even refer to something that would eventually be the foundation of a helpful modernized notion? If the seven deadly sins cause suffering, why not isolate these urges, or at least try to in some way define them in a deeper context so that practitioners may be guided to some kind of path rather than encourage to merely control oneself? The thought of just controlling desire when surrounded by temptation is frightening in itself, but repetition of an emphasis on the limited notion of sin regarding suffering seen throughout the years in Christianity has yet to present examples of an effective counter to the actual suffering.

The Bible contains examples of good deeds, but no insight into the nature of inner suffering, or how to cope with it. Instead, it promises through God wealth to those who desire, vengeance for those who suffer and an end to unhappiness if the practitioner follows religious rules. Is there some occurrence that takes places in this other realm when the believer follows these rules? What is the instant metaphysical transition if so? In Revelation 21:3-4 we are told that God will end our suffering, but the teaching itself fails to focus on the actual emotions or steps to analyze the psyche, and merely presents hope from a benevolent creator as an escape from pain, assuming they are even discussing emotional suffering and not just a local reference to physical pain. John is impressive to a lot of religious proponents in his description of advanced times in Revelation, yet not one piece of advanced kind of advice concerning suffering from Biblical scripture. This is curious, considering Revelation takes place at least in the present where modernity enjoys a plethora of technological and scientific advancements.

The expectations of any kind of helpful authorship in such a place and time are unsurprisingly not met in the Biblical authorship. It isn't as if the authors did not have enough room to add any of what we are talking about to Biblical verses. This is what happens when modern religious "philosophy" uses vague and provincial leftovers from a forgotten time. Notions evolved from shallow concepts concerning human suffering can only evolve so far when they are that local and trivial. There is only so far the authors can go with the meaning of the texts outside of taking certain liberties with them, which they do. The information claimed by religious proponents is based on a time when authors were illiterate on an infinite amount of areas.

In comparison, the basic knowledge of what is required for stable emotional states and relationships is by now a discovery which is a thing of the past for psychology, a life science in mere infancy, and with nowhere near the arrogance found in religious teaching. Clinical psychology expert Jesse Geller's article for *American Journal of Psychology* illustrates how far psychology has come regarding inner suffering. In it she discusses the relationship between pity -ideally what the religious wants from a deity- and human suffering. She contends that pity is a temporary cure for something like suffering, "a rare and fleeting virtue whose essence is freedom, to be freely given, it must remain unsought or accidental, even fought against."[46] Opinions like this are missing from the lessons of the Bible, and this opinion needed to be there, rather than encouraging false notions to the masses through verses which do not promote critical thinking.

The knowledge and proper guidance that humans are certainly capable of is clearly absent in such flawed religious notions. To hope that a deity takes pity on humans in every day plight is not only childish, but unhelpful. This small quote explains more than many the scriptural tales, instructions and songs. It deals with reality, the nature of the mind. This one quote explains more than most of the centuries of church teachings and theological analysis. It is trust-worthy and from someone qualified to give an expert opinion. This is the type explanation that is missing from scripture.

Religious exceptionalism merits no credibility. The notions that promote such a mindset do not command respect from credible institutions throughout the world or indicate any helpful messages, but instead show an arrogance and stubbornness in the face of real-life problems. This is why Pew Research Center shows that traditional Muslims internationally believe humans evolved over time and is also why religion has lost its grip worldwide. It is why even though most Americans consider the Bible sacred, they don't read it, and it is also why a Gallop poll revealed 77% of Americans believe that faith has lost its influence. The local lessons found in scripture expose religious notions and the arrogant, ignorant, limited notions they are.

As much as theologians would like to separate previous religious lessons from more modern ones, it is difficult considering those lessons were the meat to a skeletal basis of an entire religion. We would not have the basic foundations of Christianity, Judaism and Islam without the local notions of scriptures. All three religion's scriptures ignore that Neanderthals died out 40,000 years ago, that Cro-Magnon is actually the ancestor to Europeans, that man is made from the same compounds as the stars in our galaxy, that we are a social and pattern-seeking species who share similarities with other placental mammals that only mammals share (such as fur, feeding milk to our young and giving birth), and display the same physical characteristics that only primates share (such as increased tactile sensitive nerve endings).

There is exactly zero reference to the findings of human ancestral footprints and fossils in any of the three major religious scriptures, or that there are at least 21 similar species just in the human family tree alone.[47] If religion is inherited and comes naturally to us in a path that is guided by God, where exactly is the Cro-Magnon's version of God in the multiple findings of 39,000-year-old cave art?

If evolution is, according to deists, the work of God, why didn't Jesus or Muhammad or Yahweh mention evolution or something akin to it, or even a prototype that would later lead to such a notion? Did the mind-numbing locality of Psalms take precedence over explanation of human life so much as to riddle the scriptures with endless local verses? The problem with the arrogance of certain religious proponents when it comes to their life viewpoints is that they in time seem ridiculous. Not only do they not know what they are talking about when referring to a deity in explaining reality, but they assume that their point of view takes precedence over others, as if the concept of a divine entity is the validity for their notions.

If man is from the image of a god as is the wide claim among religious proponents, is that god also made mostly of water? Because this is apparently what he made us from, and ensured we were entirely reliant upon it to survive. If a god is the designer, then why do humans and animals alike display the same instinctive behavior? Why doesn't the Bible or the Koran indicate basic information like this? Does he also have a large nose to help him survive in the Caucasus Mountains? Would he not have spherical vision, or the ability to break down energy for consumption beyond the use of teeth? Why do humans have teeth anyway if we are in his image? Don't teeth rot? This entity would also be endowed (by himself) with a tail bone and feet that resemble those of a gorilla. Are these physical parts claimed to be "metaphorical" by the religious community as well? If so, the claim that humans are made in his image is either a lie or a well-intentioned, man-made myth.

A popular Christian apologetic counter to criticism of religious notions is the assertion that the Bible was not meant as a science book, but a look at ourselves, an introduction to God. Religious proponent Francis Collins stated to *Time* what many religious apologists today assert when she claimed that, while everyone looks at the Bible scientifically, it should be seen as God revealing himself and how people should act. If this is true, then why would the Bible consist of endless tales that specifically detail its local themes? Is the treatment of woman and ignorance to the effects of alcohol metaphorical as well? Why was it taken as science for centuries by the Church leaders of the time?

Another interesting point about this claim of scripture not being meant as any serious analytical text is the influence over the religious worldview that the verses have. Isn't the word of God what Christian lives and ministries are built on? Doesn't John Bevere write in the million selling *The Bait of Satan,* "the revealed Word of God is the solid rock on which we are to build our lives and ministries"?[48] The truth is that they don't know what they are talking about because that is what happens when one analyzes ignorant writings regarding a myth. They cannot answer for it because there was nothing ever there to analyze but well-intentioned notions based on limited knowledge about a great many things on a spectrum of different subjects. On the other hand, scientific discovery has come so far that the recent discovery of fossils linking humans to apes as well as the discovery of prehistoric fish that crawled on hind fins ("an amphibious ancestor of the swimming ichthyosaurs named Cartorhynchuslenticarpus"[49]) tell scientists what they already knew based on scientific inquiry, which is possibly why there wasn't a larger media blitz to the discoveries. It is almost as if it was common knowledge, the discoveries going as planned in scientific inquiry.

Consider the nature of the sciences as a comparison to such religious notions. The scientific theories adhere to strict standards and are reviewed by the brightest minds in the world, a process of how the scientific fields took shape to what it is today. The progress for science since its beginnings was slow, but, as Chet Raymo explains in the periodical *Commonweal*, these sciences have evolved into something quite impressive: "From the time of Isaac Newton (1642-1727), mathematical deduction and experimentation became the sole arbiters of scientific truth, administrated by a secular establishment anchored in local scientific societies. The new authority was international, nonsectarian, and fiercely independent. The motto of Britain's Royal Society, established in 1662, was 'Take no one's word'."[50]

With the observations of the Newtonian worldview and then succeeded by the Einsteinian universe, Dr. Richard Gerber notes in *Total Health* the reasoning behind the switch in the paradigm of a worldview from a religious viewpoint to a scientific one when he noted, "divine explanations for the nature of health and illness were no longer deemed necessary."[51] Stephen Hawking and Leonard Mludinow now share the sentiment that there was no need for a god regarding questions of reality and the universe in their book, *The Grand Design.* "It is possible to answer these questions purely within the realm of science, and without invoking any divine beings."[52] With all the painstaking processes that brought the scientific method into existence and which is maintained today by the scientific community, we can see a process that has earned the right to be called the best arbiter of truth we have. This process escapes religious analysis no matter how much is asserted by theologians.

Specifically, psychology can be used as an example of scientific analysis and the rigors involved in comparison to major religious notions and their foundations. Even today, there are different ways to view psychosis which are being discussed by experts. Psychoanalysis is one of the many sciences that saw its awkward beginnings eventually flourish by standards scientists adhered to. Discussing this growth and process, psychiatry professor George Makari wrote in his book, *Revolution in Mind* regarding the field after Freud's discovery of psychoanalysis and the eventual questioning of old notions.

> "The prewar Freudians were no more; psychoanalysts were no longer made by a simple commitment to a Freudian theory of unconscious psychosexuality. By the 1920s it became possible to pit one Freudian position against another and leverage these differences into a more open community. What was in the unconscious? Was it sexual, aggressive, both, or perhaps something else? Was psychoanalysis depth psychology or I psychology? These became generative

questions for a profession, not oaths of loyalty to a movement."[53]

Analytical psychology founder Carl Jung would eventually break away from his mentor Freud's views of as well as importance placed on myth, changing psychoanalysis drastically not long after its formation. Even though Freud invented psychoanalysis, many of his views were no longer adhered to once proven difficult to maintain. This process of holding accountable theories and conclusions is clearly different from the claimed personal where science "can't measure" the religious philosophical notions.

Clearly there is a difference between religious explanation of what we are and what science and philosophy tell us we are. Even though religion was disproved by science, there remains an exceptional tone religious teaching encourages. The preceding were examples to show the vacancy of religious notions, and why they have no place in society. Perceiving oneself as special or exceptional not only echoes other egocentric religious views promoted in Christianity, Judaism and Islam, but encourages the ignorance we see worldwide among many of their faithful in these areas. There is no enlightenment for the faithful, as the accepted and strict word of Jesus was answerless for many difficulties in life.

Pastor Chip Ingram once wrote in his book, *Culture Shock*, "God appointed humankind with dominion over the earth", and quotes Psalm 115:16, "The highest heavens belongs to the Lord. The earth he has given to mankind",[54] but if there is no deity perceived by the people, then by what right do they have to consider themselves exceptional? Religious notions fail because there is nothing behind their statements. The arrogance and self-centered worldview promoted by the barely literate thousands of years ago damages progress due to its lack of valuable information on any important subject. Humans are not special, they are not chosen by a supreme maker of life, and they do not possess a superiority to anything in the solar system, much less the Universe. If humans are so special, why is the moon landing the most significant stride humans have made yet in a galaxy that is one hundred trillion miles across, with much of what is in our solar system alone capable of destroying us all?

Not only are humans not special, but we are extremely vulnerable to disaster at any minute due to natural catastrophe alone. In fact, the only thing that is special with humans in relation to other species is our arrogance. It is true that most humans believe that there is a certain 'something-else' out there[55], but as exhaustive as the religious inspired search has been for ultimate truth, the expedition continues to fail. The sciences, by contrast, have come a long way since the philosophical principles in ancient Greece. It was only a matter of time until science took apart religious explanations so efficiently, especially now that such overwhelming facts and data have been presented which are no longer considered a crime by church rule (work which proves the explanations of the Church wrong for the ages to witness), but we have a larger responsibility to adhere to what empirical data tells us and follow through with action for the progress of society.

Chapter Two

The Unseen

Metaphysical properties have bewildered scientists to this day, as whatever lies in the realms outside of human perception has been an elusive subject to say the least. At most, humans have discovered a general blanket explanation for what lies in the metaphysical. Many have attempted to define the metaphysical ever since Aristotle, or at least describe what lies in those realms not sensed by man. *Random House Webster* gives a general definition of the metaphysical as the highly abstract or incorporeal.[1] Durkheim addressed what he referred to the immaterial as sacred, noting that it was something forbidden.[2] But whether it has been termed the metaphysical or spiritual, human beings have very little knowledge of what resides in this mysterious realm claimed by many religious proponents to contain forces, beings and places. The little that science has revealed about the metaphysical is both fascinating and, of course, contradicting of religious scripture.

In this chapter, we will discuss claims of the metaphysical by religious proponents, and how those claims represent a questionable ideology. Theist assertions of immaterial realms as well as notions of the afterlife and behavioral effects are also looked at here. This is due to concepts of invisible entities such as the holy spirit as well as angels, quasi-physical descriptions of heaven and hell are stubbornly held by the individual, a cultural and generational influence encompassing the "personal", where criticism is claimed by the religious proponent to be pointless. But as we will see, this is a mute claim given the vacant nature of religion in general.

That there is a vacancy in religious scripture is why such liberties with metaphysical interpretation are taken by many believers. With tens of thousands of Christian denominations in existence, it is easy to see why each denomination can take the vacancy to mean what their respective views are. False claims of metaphysical forces being evident when one follows the doctrines of their religion is problematic because nothing is known or has been revealed regarding what to actually follow. The faithful rely on their "spiritual" fathers for guidance who are also just as ignorant as the flock concerning even the basic of different realms, much less on how to navigate in concert with these realms as they claim. If it seems unfair to hold accountability for such religious claims, it is important to keep in mind that the Bible includes a physical measurement of heaven, what was inside, and what its function was.

It has been discovered many times over that there is no significant link between religious teachings and an ethereal substance of influence that is beyond the senses. This appears in many quotes and studies. Most cultural anthropologists and those who analyze behavior can attest to this, as they do not see any fundamental difference in the practices of the religious and those who are not religious.[3] Sociologist Reginald Bibby, for example, illustrates this point when "specialized" and "inconsequential" were the words he used to describe the effect religion has,[4] and sociologist Emile Durkheim once criticized the vacancy of religion in his claim, "there is no church of magic. There is no possession of souls or other stuff of mere folk religion." Thomas Hobbes wrote in the 1600s, "seeing there are no signs, nor fruit of religion (italics), but in man only; there is no cause to doubt, but that the seed of religion (italics), is also only in man; and consisteth in some peculiar quality, or at least in some eminent degree thereof, not to be found in any other living creatures."[5] Arguably the greatest mind ever, Albert Einstein, while embracing the warmth of Jewish culture, also admitted to its vacuous nature and lack of any ethereal substance in a correspondence:

> "For me the Jewish religion like all others is an incarnation of the most childish superstitions. And the Jewish people to whom I gladly belong and with whose mentality I have a deep affinity have no different quality for me than all other people. As far as my experience goes, they are no better than other human groups, although they are protected from the worst

cancers by a lack of power. Otherwise I cannot see anything 'chosen' about them"[6]

The same could be said of the personal relationship one has with Christ, or the "message" of the prophet Muhammad. What is the basis for the foundation of religious metaphysical claims? What is any math to prove or disprove? Where is the work to be scrutinized as Copernicus did with Aristarchus' work about 2000 years previous with the heliocentric model?

A Christian denomination can assert any offshoot notion since the realm the notion regards cannot be perceived, therefore disproved. Mormonism, an American-based denomination, includes strong Native American undertones, and Native American influence is throughout Mormon history. The different sects of Christianity remain to this day a testament to this void in the esoteric, and the lack of guidance from the metaphysical allowing for the thousands of sects to interpret the "word" of god any way they choose is a result. The fact that these practitioners are not aware of just what is the ultimate "truth" is what allows for them to be influenced, and in most cases wind up nowhere with their assumptions about the metaphysical. When there is no substance claimed to be measured regarding any of the personal or metaphysical causes and effects of religious practice, what is to stop any of the thousands of different metaphysical religious claims?

Who, for instance, can prove that Mormonism is the wrong denomination? If Mormonism is correct, doesn't that make every other denomination wrong? Because if this is so, and it was to be determined that a Native American influenced offshoot of Christianity formed in the middle of buck America is the correct religion, then we have what is a pesky recurring theme in religious history, and that is utter indifference towards human plight. The other millions of Christians who are not Mormon might have a hard time discovering that Mormonism is the correct version due to the strict adherence to religious "laws" of each denomination that literally fences in thought and forbids an open mind towards even other denominations.

Not that proponents of religion would want to use the religious pluralism argument anyway. This is one example where religious claims of the metaphysical are from a vacant premise. That there still is a religious debate among theologians of religious pluralism and exclusivism is an example of where the lack of progress in theology has led the religious perspective, this after 2 millennia following the claimed death of Christ. Professor of religion Glenn Siniscalchi admits that religious pluralism is a problem for religious claims. He writes the following in *Journal of Ecumenical Studies*:

> "The problem of religious pluralism de jure is one of the most daunting problems that Christians are now facing. If the fundamental beliefs of Christianity are true, then any beliefs in opposition to them must be false. There can be no denying this obvious fact. If persons can be saved outside of Christ, then the church has obviously erred for centuries about its central belief in the one mediator between God and humanity, casting God's sovereignty into serious doubt."[7]

In a way this presents a paradox. How do those of different religions even get along without casting aside long-held prejudices regarding those of other religions? Don't the religious have to break the rules of their respective belief system to even get along? According to Sam Harris, almost every page of the Koran contains instructions of despising non-Muslims.

Another example of mere guesses regarding the metaphysical by the religious community is the personal claim to spirituality. A person experiencing a "religious" moment becomes, according to his/her testimony, aware of notions concerning his/her religion. We will ignore the possibility of a different experience occurring from a religious figure with a believer of a different religion. That the experience is claimed to be personal can be disregarded right away. Claiming something is personal does not make it valid, not to mention the vague definition of the "personal" being claimed. What exactly is personal about it?

John Torpey's piece for *Social Research* points this false claim out when he writes, "It is not entirely clear what it means to say that religion is 'privatized'; does such privatization refer to the inner life only of the individual, to that of a family, to small conventicles of believers who shun public relevance or indeed the outside world as such?"[8] Also, the "internal testimony" the religious refer to should have real internal effects from the metaphysical. The claim of the personal is rampant in Christianity, but what exactly is the personal that they are claiming? What is the criterion of anything whatsoever involving the unseen personal, much less a relationship with a creator? What type of relationship is it?

While a claimed spiritual experience of the Christian is often the result of an actual metaphysical occurrence (i.e. an out-of-body experience), the notion that Christ, Allah, or any other religious figure intervened in the life of the individual is perceived rather than what actually occurred. Soon the individual will imagine all sorts of scenarios based on his/her exposure to certain religious notions. Such claims and guesses of the unknown are in every religious culture. In Judaism, Rabbi Brad Hirschfield, for example, writes in his book, *You Don't Have to Be Wrong for Me to Be Right*, the importance of the circumcision ceremony:

> "The baby is placed in what we call "Elijah's chair," because in Jewish tradition it is Elijah the prophet who announces the coming of the Messiah. By putting the child in that chair, we're saying that maybe this child is the one. That tradition has been expanded in many Jewish communities so that daughters are placed in Elijah's during naming ceremonies because maybe the Messiah is female."[9]

The fact of the matter is that the religious have no idea what they are claiming because the metaphysical is almost entirely unknown to everyone except for the surface-scraping fringe sciences. To claim anything else, especially with the dangerous conviction many believers are known to have, is counterproductive to a society trying to progress.

Another example of religious proponents claiming the metaphysical is asserting the argument that validates religion. It usually is placed where science cannot disprove the argument. In a *Time* cover story, religious proponent and geneticist Francis Collins provides an example of this modern inarguable premise when he asserted, "God's existence is either true or not. But calling it a scientific question implies that the tools of science can provide the answer. From my perspective, God cannot be completely contained within nature, and therefore God's existence is outside of science's ability to really weigh in."[10] In this example, Collins inserts a classic god-of-the-gaps argument: because science is mute on this subject, proof of a deity is asserted. In another example, Dan Peterson contends in *American Spectator*:

> "But doesn't science admit only materialistic or naturalistic explanations? In the ordinary course, yes, science seeks to explain observed phenomena by reference to natural physical laws. But the creation of the universe (where did the laws come from?) and the origin of life (how did complexity that is vanishingly improbable come about?) are rather special questions, and the answers maybe special as well. Materialism and theism answer them in very different ways."[11]

This is a recurring theme in theology, a repetitive variation of "the existence of a creator is by definition outside science's domain."[12] Patrick Glynn delivers a harsher sentence to science when comparing scientific analysis to theism in his book, *God: the Evidence*:

> "The modern secular psychological paradigm- the effort to give a complete account of the workings of the human mind without reference to God or spirit-has crumbled. Modernity failed to achieve its ambition of a comprehensive, materialistic alternative to the religious understanding of the human condition. A purely secular view of human mental life has been

shown to fail not just at the theoretical, but also the practical, level. The last thing Freud would have predicted as the outcome of more than a half centuries' scientific psychological research and therapeutic experience was the rediscovery of the soul."[13]

In this sense, it is true that the overall "claim" to the metaphysical by the sciences is overwhelmingly small, and next to nothing. So new is the advancement of science, so immediate are reminders of how the scientific revolution is a fairly recent event (one which can be *accurately* described a phenomenon) that science can't fully describe the definition of the word 'knowledge', properly define a thought, or how they are conjured by the mind from the immaterial (a process referred to by the Chinese as "dragon veins"). However, this claim of ignorance from the scientific community does not validate religious arguments. Religious claims and explanation of the metaphysical still appear incredibly insignificant when considering even the smallest bit of confirmed information science has acquired regarding the metaphysical, and it appears only a matter of time when more evidence is revealed.

In another example of religious proponents taking advantage of gaps in science with regards to the metaphysical, religious authors Mario Beauregard and Denyse O'Leary criticize evolutionary biologist D.S. Wilson's argument that factual realism is the ideal arbiter of truth in their book, *The Spiritual Brain*. "The main difficulty with his thesis [this] is that mystics who found religions are in fact seeking factual realism. That is precisely their purpose. Based on their experiences, they tend to describe ultimate reality as suprarational, not as subrational." The authors also claim that science has no serious evidence which proves science is right and mystics are wrong.[14]

While the authors are correct that the search for factual realism is considered the purpose of a so-called mystic, it does not mean that the interpretation of the metaphysical by the mystic is correct by any means and in any area. It also doesn't mean that they can even claim to be correct. If this were so, would not every qualified mystic be correct? What exactly is the qualification to be considered a mystic anyway? The problem with claiming the unseen, or claiming it belongs to a religious system is -once again- due to the complete vacancy of religion. The religious notions concerning another realm not sensed comprise of forces that simply do not exist. There is no ethereal substance in the religious context, or even knowledge of what lies in this other realm. Not only does research on the immaterial present information not mentioned in traditional or even modernized views of religious scholarship, but provide a more stunning portrayal of the truth, as will be discussed later in this chapter.

This lack of substance in a religious-claimed metaphysical is what leads so many to turn from religion. It also has taken a toll on the practices of the religious worldwide, and there are countless studies on this topic. This is why physics professor Chet Raymo wrote of his personal discovery of science in his youth in *Commonweal*, "Science made no use of irreconcilable polarities. 'Matter' and 'spirit', 'body' and 'soul,' 'natural' and 'supernatural' denoted meaningless distinctions."[15] His awakening did not involve a meeting of a deity that one automatically knows and then serves. It did not consist of something that requires one to blindly guess, because that is what mystics do, regardless of what they claim is "revealed" to them from the metaphysical. Raymo's experience did not contain a conversion to what binds, but a freedom, an opening of consciousness.

This is also why Spinoza once wrote of how man interprets nature, "upbraiding reason as blind, because she cannot show a pure path to the shadows they pursue and rejecting human wisdom as vain; but believing the phantoms of imagination, dreams and other childish absurdities, to be the very oracles of Heaven." Unfortunately, many have this same religious influenced view of nature today. The general notions suggesting that by following Biblical messages one will somehow lead a different existence, or that changing to one of the thousands of Christianity's denominations, the believer will somehow lead a separate life and afterlife than those who do not is impossible to take seriously considering they all generally have nothing esoteric to show. If there is something concrete that religious proponents can present regarding personal experiences, why dance around what has yet to be proven in science? Why not just present that one piece of evidence that will prove religion? Not a claim of the personal, not a claim of faith, and not a claim of a designer too complex for scientific analysis.

Not just claims of the metaphysical, claims of places and beings in other realms have also been frequently made by the religious. So detailed are accounts of the metaphysical by religious proponents, that beings and places claimed to be in these realms also have had their own history and variations throughout time. More than just a general belief in the unseen, the religious subscribe to figures, places, and even lifestyle in the metaphysical with conviction, and it has been so for numerous generations. The guidance and messages from claimed angels and a holy spirit, as well as notions of an afterlife, heaven and hell are all promoted throughout religious communities in their limited splendor and will be briefly discussed here. It is important to keep in mind the influence that the notions in question have on the religious masses, as these claimed places and figures permeate even the modern religious vernacular. As we view the gods of Rome and the crystal mansions of Zeus and his court on Mount Olympus in ancient Greece with the same curiosity that our descendants a few thousand years from now will look on our religious cultures with, the beings and domains claimed today -as always with time- will see many road blocks that facts and reason will present in the coming years.

Although the number of beings claimed in the metaphysical by the religious is impressive, one notion that has managed to survive centuries of editing is that of angels. While there exists a plethora of versions concerning the concept of angels in different cultures, it is not uncommon for the religious to refer to angels in a general and vague description. One of the popular schools of thought on the idea of angels is that it began in Greco Roman times, human-like messengers from the heavens being the focal point of such notions. Since ancient Greece, we have seen the spread of meaning in referring to its descriptions. In his *Angels: A History*, David Albert Jones gives a fairly accurate description of what many religious today would perceive angels as. "We all know what they look like. They have wings and halos. They appear in children's nativity plays. They wear long white robes, apart from cherubs, who are like naked fat little children. They live in heaven on clouds but come to earth to guard or guide."[16] He also documents in the book how verses in Exodus, Isaiah, Samuel, Psalms and the Koran portray angels to be winged beings with halos.

Concepts of angels portray them as benevolent and wise entities, but they were not always perceived this way. Awe and fear permeated notions of them much more than today. Examples of this include Exodus 23:20 where an angel is sent by God to his people for the purpose of leading them to safety. God commands them, "Pay attention to him and obey all of his instruction. Do not rebel against him, or he will not forgive your sins. He is my representative - he bears my name." Job 33:22 describes angels of death in wait for misbehaving people. God dispatches a band of destroying angels in Psalms 78:49 and Jesus warns in Matthew 16:27 that he will, with God's angels, judge people, "according to their deeds." Yet in all the centuries of literature on angels – like other religious notions- the nature of them, or even a general concept remains vacant. This is the reason why the differing notions of angels are found in different times and cultures: no one can be held accountable for what is not sensed by humans in the first place. The claim cannot be disproved no matter how ludicrous it sounds.

As far as the nature of angels, we find a modern attempt at an explanation by Biblical scholar Stephen Binz in *Catholic Digest*:

> "Angels are pure spiritual beings created by God. Like human beings, they are relational creatures and they have minds and wills. This means that they can interact with other creatures, think, make choices, and love. But unlike human beings, they have no bodies. It is difficult for us to imagine creatures that are not part of the material world. We can't study them scientifically, as we can rocks and plants and whales. They are invisible, even with microscopes and telescopes. The only way we know of the reality of angels is that God has revealed their existence to us."[17]

Binz goes on to attempt to describe the apparent lifestyle of angels, which, it is claimed, can be revealed by God to the religious as well. "They were created immortal, so even though they had a beginning, they do not have an end. Because they do not have bodies, they do not have gender, nor do they participate in the sort of living that requires nutrition, growth, reproduction and sensation."[18] It would be interesting to see just how Binz is aware of all this. What school of thought is he subscribing to when summing up such notions? What field of the metaphysical exactly? How does he know that angels would not have a physical body? Is it the same school of thought that directly contradicts David Albert

Jones's physical description? Also, the claim of the personal cannot be made by religious proponents in the sense that angels are outside the realm of scientific discovery because the concept of religion being personal is hard enough to accept something so illogical for most scientists, much less the claim of mythic super beings *inside* that personal mythic realm. This vacancy reminds us that, if there is nothing in another realm that we have proved in religious terms to be sensed, what is to personalize aside from one's own subjective viewpoint?

The holy spirit is another claim of the metaphysical from the religious. Although the holy spirit is mentioned only three times in the OT, the NT is filled with the term, including various versions of its name such as "glorious Spirit of God". 2nd Century authorship would eventually include an emphasis on the notion that human souls are not naturally eternal,[19] but will obtain entrance and participation in God's eternity from the holy spirit. However, in the first two hundred years after Christ, as Clint Tibbs admits in *Catholic Biblical Quarterly*, "there was no clear statement of the theology of the Holy Spirit."[20]

The vague concept of holy spirit would continue throughout the years without a concrete notion of even what the holy spirit is, at least not one which could be agreed upon. This general concept of the holy spirit continues today, as it is referred to in earnest. But it is without description, as Francis Chan and Danae Yankoski happily admit to in *Forgotten God*. "Come Holy Spirit, come. We don't know exactly what that means and looks like for each of us yet, in the particular places You've called us to inhabit. But, nonetheless, whatever it means, we ask for your presense. Come, Holy Spirit, come."[21]

If it is through revelation that theology obtained descriptions of the holy spirit (starting about 1800 years ago) then we might as well not bother relying on theological writings for other explanations given the credibility of that field, but certain points on notions of the holy spirit are still worthy of noting. According to many believers, the claimed reality provided by the individual religion is discovered through faith, revelation and obeying religious law. The teaching is that the magic -the holiness- will enter the believer and become a part of their lives, affect others, and produce significant personal change if one believes in the creator. A holy spirit enters the person in Catholicization and is a part of a Triune of Christianity. The Jewish version of the holy spirit promotes a well-being among the believer, and Allah, according to Islamic tradition gave his followers sakina, or an inner peace.

Christian writings indicate the holy spirit as the essence -a trinity- of the divine. This trinity, Father, Son, Holy Ghost, enters the person based on his or her faith, repentance, and overall morality. According to the Holy Roman Church, the holy spirit fills priests, bishops and cardinals. We are told that the holy spirit will enter us if we were truly men and women of God. The problem is, how does one judge if a person is filled with the holy spirit? What makes someone holy, and what are the attributes of the person who has repented, accepted Christ and has a sizeable amount of faith in him as Lord? What exactly consists of a man of God in the Christian worldview? Were the masses of Church followers along with the church clergy all mistaken when judging the holy spirit of the gay clergy who were elected to positions of power in the Church? This is something that is not accepted in Catholic tradition. The broad term holy is something that should encompass more than generalities and vague descriptions. So far what we have been shown through scripture as well as theology has proved to be vacant. It is not just the vague idea of the holy spirit that is alarming, or how it supposedly influences humans (Christians might also want to be aware of the unforgiveable crime of insulting the holy spirit and the punishment that awaits them no matter how they repent according to Matthew 12:32), it is the requirement of faith encouraged to put into this unseen realm. Faith cancels out critical thought.

Another claim of the metaphysical by religious proponents, the notion of heaven, has been a popular one held by the masses and religious leaders alike. It also is misguided. In general, a promise of life after death to the world's suffering[22], the Greek translation of the word heaven appears in both Testaments. However, ominous signs of the same locality as verses elsewhere in the Bible concerning a different realm splatter the verses on heaven. According to Revelation, a physical description of heaven, is the equivalent to 225,000 miles squared and cube shaped depending on which apologist one asks. It is also not lit by the Sun but by the "glory of God" in Revelations 21:23. Revelations 22:1 explains a "river of the water of life" running down a street made of gold that is located the middle of Heaven. A tree of life on each side of the river bears fruit once a month and healing leaves for all nations.

The locality of such a description is typical of the times. Apologists tell us such verses are metaphorical for something different. They tell us that the verses are of the personal and faith-oriented, not to be taken literally. But the metaphorical meanings have yet to be discovered, missing anything resembling concrete descriptions, much less any agreed upon notions. If the metaphors are meant to indicate faith-based notions rather than literal ones, couldn't the Biblical authors have given us what the metaphors mean? Why was there a need to produce such long and trivial tales to represent metaphors for something different?

When it comes to Biblical interpretation concerning heaven, the locality in the promises of comfort or security to a fearful human race is abundant. According to Jonathan Aitkan, the message of Psalm 48 and the ensuing verses, which describe heaven as strong, secure and invincible is, as he puts it, "a theological way of saying that man's power on earth offers no security, whereas God's power in heaven gives total security."[23] This sounds comforting, but security from what? Suffering? Fear? In John 14:2 Jesus tells his disciples, "In my Father's house are many rooms. If it were not so, would I have told you that I go to prepare a place for you?" Why does this verse exist? What purpose could it possibly serve aside from the abstract? Also, this is a concrete description which does not necessarily invite metaphorical "interpretation". Even if this quote was meant to be a metaphor for something else, the idea that the teachings are meant to be perceived differently becomes exhausted at some point. Surely not all his teachings were meant as something other than what he said. How many positive verses are metaphors for something negatively perceived?

Religious author Nathan Eubanks writes in a piece for *Catholic Biblical Quarterly* of the Bible regularly promising treasures in heaven,[24] but he does not provide an ample expression or even suggest verses in the Bible that provide explanation and description beyond the material (He also quotes fellow religious author Gary A. Anderson's work in showing a switch in referencing deeds in terms of weight in the OT to finances by the NT). This guessing regarding the metaphysical continues without regulation or any governing body to give credibility to religious claims. Anyone who argues is deemed by religious philosophers as not educated enough in theological matters. Never mind the shallow and hedonistic viewpoint the notion of "treasure" has, enlightenment and becoming self-aware clearly giving way to financial security in Biblical verses.

Other examples of locality regarding physical descriptions of heaven are in Revelations. It is said to be a complex and impressive book entailing mysteries and epics, but includes verses like the description of the throne of God in heaven and the spring where those who suffered the hardships of the Great Tribulation are led by the "Lamb" to water that gives life ("And God will wipe away all their tears"). One can only wonder what the metaphorical interpretation of tears is by religious proponents to explain away the locality of the verse. Revelation also says that believers "will never again be hungry or thirsty, and they will be fully protected from the scorching noontime heat." (Revelations 7:16-17) Does this mean the Sun's rays cannot penetrate the protective shield of an invisible heaven? Can those in the metaphysical even feel the sensation of sunlight rays?

Jesus mentions the physical descriptions of heaven as well, but they are just as local, such as when discussing treasures in heaven in Matthew 6:19-21:

> "Don't store up treasures here on earth, where they can be eaten by moths and get rusty, and where thieves break in and steal. Store your treasures in heaven, where they will never become moth eaten and where they will be safe from thieves. Wherever your treasure is, there your heart is and thoughts will also be."

Hints of discouraging the materialistic in this lesson become problematic when he apparently leaves the happiness or "treasure" to be of the choice of the individual. What exactly is the practitioner supposed to seek? What type of treasure, happiness? Righteousness replacing happiness is not valid when interpreting the verse. Even if it were, that is vague and ridiculous, as if righteousness is something that just happens. There are no steps to guide the practitioner to what is being discussed, no path to wisdom. There is an indication that Jesus might not even have been aware of what to seek in personal fulfillment comprising of anything deeper than the shallow.

Although NT messages of atonement and forgiveness differ from the harsh treatment in OT scripture, the reader can also count on the same localized references of punishment in the NT such as the "weeping and gnashing of teeth" outside Heaven's gates according to Jesus while others "feast" with Abraham and others in Matthew 8:11-12. Even though he is claimed to have spoken in parables, the meaning of the parables about heaven were just as local. For instance, in Matthew 5:11-12 Jesus says, "Blessed are you when people insult you, persecute you and falsely say all kinds of evil against you because of me. Rejoice and be glad, because great is your reward in heaven, for in the same way they persecuted the prophets who were before you."

In this verse, the suffering of the ignorance of others is what allows for a greater reward in heaven, although it is not known what the reward is. The "riches" in heaven, which are constantly encouraged by Jesus rather than the material riches on Earth, are not expanded into something that would disassociate from the hedonistic, materialist worldview.

There is no transcending, no 'beyonding' as sociologist Robert Bellah put it. It would be interesting to see what type of wealth Jesus was talking about, and it would be interesting to see if that would be something beyond the mind-numbing pursuit of the monetary, and even something beyond the usual "faith" and "righteousness" claims in order to promote even deeper thinking. Yet, there is nothing. A stale reminder of a time before the advancement of modernity. The meanings are also contradictory. Is Jesus encouraging following the will of the Old Testament, or the New? If it is the will of the Old, then murder and stoning is called for in many everyday scenarios, if it is of the New, following the path of Jesus, then it contradicts his demand to follow his father's will.

These localized themes of heaven are prevalent and are found in the Koran as well as the Torah. Despite the nature of verses and meanings, there is no such confirmation of such claims of the religious. What can be learned today from the notion of an unseen realm described by people of ancient times, other than the fact that the scriptural authors clearly hadn't been introduced to something like existentialism? Finally, a new Earth and a new heaven occurs according to Revelation 21:1-3, but what exactly will be involved? Will there exist human servitude like the ancient Egyptian and older Christian teachings? What utterly trivial description would have been etched out in the Biblical verses had the authors delved deeper into the subject of a new heaven and Earth?

Notions of hell are less complicated and just as vacant as concepts of heaven, as old variations of the notion itself are becoming more distant in the collective consciousness due to its strict locality and the convenience of modern practitioners. Sheol, the original Hebrew word for the place where everyone enters after death, would be eventually translated into hell or "grave" in the King James version.[25] According to *Reuters*, the offshoot notion of limbo (Latin for border or edge) was, "considered by medieval theologians to be a state or place reserved for the unbaptized dead, including decent people who lived before the coming of Christ."[26] The notion of hell also appears prevalent in Christianity: as much as Jesus talked about heaven, he talked about hell more.

But questions regarding the validity of notions like hell surface when considering religious concepts of the metaphysical, especially considering the harsh punishment as well as an overall theme of locality in Biblical verses. Revelation 20:15 tells of all names recorded in a Book of Life based on their deeds, and whoever is not recorded in the book is "thrown in the lake of fire." The metaphorical rebuttal is often presented for such verses but can hardly be taken seriously. What is metaphorical about Numbers 16:33 where it reads, "So they went down alive into the grave with all of their belongings. The earth closed over them, and they all vanished."? In this verse, the possessions of the dead might represent something other than belongings, but what are they for metaphorically? Equally questionable in its metaphorical interpretation is a story that warns of hell told by Jesus in Luke 16:25-26:

> "There was a rich man who was dressed in purple and fine linen and lived in luxury every day. At his gate was laid a beggar named Lazarus, covered with sores and longing to eat what fell from the rich man's table...The time came when the beggar died and the angels carried him to Abrahams side. The rich man also died and was buried. In hell, where he was in torment, he looked up and saw Abraham far away, with Lazarus by his side. So he called to him, Father Abraham, have pity on me and send Lazarus to dip the tip of his finger in water and cool my tongue, because I am in agony in this fire."

What exactly is metaphorical about that? Even if it is metaphorical, why would there be an entire tale about the metaphor? Does every sentence of the story mean something other than what was spoken? The argument that one day these metaphors will be deciphered based on a faith-inspired interpretation is one that has been made for some time now, yet here society is without any real depth interpreted from verses written by near-savages about basic daily life.

The locality concerning hell is on special display in 2 Peter 2:4: "For if God did not spare angels when they sinned, but sent them to hell, putting them into gloomy dungeons to be held for judgment..." In Matthew 5:22, calling someone a "fool" or being angry with someone lands them in hell. James 3:6 states, "The tongue also is a fire, a world of evil among the parts of the body. It corrupts the whole person, sets the whole course of his life on fire, and it itself set on fire by hell." Since many including Pope John Paul II argued that hell was a state of existence rather than literal, why would so much physical agony be described with repeated references to fire? If this were all metaphorical, why would Jesus use those words, why didn't he just describe the correctly perceived state of existence? If this is a metaphor for a fear-based lesson in misbehaving, why all the nonsense about fire? Is fear of physical burning the best analogy he could come up with in his lessons?

Regardless, theologians and others are still unsure of any concrete description of hell. This is why the Catholic church ruled against the idea of limbo recently, and, according to *Catholic News Service*, the notion no longer plays a role in contemporary Catholic theological thinking (even though it also asserted in the same release that their conclusion, "should not be interpreted as questioning original sin or 'used to negate the necessity of baptism or delay the conferral of the sacrament'.")[27] It is also why popular evangelist Billy Graham in *Time* publicly pulled back from notions of hell when he claimed, "When it comes to literal fire I don't preach it because I'm not sure about it. When the Scripture uses fire concerning Hell that is possibly an illustration of how terrible it's going to be -not fire but something worse, a thirst for God that cannot be quenched."[28] Smart move. That "something" he refers to has eluded religious scholarship for countless centuries now.

Claims by the religious have been made for some time now that their religious relationship, what they subscribe to, exists in the metaphysical, something they claim science can't prove. They often claim that their respective religion has answers for this world from another realm, another plane of existence. Studies show that this is not true, however, and certain studies conducted on near death experiences, specifically on deathbed visions (DBV), reveal a contrast to the religious view of the afterlife and metaphysical notions. As with all subjects which prove traditional Church interpretations of existence wrong, the facts are stranger and more wonderful regarding DBV than with traditional religious metaphysical claims. Although the study and discovery of what DBVs entail are not many, there already exists more evidence of the phenomena than what is claimed to exist outside the material in all three major religions.

Throughout history, humans have recorded in tales and accounts visions by those near death. Patients who are in-and-out of consciousness and about to take their last breath are witnessed by physicians and nurses to change noticeably. For a moment, a joyful expression, a peaceful state and painless movement are recalled. In a flash, that moment is gone, the patient continues into coma or previous state. This phenomenon has been told time and again by doctors, nurses and others beside those near-death. It generated enough inquiry for the first scientific analysis on the subject in 1926 by physics professor Sir William Barrett. Barrett wrote in his book, *Death Bed Visions* regarding the occurrences and what separates them from other phenomena:

> "It is well known that there are many remarkable instances where a dying person, shortly before his or her transition from the earth, appears to see and recognize some deceased relatives or friends. We must, however, remember the fact that [hallucinations] of the dying are not very infrequent. Nevertheless, there are instances where the dying person was *unaware* (emphasis in original) of the previous death of the spirit form he sees and is therefore astonished to find in the vision of his or her deceased relative one whom the percipient believes to be still on earth."[29]

Barrett's work provided a starting point from which to continue serious case studies on the subject. Interest in the phenomena increased, and in 1961, Dr. Karlis Osis released his book, *Deathbed Observations by Physicians and Nurses*, a case study consisting of testimony from hundreds of nurses and doctors witnessing some 35,000 near-death patients. Testimony also indicated a pattern of deceased family members and loved ones, beings of light, and experiences of a calm and painless state. Dr. Osis released another book in 1971 from a 14-year study on death bed visions called *At the Hour of Death* with a co-author. According to an interview he gave to Dr. John White, "The experiences of the dying are basically the same, regardless of culture, education, sex or belief system, and their experiences cluster around something that makes sense in terms of survival after death, and a social structure to that afterlife." Of his analysis of the patients, he cited mood elevation in those who were not under the influence of medication or sedation. These patients did not lack oxygen being sent to their brains. It also didn't matter what their illness was. The claims were peaceful passing of patients, "a strange contrast to the usual gloom and misery commonly expected before expiration."[30]

Describing the typical experience of a DBV, Dr. Osis explains in more detail what one might witness:

> "These visions were of two kinds; one was where they would see a person or a religious apparition – a hallucination that no one else could see. An invisible visitor would come into the hospital and the patient would talk with it. Usually it was a close relative or friend, but it might also be a religious figure such as Jesus or Krishna...The other kind of visionary experience was where the patient saw surroundings as if it were another place, another reality. You could call these scenes non-human nature. In almost every case, whether it was a figure or a landscape, the visions were of a positive sort. The hell-and-brimstone sort of place simply didn't appear."[31]

Since these initial books covering DBV, many more have been released with similar experiences reported to hundreds of doctors and nurses.

Near death experiences appear universal. One example is, according to Dr. Raymond Moody, those who are near death sometimes experience the same phenomena as others who are near death, giving further credence that the phenomena is not due to illusion presented by a medically dying brain. As far as any religious influence during a DBV, Douglas Fox notes in *New Scientist*, "The identity of the person seems to depend on your religion. Christians, for example, often meet Jesus or a dead relative while Hindus may see Yamraj, god of the dead."[32] Other near-death experience case studies corroborate these differing accounts taking place. This indicates one's perception of their respective religion. Since religion promotes hope and comfort, it would make sense that the individual would experience something akin to his or her religious beliefs regardless of the religion's validity or exclusivity. Another example of the universality of DBVs is the common experiences of a euphoric state, but a culturally different perception of the experience. A team of Australian researchers report, for example, that Chinese near death experiences are dominated by feelings of bodily estrangement without a sense of peace, and that the Japanese see caves rather than tunnels.[33]

We have a couple of problems here with regard to religious contentions and the metaphysical. Concerning religious exclusivism, people of religious faith are seeing religious figures of their own religion. The fact that an Indian woman will in most cases see a Hindu entity contradicts Christian doctrines prohibiting false idol worship. Also, the Bible, Talmud and Koran do not once indicate that we see deceased relatives and deceased loved ones during near-death visions. This seems like an especially important notion left out from scripture, considering there is a real chance that we are being observed on realms not perceivable by us and what that may mean.

To give an example of the nature of DBVs and how religious concepts of the subject do not relate to them, British neuro-psychiatrist Peter Fenwick's *Truth in The Light* includes testimony that he took from a witness concerning a patient's DVB. It involves the personal, but in a more surreal, if not dazzling form, one that the Biblical scriptures cannot compare to in detail of wonder and strangeness. In it, the witness describes the remaining seconds of his brother's life before passing away beside him:

> "My brother was in hospital dying from emphysema. His breathing was very laboured, when all of a sudden he stopped and his breathing suddenly appeared normal. He looked at about 45 degrees upwards and smiled broadly, as if at something or someone: he turned to me and died suddenly in my arms. I am positive to this day that he wanted to tell me what he had seen. Those few seconds before he died will live with me forever, it was so powerful."[34]

This testimony from a witness describes an experience that can be verified to validate the claim to the point of scientists recognizing patterns directly associated with the phenomena. This is a process which has come to countless people for ages, and simply does not exist in the Bible. This is odd, considering how many other detailed featurettes are included in religious metaphysical claims. It isn't as if the concept of DBVs were not simple enough to interpret.

Before modern times, we could only imagine what the real afterlife was like. The question of one has been debated, particularly concerning religion. Until studies conducted on the subject, humans could only guess what occurs. Now we have a reference point. The cases are documented, universal, and analyzed by doctors and scientists. In contrast, the Bible doesn't even mention DBVs, at least not in the literal sense. We can make a metaphorical claim that some DBVs are in the Bible, but let's be realistic. There is nothing whatsoever in the Bible that coincides with DBVs.

Religious proponents aren't entirely unaware of phenomena like DBV. Books involving the experiences have come out recently. Books with titles such as Mary Neals's *To Heaven and Back: A Doctor's Extraordinary Account of Her Death, Heaven, Angels, and Life Again* by the Christian book distributor Waterbrook Press, *Heaven Is for Real: A Little Boy's Astounding Story of His Trip to Heaven and Back,* told by a man named Todd Burpo and released by Christian book distributor Thomas Nelson, and Pastor Don Piper's book *90 Minutes in Heaven*, published by the Christian book distributor Revell are all examples of Christian authors' most recent attempt at hitching a ride on to modern scientific discovery.

Assertions on DBV made by religious proponents do not matter. Theists are not credible, and -without surprise- take liberties in their assertions on DBV in their work. For example, the reason author Mark Galli in *Christianity Today* uses the phrase "near Heaven experience" throughout the article in describing the event rather than calling it near death? The rise of near-death books written by orthodox Christians. As if this were a legitimate reason to do so. With this type of reasoning, should it matter that a word used to demean women is used in hip hop culture, and therefor is validated due to so much use of that word in popular culture?

It most likely won't matter that the distributor of *Heaven Is for Real* which sold 8 million copies pulled the book after its subject admitted to lying about the whole thing: theologians will likely claim that the "essence" of the meaning is what is important, and the show will go on. That is the sad part with remarkable subjects like this. It doesn't even matter that the author of the book Burpo didn't know that a child was lying to him the entire time: the reality is that people wouldn't have been able to disprove it if he did know the boy was lying.

Whether it is claiming a force or entities of another realm, proponents of the three major Abrahamic religions not only assume to know what resides in the metaphysical, but that the unseen somehow hosts the nocturnal breath of life from *their* religion's doctrines. Unfortunately, notions from the religious discussed in this chapter are what many around the globe believe in regardless of credibility. As we can see, even in different interpretations, metaphysical claims by the religious come across as stale and of the same trivial ilk as other Biblical or religious meanings. This is found in every aspect when dissecting religious claims. Literally in every assertion, the results are the same: interesting sounding claim, zero validity. The explanations of the metaphysical afterlife in religion even have the same tone as the explanations of daily life occurrences of the physical world in religion, complete with similar themes of mistreatment, judgment, punishment and a physically relaxed and luxurious afterlife.

One of the strengths in claiming something in the metaphysical is that the claim cannot be sensed in the material, so it cannot be disproved in the material. This is the basis for many claims regarding the unseen, and anyone can make that claim. Anyone can claim whatever they want in the metaphysical, and it cannot be disproved because it cannot be so easily sensed by any material instrument. But, if the religious assert claims like the god of the gaps argument, why also subscribe to the same school of thought that includes angels, demons and a physical description of heaven? One cannot subscribe to this school of thought and be taken seriously outside of their own circle, in this case, theism. Either one can choose the complex and multi-layered modern theories attempting to validate religion, or they subscribe to the local and near illiterate world (and outer world) viewpoint of Biblical authorship. One of the choices almost has one fooled, and the other is easily categorized in the same section as every other religion because of the absurdities involved.

In many ways, religious teachings concerning the metaphysical have created an impregnable and impressive dome of ignorance throughout the masses generationally. Even though religious doctrines differ from one another, the notions are still deeply held by the modern practitioner, blinding them to the reality that there is something else out there that religion does not and cannot explain adequately. The very least that Christianity can provide with its mystical claims is one metaphysical prophecy or observation that doesn't have to do with local tones or the nonsensical, something that speaks to us. But it cannot provide that.

There is nothing in Christianity like the beliefs of the Hopi and Suni, for example, who claimed civilization has been destroyed three times over, or that those two tribes, along with the Pueblo believe that greed is the ultimate reason each time, that "greed destroys worlds".[35] These beliefs tell us something based on human behavior, indicate a deeper message about ourselves that we can relate to as real problems to identify, rather than the vague "sin" referred to so many times in scripture, or Satan, demons and a trinity which absolutely zero people can relate to on a human level because of their inhuman notions and detachments from humanity.

Rabbi David Wolpe said once in a debate, "it is not scientific to believe there is something eternal inside of us", but shouldn't there be some responsibility, an urge to truthfully discover what that something is instead of merely succumbing to unverifiable rules and tales? Clearly there is little known outside of invalidated claims regarding the metaphysical, but relying on this unseen realm for guidance in life without evidence is limiting to the otherwise larger potential of human ingenuity. Thought-policing notions like these limit one to perceive a truer spectrum of human life and ultimately consciousness. The religious claim figures like Shakespeare and Dante and Homer among the great authors whose works were inspired by religious notions of the metaphysical. Imagine what their works could have been had death bed visions been in the mainstream consciousness in their times. Imagine what they could say about humanity if their writings didn't involve disproved myths.

This general notion so many religious hold of a metaphysical based on their loose and vague religious concepts is a problem. Did the world need the recent ruling by the Catholic Church to oust the notion of limbo forever as a place where unbaptized children are sent upon death due to an "unduly restrictive view of salvation"[36] to think that it was not true? Why is it not true now, because the historically wrong Church admits to it finally? Why would it be restrictive now? It is assumed Augustine knew limbo was false the whole time he was writing about it.

Research and breakthroughs on the metaphysical will continue. Cognitive research alone relating to the metaphysical is due for tremendous discoveries. In a lecture, neuroscientist Vilayanur S Ramachandran once proclaimed as much when he wrote, "We are poised for the greatest revolution of all: understanding the human brain. This will surely be a turning point in the history of the human species."[37] Then president Barack Obama unveiled "a 10-year, $3bn "brain activity map project", billed as the neuroscience equivalent of the human genome project."[38] and recently scientists have made a breakthrough in mental telepathy.[39] This shows that one-day science will discover what is currently unknown in brain activity and will continue to shed light on many related subjects in an unseen reality. On the other hand, the views of this realm by religious proponents are littered with texts and 'translations' that prove time and time again to be at best false and at worst a stifling paradigm through which we limit potential.

Chapter Three

Limitations

The first verses of the book of Genesis read as follows, "In the beginning God created the heavens and the earth. The earth was empty, a formless mass cloaked in darkness. And the spirit of God was hovering over its surface. Then God said, 'let there be light.'" This is how one of the most revered, highest selling books of all time describes the creation of our solar system's Sun and home planet. And while this passage from the *New Living Translation* might be said to contain metaphors and different translations other than the real meanings of what was intended, it is important to note that this version is the end result of 90 evangelical scholars working for seven years to revise its predecessor, *Living Translation*, the popular and lay friendly version considered outdated.

The limited messages and understanding in the scriptures along with the lessons in the three monotheist religions are only too noticeable to ignore as the influence of such authorship stumps growth. As encompassing as the scriptures, Catholic doctrines and Western theology are, there also lies a harsh reality that the focus of these works is of thin air, thought of long ago and not by the most imaginative of men. The limitations of religious works like the Bible prove only too obvious, especially today, as do the inadequate guidance from centuries of promoting such insufficient information on reality.

The fact that we live in a world that permits something like religion -an institution that governs more of our lives than we may know- is unsettling. The scriptures (and teachings inspired by them) are without necessary information needed in life for growth and progression. A look at the empty and local nature of the scriptures continues in this chapter. One of the reasons why atheists keep bringing up the fact that religion is a man-made myth, it is difficult to maintain the credibility of something that has aged as poorly as the Bible. The shallow and materialistic perceptive view of daily life in the Bible is obvious, promoting not much when it comes to real help in today's society (or their own society then). As well-meaning as Biblical lessons and messages are, they represent something encapsulated in a time long ago, forcing the most ardent of followers to shrug their shoulders when it comes to actual advice given in scripture concerning daily life.

Other verses attempting to provide explanation of creation fall similarly flat the moment logic is considered. Regarding the physical dynamics of Earth in relation to space alone, I Chronicles 16:30 reads, "The world also is firmly established, it shall not be moved", Psalm 93:1 states, "Surely the world is established, so that it cannot be moved." Psalm 96:10 states, "Yea, the world is established, it shall not be moved..." and Psalm 104:5 reads, "the Lord set the earth on its foundations: it can never be moved." Regarding the explanations for the image of a rising and setting Sun, King James Bible includes the following from Ecclesiastes 1:5: "The sun also ariseth, and the sun goeth down, and hasteth to his place where he arose."

The Sun and moon are ordered to stand still in Joshua 10:12:13. Revelation 7:1 mentions "four corners of the earth" as does Isaiah, the description even being depicted in different artistic forms through the centuries including ones with angels guarding each corner. It can be said that they all were metaphors for something else, but if this is the case, then why did the Holy Roman Church viciously punish anyone who did not agree with certain explanations? What a surprise that those in the Church were not aware that the Earth is actually hurling through space at about 18 miles per second, and that the Sun actually doesn't move at all in relation to Earth's orbit at all.

Apologists may quote Isiah 40:22 -which calls the earth spherical in defense- but why then do the verses claiming such limited physical characteristics in the text exist at all? What stupid metaphor do those verses represent? Even suggestions of a flat earth are assumed in creating the imagery of other backdrops: verses like Daniel 4:10-11, which describes a great tree arising from the earth's center, visible until the earth's "farthest bounds", or Matthew 4:8 which states, "Once again, the devil took [Jesus] to a very high mountain and showed him all the kingdoms of the world in their glory." This verse suggests that somehow by the height of a mountain that the whole view of earth's surface containing every global kingdom would be visible.

Again, even if it was not the intention of the authors for us to interpret this verse as a literal meaning of a flat earth, why would they even imply something as trivial as that? Why not just write about the spherical earth, and involve that description as a backdrop or context for other verses? This also suggests that, not only were the Biblical authors not aware of science yet, but they weren't even aware of the basics concerning the world, even referencing these trivial and false notions when regarding other notions of the same local tone. Apologists may try to protect the Bible, and may claim whatever they want regarding the literal meaning of scripture, but these are verses which cannot be ignored, cannot be passed off and be free from mainstream consciousness like theologians would prefer.

This is what is meant by shortcomings regarding scripture. If these are not the real meanings of the verses, why doesn't the Bible simply indicate that earth does spin, or that the Sun is the equivalent to 865,000 miles wide, or the equivalent to 110 times wider than the earth? What were all those verses about the physical solar system for? Religious proponents claim that the Bible's intended purpose was not a science class and rather an introduction to God, but couldn't it have displayed some knowledge beyond what anyone in the Bronze Age could come up with?

The Great Pyramids were made before the OT and baffle scientists to this day. No mention of Venus's atmosphere, or that the light at night is not current star light, but actually shone ages ago, or that we won't see something akin to a hypernova until it actually hits us. Even the description of physical objects like our Sun or its inner dynamics is unsophisticated, further leading one to believe that if the authors really were aware of these correct explanations and remained silent about them, they certainly weren't suggestive of that in the referencing of the objects explained in other verses for imagery or overall tone.

Aren't objects used in the Bible to describe even deities? Doesn't a bull calf represent God among many in highly religious times? Religious author Tim Callahan admits so much in his book, *Secret Origins of the Bible*: "That Yah was not only represented as a bull calf but that the god was not solely the god of Israel is attested to a number of ancient artifacts and records."[1] Yet the fact that so much time is spent on something as trivial as a bull representation is curious considering time could have been spent warning of cancer, having been discovered in humans as far back as 3200 years ago. What could something like a bull calf possibly represent in any real-life help for people who need answers?

Religious proponents may downplay the priority for the well-being of humans in scripture to avoid criticism of the verses, but there are clearly passages promising the destruction of enemies and "riches" for obeying God's law. Doesn't Jesus mention money more than any other subject in the NT? Are these superficial and materialistic pleasures merely hung in the face of humans as a tool by a god in this Christian view of reality? *That* is the paradigm of thought the Biblical god wants us to view our lives through? Although there might be theologians who question the interpretation of the Bible in this chapter, they would do well to consider that the examples presented here are examples ministers use in front of their congregation on a weekly basis and are even emphasized by prosperity preachers like Joseph Prince and Joel Osteen. They are also notions which the religious masses live by and draw hope as well as comfort from via their perceptive views on life.

Hydrologist Vit Klemes in a letter to *Physics Today* encapsulated what many skeptics feel with regard to the lessons presented by the scriptures when he wrote, "Altogether, I can't believe these special stories that have been made up about our relationship to the universe at large because they seem to me too simple, too connected, too local, too provincial."[2] The simplicity of the Biblical lessons is the problem here. It is this disconnect regarding personal meaning, this vacant nature of scriptural doctrine that is felt universally regardless of what is claimed or believed about the verses. It is with this notion in mind that we look at the examples below.

It isn't as if theologians have not had time to analyze scripture. Of the thirty thousand Bible verses, little is to be said of them above the near illiterate level after all these centuries. This is not surprising, as theologians themselves admit to not being able to interpret scripture beyond such a remedial level. Modern examples of this known fact include theologian Phillip Moller in *Theological Studies*: "We could hardly maintain that theological interest among Catholics today is focused upon the problem of the inspiration of the Scriptures. To be honest, we must admit that the average Catholic exegete, while not denying or questioning the inspiration of the Bible, simply leaves it aside in his exegetical work; he seems unable to make it relevant to his own labors."[3] Theologian Douglas E. Christie admitted the subtler contention:

> "There is something beautiful and moving in this account of our capacity and obligation to learn how to see 'reality.' And it strikes me as being analogous to the sensibility that we often find so compelling in the spiritual texts and traditions that occupy the center of our work and in the scholarship that seeks to elucidate their meaning and significance."[4]

Theologian Alvin Plantinga admits that the messages such as those in *Genesis* are ultimately "unclear" and have been for hundreds of years, and Robin Young admits in *Commonweal*, "to call forth a fuller sense of the mysteries of the church and its sacred writings have also thus far failed."[5] Not only does this tell us that theologians are not any closer to discovering a deeper truth to Biblical verses, but what should provide inspiration and a guide to life instead appears as not more than writings and lessons which require a suspension of disbelief and a dismissal of basic facts. The sad part about such admitted failures of interpretation is that they come about 2000 years after the death of Christ, claimed divine messages which should have likely been discovered by now.

It is no surprise theologians have difficulty in interpreting scripture given the process that finalized the Bible. 2nd century theologians literally made up the teachings from apostle letters and writings which were converted to parts of the NT,[6] apparently taking a long time for religious scholarship to even begin the practice of actual "Christianity". Even different forms of teaching Christianity that included a separation from the Judaic texts like the Torah were introduced, although rejected. The current form of Christianity was clearly not recognizable yet, as Roman teacher Justin and other Christian teachers were accused of "kisses of peace" with women in dark rooms at night, and cannibalism in a ritualistic consuming of the "body and blood" of Christ. The latter is something unthinkable with modern Christians, but evident in Christians of an incomplete religion where the separation of OT absurdities had not yet occurred.

The vacancies are obviously the reason for the uncertainty of interpretation. What occurs is a universe of subjective interpretations and offshoot delusions due to this vacancy: no one can dispute what cannot be seen. It is why anyone can assert anything into ancient Bible verses, as there is no way to disprove the claim. People can insert possibilities no matter how remote. People like Marshall Shelley can say that Bible verses do not exclude possibilities of dinosaurs[7] because of this vacancy, but despite the likelihood that such a statement on dinosaurs also might have gotten him killed if his quote were published in the Middle Ages, this can be said of many documents. The work of Nostradamus is filled with what could be taken as prophesy if "interpreted" a certain way.

Theo Hobson's account that a supreme being "detaches from state power and rejects theocracy" can be claimed,[8] but if the authors purposely left out such important material, ignoring these sociological and economic aspects was an unwise move, as the awareness level of such dire importance regarding those subjects is embarrassingly self-evident throughout global societies, ignorance from such a subject rendering civilization vulnerable to any event capable of destroying it. Events like a nuclear holocaust or irreparable damage to our environment which are set to occur globally because of human carelessness is the consequence for such vacancy. It is a shame the authors of the Bible chose to stay away from real subjects like state power and theocracy, because it could possibly have saved countless lives and civilization as we know it. What infant-like tale is more important to address in the Bible than those two subjects? What psalm praising a deity for the brutal punishment of an enemy was too important for the authors of the Bible to elbow out the subject of state power from the texts?

Writing of the staleness of Biblical verses, John Hopkins University Professor of NT Greek Gary Wills asserted regarding how people should interpret the gospel of Mark. "Mark's Gospel was written in, with, and for a particular community. It has references that would be meaningless outside a local context- references not picked up by either Matthew or Luke when they are using material from Mark."[9] If the Bible is claimed to be the perfect word of God, why the local context? Why insert something meant for only the readers of that time unless the authors were clueless of existence outside of that context? At some point the question of whether those local tales were purposely intended by authorship for a divinely wise and incomprehensible reason gets tiresome.

Plagiarism can also be added to the list of criticism regarding the scriptures throughout the centuries. As if theologians do not have enough to answer for in religious texts, the plagiarism found in the Bible is an important aspect, as it shows another chink in the armor of religious validity. For one thing, the number of similar stories preceding Christ's own is numerous, as other figures died and rose from the dead long before Jesus, and most scholars agree that the four gospels were not even written by the disciples. One of the most glaring examples of plagiarism, however, is the OT Adam, Eve and Noah in Genesis taken from the Assyrian/Babylonian poem *Epic of Gilgamesh*. According to researchers Elizabeth and Paul Barber, distillation is what happens when the story of Noah contains fewer characters than the Gilgamesh tale. "Stories with more characters typically have stayed in the oral pipeline a shorter time than stories with fewer characters, which have been distilled down to essentials."[10,11]

If a student were to turn in a college paper with the amount of ideas taken from previous course papers, especially word-for-word, that student would likely be either suspended or flunk the course. No such accountability is laid on Biblical literature in religious institutions. Christian apologists would argue that the Bible was written in different times with a different vernacular, and the 'borrowing of stories' from other texts are to move the story along. This is an acceptable counter if this was merely a question of originality, but it is not. It is a matter of questioning the vacancy of a paradigm that insists it knows about existence, how we should live, and what we should think. It is a matter of everything that is claimed by religion. If the Bible is not original, why accept its word when it comes to subjects it gives advice on?

It is understandable why theologians want to shade this aspect of religious scripture. The reality, however, is that the claim of plagiarism, like other claims of Biblical fallacies is real, and it is legitimate. Although the masses ignore this fact now, plagiarism is yet another indication that the scriptures do not represent "truth" in any deep sense of the word. Expecting us to accept something and take it to heart when it is not even real, when it is not original, is to ask us to believe in a lie. There is so much literature documenting the plagiarism in the Bible that anyone who takes the time to research for about five minutes can find some. Whether or not they want to accept it is up to them.

As vague and trivial as the Biblical texts appear, the overall tone suggests nothing different. The tone, consisting of thematic style and cultural context, represents a deeper look at Biblical verses containing locality with verses that are physical settings and backdrops along with cultural settings. References of material objects and desires and even states of mind reflect this similar tone in the cultural context of both testaments, as the mindset is of a shallow, materialistic one. Even in these verses, there are no hints at what might later be discovered and verified, no thematic settings or undertones or subtext-based assertions in any of the books to suggest even an awareness outside of their own little world. This obvious combination of the almost illiterate view of existence along with the same explanation of reality and ultimate reality provides us with scriptures which may as well be accompanied by a giant arrow in history that points directly to the time and place of the writings.

Just one example, glaring in its local tone, is literature of the Bible. The overall writing of the Biblical tales seems harsh, flat and in a dictatorial theme. This rather unpleasant introduction by a supreme being is clearly disengaging literature, fear-based in nature, and not exactly Hemingway in composition, with such words as "good" to describe events or states of being. Although apologetics might add that these words or references have been changed throughout the millennia, if the meanings of words or verses are changed, won't this also change any intended literary flow, style, theme, and tone of the story? If some poetic narrative existed, wouldn't an echo of some concern for such an important feature exist as well? If the tales of the Bible were the absolute word of God and admired as such, change was not necessary of words, verses or interpretation. Won't metaphors be changed as well if the words change, or is that not the case in theology?

If any doubt is held concerning the locality of such Biblical tone, the book of Psalms will compensate. Despite what advanced, above mere mortal meanings and goals are claimed by theologians concerning the Bible, the songs paint a stunning picture of exactly the same tone and meanings as other verses. For instance, this is what Psalm 137 reads as far as Babylon and Jerusalem,

"By the rivers of Babylon we sat down and wept
As we remembered Zion.
On the willows trees there,
we hung up our lyres
for there those who had carried us captive
asked us to sing them a song,
our captors called on us to be joyful;
'Sing us one of the songs of Zion.'

"How could we sing the Lords song
in a foreign land?
If I forget you, Jerusalem,
may my right hand wither away;
let my tongue cling to the roof of my mouth
If I do not remember you,
If I do not see Jerusalem above my chief joy.

"Remember, Lord, against the Edomites

the day when Jerusalem fell,
how they shouted, Down with it, down with it,
down to its very foundations!'

"Babylon, Babylon the destroyer,
happy is he who repays you
for what you did to us!
Happy is he who seizes your babes
and dashes them against a rock."[12]

Presenting the same exact mindset as other verses, Psalms speaks of a perceptive worldview that has long ago been forgotten. If other sections of the Bible are to be revered in their claimed incomprehensible form, why does the literature of Psalms indicate the same exact material world and the same promises of vengeance? This overall tone of the shallow shows the authors of these verses might not have even been aware of an existence outside theirs. The truth is that, not even a hint of depth is to be found among all three major religious scriptures, with locality consistent throughout the NT, the Torah and the Koran. Even the definition of a supreme being by authors of the Bible as well as that of modern theologians are of the same ignorant worldview. Why a supreme being wants the total adulation of people who are to be considered beneath and separate from him stemming from some need or insecurity appears just as local as the other notions on him, yet we are to believe this Iron Age deity is complex beyond comprehension?

Metaphors are often claimed by religious proponents, and a couple of examples will be presented in this chapter section. As many may know, these proponents have been known to claim that many of the questionable Bible verses under so much criticism from atheists are metaphorical and are not to be taken literally. *Christianity Today* Vice President Marshall Shelley, for instance, once indicated that as human beings, we were incapable of understanding Biblical texts. This and other notions like it have been asserted on behalf of the idea that the writings suggest a "complexity" which makes human understanding impossible. Speaking of this, Shelley once stated to the periodical *Ignite Your Faith*, "we can't as humans fully understand it". He goes on to say that if the Bible is understood *correctly*, we will figure out what was "meant".[13] Minister John Buehrens also writes of this proposed notion from the religious that verses are to be taken metaphorically in his book, *Understanding the Bible*:

> "Human experiences within history demand metaphors that transcend that history in order to interpret what we have experienced. In the Biblical tradition, God is, at the very least, the ultimate such metaphor. We may be complete agnostics about God and skeptics about the natural historicity of events like the exodus from Egypt or the resurrection of Jesus. These two may partake in metaphor. But to

understand the Bible requires that we try to understand, at the very least, what it is in human experience that brought forth such transcendent metaphors as creation, liberation and resurrection."[14]

Although Buehrens' conviction is to be admired, this, along with all other notions about metaphorical meaning is false and, here is why. Metaphors do exist in the Bible, and there are quotable verses regarding which can be perceived as such. One is in Matthew 7:15-20 where Jesus said:

> "Beware of false prophets who come disguised as harmless sheep but are really wolves that will tear you apart. You can detect them by the way they act, just as you can identify a tree by its fruit. You don't pick grapes from thorn bushes, or figs from thistles. A healthy tree produces good fruit, and an unhealthy tree produces bad fruit. So every tree that does not produce good fruit is chopped down and thrown into the fire[.] Yes, the way to identify a tree or a person is by the kind of fruit that is produced."

Forgetting the ridiculous threat of fire for schemers, this can be considered a metaphor. However, there are many claimed metaphors that are questionable. The following from Psalm 92:10 is an example. "But you have made me strong as a wild bull. How refreshed I am by your power! With my own eyes I have seen the downfall of my enemies: with my own ears I have heard the defeat of my wicked opponents. But the godly will flourish like palm trees and grow strong like the cedars of Lebanon." Taking away the obvious metaphor of the godly growing like Lebanon, the beginning is not a metaphor. it is local and trivial praise for the destruction of "enemies".

What is incomprehensibly metaphorical about God crushing the enemies of Israel? Is the local treatment of women and animals not considered metaphorical as well? If questionable verses are metaphorical for something else, what is the metaphor? No one knows, or no one has an agreed upon opinion. On the other hand, scientists have agreed for some time now on certain scientific formulas. These metaphors cannot *all* stand for faith and recycled social skills taught in the OT, the abandoned word by many Christians and theologians, can they? In the very least, the metaphors can resemble something helpful regarding humanity and real life, something beyond the same tired tones of the Bible.

Not that it matters anyway regarding the contradictions of verses. It seems theology will no doubt take it upon itself to change the meaning of these verses to something more plausible in the future anyway. That other Bible versions and the more modern *New Living Translation* differ already in meaning to this generation concerning verses shows this. For instance, *New Living Translation* changes words which suggest an immoveable Earth, rearranging the word "moved" to "shaken" in all but one of the verses that originally includes "moved". Another translation supporting more scientifically compatible verses occurs in Ecclesiastes1:5 which states, "And the sun rises and sets and returns to its place." *New Living Translation* version reads, "The sun rises and sets and hurries around to rise again." These convenient changes in script to support a more scientifically plausible explanation of existence will only continue, as there will be an increase in the case against religion with more scientific discovery.

Apologists also claim that translations through the years have tainted the essence or meaning from the scriptures, that the translations have been compromised. But haven't humans told for centuries in oral fashion the epic stories of Homer with an aesthetic that surpasses literature like the Bible? If Homer's *the Iliad* and *the Odyssey* were passed on to generations orally while not affecting the literary flow, the effectiveness of the teachings Jesus gave should not have been compromised in the way religious proponents claim, and it is highly doubtful that people held on to Homer's tales at heart the way people respond to the Bible. Even the orally translated Koran displayed the essence of Muhammad's experience,[15] no matter what critics say about the document. In fact, so accurate is the oral tradition of transferring information, the Greco Roman era banned all texts in all classes of society with the exemption of skilled trade to avoid flawed translations, and William Schniedewind noted the influential Roman physician and philosopher Galen's disdain even for "those who —according to the proverb- try to navigate out of books."[16]

The religious Vedas were also verbally passed to students by teachers for many years, and when an alphabet was finally introduced, strong opposition met the written text form.[17] If God and Jesus were aware of this flaw in written translation, why leave the divine messages to those who will not understand, why not just command oral translations? If the lengthy verses were difficult to memorize, were the long tales and metaphors in each book that important to detail? Why not just give direct instructions or show a more enlightening path with the verses given? Also, scientists have to go through so much tedious time to make their discoveries. Shouldn't the discovery be a little more instruction-based to at least the point where the direction can be fully grasped of where to go? Why bother giving us a goal with a directionless path to get there?

Why did Jesus not write what would be the most famous books of the NT? Wasn't he a teacher? He had about 30 years before he started teaching to do so, and it would have likely prevented countless murders and genocides. These vague texts could have been directly written by him, and the confusion and deaths throughout the millennia -which he must have known would occur as a result if he was all knowing- could also have been avoided. What kind of master plan includes the holocaust or slavery? Do we want to put our lives in the hands of him because of his grand plan? Foreseeing that this would occur along with other catastrophic events influenced by religion, why would God appear to have his story told in such a limited form?

Perhaps the different meanings of the Bible that people have taken on add up to a good thing for the survival of Christianity: The Koran has not been significantly changed, and we see the ridicule towards its locality worldwide because of it, namely the disdain for non-believers. But if God, Jesus and Muhammad wanted to create a following, couldn't the clarity of the lessons be more evident? If they wanted the world to receive their message, shouldn't it be one message? Did Jesus create and then spread a religion knowing how people would perceive an apocalyptic movement and almost be welcoming of end-times scenarios? Did he mean for his message to be documented by four disciples? What is there to follow, aside from rules which obviously make a perfect recipe for controlling the masses?

Yet despite this confusion regarding the Biblical "real" or truth, it is important to remember that, throughout the history of Biblical analysis there have been more people studying the Bible in the twentieth Century than all of the centuries since the NT, and still no success has been achieved with regard to discovering any deeper lessons from the document, much less provide deeper meanings in "metaphors" than ones supposedly originally intended by Biblical authors. Religious proponents may change the meanings all they want, but the eventual meaning will be just as meaningless, just as empty regarding any real answers about life or about pain, or anything to do with our everyday lives.

Preachers always say the words, "if we understand a verse in the Bible this way", but if we are honest with ourselves, we can view an obvious void in this type of philosophy. The vacancy of scriptures is a theme that pops up again and again when discussing the Bible, including tones and subtext. It does not matter if apologists today disagree with the literal translation of the Bible, because for nearly the past two millennia not only were the literal meanings taken as truth, Holy Roman Church leadership would viciously enforce these notions.

Not just a few aspects in life, examples of vague and local subject matter void of a deeper level in any aspect in life permeate the scriptures. Notions which would later be sociology or what would later be psychology, or any other life science are nowhere to be found, and neither are ideas revolving around a more complex reality, or any philosophical subject. It is as if the scriptures are a relic and for a time of a different existence. Striking (as well as noticeable among the faithful of the three major religions) is the lack of overall *awareness* in life sciences displayed. The perception, understanding, and knowledge of self and others in the scriptures all are examples of this. This section looks at New Testament models as well as their modern-day reflection among practitioners.

When it comes to lack of depth, the New Testament is definitely generous to its readers. The most important lesson or commandment according to Jesus himself? -Loving God with all your heart, followed by loving your neighbor. Not following the will of God, according to Jesus, will keep the follower out of Heaven, so will not acknowledging Jesus in front of men in another verse. Even the laws of God in the NT are vague and difficult to understand. Is Matthew's insistence on obedience of orthodox Jewish law to be followed or is Paul's view of detaching from the law for the sake of salvation to be followed?[18] It wasn't even agreed among 1st century Christians that Jesus named Peter his main successor,[19] and *no one* knows who wrote the NT or the five books of the Torah.

This is all very odd, considering the scriptures throughout appear to indicate a divinity unparalleled in stature or in wisdom. The lessons provided by them have been held for thousands of years as holy and above human comprehension by many. Those in the Holy Roman Church who would maintain an academic stature unlike no other for centuries would claim that this Biblical knowledge handed down to humans is the ultimate in divine knowledge. However, the utter basics of human behavior are not only excluded in the entirety of Christianity other than what is the boiling down of the trivialized "sin", but there are also no proven steps to progress, to go beyond an ignorant mindset. This is the case in all the major Abrahamic religions.

Falling short when it comes to promoting a personal well-being, the Bible discourages unhealthy human urges like pride, insecurity, greed and wrath, but it doesn't exactly provide any way of understanding those notions in depth. It doesn't go into detail of what they are, how to manage them personally. For example, it ignores the difference in the nature of our two forms of happiness, eudaimonia and hedonism, and the two different perceptive life views each bring. Instead, commands on behavior are given out as if the flock are doing chores. The process on how to achieve basic mental and emotional health is treated as if it were obvious or were given by a god through osmosis if one obeys him.

The notion that God is the one who should be concerned with such subjects also permeates throughout both testaments. Stress and anxiety are, according to psychology professor Tracy Dennis, "the most pressing and far-reaching public health problems we face today."[20] That there is not one in-depth piece of advice in the scriptures to offset such problems is curious considering the fragile state of existence humans find themselves in even regarding basic survival from catastrophe, not to mention from ourselves.

If these scriptures were not meant as a science or medicine book, and were for a different, personal reason, why are there endless tales about the trivial? Were these tales absolutely necessary considering the most desperate of times humans have had to endure to attempt to secure survival? Instinctive behavior deemed unhealthy by social scientists combined with lack of proven guidance from a support system or lack of education almost guarantees an individual access to limited resources in the pursuit of mental stability and a healthy life no matter which of the three major religions the individual accepts. Plato wrote about this three hundred years before the events of the four gospels. When what is required to better oneself or face difficult challenges is to put faith in a supreme being and follow religious law, a predictable pattern of ignorance occurs, the practitioner unaware of the void, unaware of the ineffective nature of the teachings.

So much more wisdom could have been gained from both books of the Bible if it only included a few advanced notions on a mentally healthy life or healthy society. Consider the possibilities of increased chances in achieving some sort of future for human survival if such notions were included, or how much more peaceful, meaningful and fulfilling someone's life would be. Is the impression that many have of the use of luxury or wealth or pleasure due to some understanding of the text not known outside of theological circles (suggesting happiness in the Bible is linked to something incredibly shallow)? Because the "examples" set by Jesus in the NT are also filled with little information on exactly how to be Christ-like, and without these specific steps the practitioner is stranded, uneducated about his or herself. He taught poverty, love and selflessness, but what are the actual teachings of *how* to be selfless or at least self-aware? Instead his lessons are generalized, even the meaning of parables are basic in nature and do not, as Durkheim stressed, "equip one with the tools necessary for life's challenges."[23]

There are no ground-breaking lessons in his work, no mention of the nature of the mind, the nature of reality. Nothing whatsoever on how biological functions dictate behavior. In all, Jesus did not mention anything beyond what the average wise man would know at the time, despite his claims of divine wisdom. This is why *the Measure of God* author and religious proponent Larry Witham admits in his book that the discovery of life science-related fields like sociology, society saw less of "God's mysteries."[23] It is because sociology relied on more practical view-points based on what was known and verified.

To give an example of the teaching from modern life science compared to the teachings of the Christ, the following list is from Dr. Gerald Lampolsky's book *Love Is Letting Go of Fear*. The list, designed to offset aggressive and angry thoughts, is one which is simple, helpful, and was definitely needed in Biblical times. "I am never upset for the reason I think. I am determined to see things differently. I can escape from the world I see by giving up attack thoughts. I am not the victim of the world I see."[23] These instructions are based on empirical research and clinical studies notating certain behavior. It is based on what actually happens with the human mind based on certain experiences. Christ's teachings do not reflect anything of this nature. So local and *immediate* were Jesus's teachings that he did not bother to mention what would arise in humanity as a direct cause of religion.

An example of what religion has evolved into regarding influence over society is Julie Hanlon Rubio's piece in *Theological Studies* when she ponders our society and basic social needs. "Asking what can be done to decrease domestic violence, treating children as moral actors in their own right, discerning the responsibilities of parental and domestic caregivers, and encouraging a new generation to embrace the challenge and beauty of marriage..."[24] These questions can be pondered, and it is a good thing that they are considered, but they should have been addressed a long time ago in religious scriptures. Unfortunately, they could not have been addressed because if they were addressed by Biblical authors, they would be wrong. The instruction in Matthew 18:10 to be kind to children as the angels of the children report to God is little more than fear-based finger wagging, similar to threats of telling someone's strict parents if he or she misbehaves. No comparisons to what would later be known as child psychology. No mention of how traumatic experiences significantly shape the personality of the child when he or she becomes an adult.

Even the fear-based threats of Biblical verses are indicative of the awareness, which fits right into the mold of awareness from thousands of years ago. Regarding specific areas in life, why did Jesus not give in-depth lessons on how to maintain relationships outside of admonishing divorce and other generalized and ridiculous orders? Consider Jesus' words in Matthew 5:27 where he gives instructions on behavior:

> "You have heard that the law of Moses says, 'Do not commit adultery.' But I say, anyone who even looks at a woman with lust in his eye has already committed adultery with her in his heart. So if your eye-even if it is your good eye-causes you to lust, gouge it out and throw it away. It is better for you to lose one part of your body than for your whole body to be thrown into hell. And if your hand-even if it is your stronger hand-causes you to sin, cut it off and throw it away. It is better for you to lose one part of your body than for your whole body to be thrown into hell."

For such a long description of avoiding lust towards other women, the lesson does not reveal a sense of direction on *how* to control the self, why humans should ignore what amounts in reality to not much more than the basic instinct to populate the Earth. He also doesn't bother to reveal the nature of these traits in humans so that we can actually understand them. In another verse, Jesus states in Matthew 5:32, "And anyone who marries a divorced woman commits adultery." How were these lessons perceived as spellbinding and awe-inspiring from the unknown divine? What could possibly be wrong with marrying someone who is divorced? Why even bother mentioning something so basic when cancer alone, or the cure of, could have been mentioned once? How to maintain a healthy marriage could have been addressed, along with a host of other subjects pondered by humans.

Not only are these important subjects not discussed, but the NT is even without a tone of those subjects. Of course the Dead Sea scrolls are also of the same local and trivial themes, not once deviating from the local tone of the Old and New Testaments. Of course the lost gospels are of the same mind-numbing perception of materialism and the cares of the immediate. This is to be expected in a religion lacking awareness in anything above the lowest common denominator, and this tone clearly spans all throughout anything to do with Abrahamic literature.

The Bible not only reads as entirely ignorant of anything scientific, but the overall tone of existence and daily life, instructions, promises and narration in the Bible lacks even any awareness that science will ever exist. It doesn't even hint at anything relating to critical thinking or love of wisdom, despite the claims of profound wisdom that is perceived as almost unworthy of human contemplation. Not one recommendation for a rigid study of the mind, or how humans can achieve and maintain mental and emotional strength through adverse times besides "God". The scriptures, while mentioning salt over 30 times, fail to mention the concept of the human cell one single time, or that there is the equivalent to a trillion of them in the human body, or that they all perform multiple simultaneous functions in order to maintain health of an individual. The scriptures don't mention the atom, while Democritus was forming the atomic theory of the universe four hundred years before the events of the four gospels. That there is none of this in the Bible further shows that either Jesus simply did not know, or that his ministry and legacy are man-made.

Even the hidden gospels, while slightly varied from the Old and New Testament, carry the same tone, the same referencing of the shallow back drops in an elaborate and rather ridiculous production. It is no surprise that documents found later resemble the same locality and shallow perceptive worldview. Jesus' half-brother James is claimed to have written regarding wisdom given to humans, "But the wisdom that comes from heaven is first of all pure. It is also peace loving, gentle at all times, and willing to yield to others. It is full of mercy and good deeds. It shows no partiality and is always sincere. And those who are peace makers will plant seeds of peace and reap a harvest of goodness."[25] But again, are these the best examples that can be made? What exactly is the benefit of heaven's "good" wisdom? How is the wisdom merciful specifically? We also see the same exact one-liners and "see-God" references for everything in life that is complicated elsewhere in the Bible. The local and general tone never ends in Abrahamic literature.

Apologists today might argue that Jesus did not come to warn of the suffering ahead, that his message was instead of a different nature, not the future socioeconomic situations of the Jews, but of what lay inside his followers. In this respect, his teachings can be categorized as a failure. Not only are his teachings a vacuum regarding anything deeper than encouraging "good", those who follow these empty instructions merely become trapped in what Sam Harris referred to as a "desperate marriage of ignorance and hope". What is empty cannot be claimed as personal, as it never affected the individual (This also despite the fact that Jews to this day reject Jesus due to inconsistencies with his story and OT prophesy).

David Van Biema and others contend in an article for *Time International* regarding popular theologian Augustine's advice on Biblical interpretation, "[he] wrote that basically it is not possible to understand what was being described in Genesis. It was not intended as a science textbook. It was intended as a description of who God was, who we are and what our relationship is supposed to be with God"[26] And how that process is coming along? There has yet to be one single shred of evidence indicating anything deeper than the remedial lessons of the Bible since its authorship. The notion that the Bible chooses to ignore science, as we can see, is questionable at best and suggests that a deity chose to ignore certain important subjects concerning humanity, replacing them with far more trivial subjects and narrow childish rules which have been given to us in authorship by what Bertrand Russell referred to as savages.

The only thing evident throughout the years since Biblical times is the utter locality in Biblical authorship. Whether it is Jesus giving us one-liner instructions in the NT, or the remedial and stern messages in the OT, the result is of the same tired and local theme regarding life ages ago. Rituals, convictions and awareness are based on the texts and 'lessons' throughout the centuries which simply do not reflect a realistic interpretation of anything relating to the personal nature as claimed by religious proponents. This vacuum is why individuals often replace religious ideas when one does not work for them according to religious author Karen Armstrong's work.[27] The Christian, finding no fulfillment in the religious system, looks to fill the personal void with ideas that have no religious bearing. "Soul mates", idolatry and other non-religious notions are accepted outright to fill the personal void, even though this lies outside the religious instructed realm.

It appears obvious in every way one dissects the scriptures that they are of the local and did not contain any complex system or guidance, regardless of translations and regardless of metaphorical claims made. Religious proponents may assert all the modern theories they want regarding Biblical locality in apology, but obviously we live in a reality more complex than Biblical authors could have possibly addressed. Ignoring basic facts of survival in dire circumstances such as our own, the case can be made that the authors of the scriptures were clearly out of their league when making attempts at explanation of reality or who we are and how to survive, much less what our purpose is.

There have been plenty of concepts relating to who we are on a deeper level than Christianity and before the Christ. Aristotle's contemplation on man and hedonism which reads, "I count him braver who overcomes his desires than him who conquers his enemies; for the hardest victory is over self" alone came about 300 years before Christ and is deeper and more meaningful than most psalms and tales of daily life found in the Bible. Not only do the scriptures right along with all their proponents try to deal in subject matters which are unknown to them, but the casual acceptance by the masses that this other world exists as if it were somehow part of a legitimate foundation for a philosophy is noteworthy for its tossing aside reason. This other world that religionists operate in would probably be harmless and not be such a concern if the influence were not so strikingly limited, especially intellectually, but it is.

Some would advise not to be too harsh on religion, to let it run its course. But one of the reasons why religion should be critiqued is because of the overwhelming influence of this claimed reality that ultimately shapes society's perceptive views. The shortcomings are claimed to be a purposely written theme that ignores or "detaches" itself from any modern notions of humanity, but not even hinting at them in metaphors or providing a backdrop that even indicates anything deeper ensure a lack of awareness in practitioners that stifles individual potential as well as that of society. These texts along with religious scholarship show that religion, if nothing else, is man-made at best, and at worst a silent weapon used on the masses, as many scholars today claim. The Bible is so flawed to the very nature of its core that it can't be taken seriously, it doesn't deserve intellectual heavy weights analyzing it throughout history for meaningful lessons. Theologians will admit to this locality themselves. If the Bible did contain any advanced messages, they would be there, and the lessons would be verified by something tangible and their complexity would be marveled at to this day. This is clearly not the case at all, however. The scriptures are laughed by intellectuals and are shrugged off by many theologians themselves as being too embedded in the local to be dusted off.

The New Testament, while it is to be praised for the general idea of promoting more compassion than the seriously dated OT, is just as local. For all the love talk, there is little talk of understanding to become compassionate, or of how to love. This vacuum of mere words of love is without depth and is typical of the isolated desert life that was the time. Although the once dominant -religious forms of thought were seen as truth at times- they can simply no longer acclimate themselves to the complexity of our reality. If Jesus wanted to truly change the world, he might as well have used his effective teaching to focus on social theory like Aristotle, philosophy like Plato or the nature of the mind like Lucretius, all before the time of Jesus.

So limited is the Bible that it can only be attributed at the time to the persons who wrote these books. The authors were clearly of the same geography and culture which can be mercifully described as limited in awareness. Knowledge is power, and religion specifically influences not to seek knowledge. If anything, Christians should be angry at Christianity for not effectively teaching how to deal with gossip, social status, judging, vanity, pride and alcohol use. What is sad about the limitations of the scriptures is that if there is no effectiveness as well as nothing to analyze, then not only is the person left stranded without any knowledge of his or herself, they will be unable to seek outside influence due to strict guidelines set by scripture.

Considering all of this, to not hold religion accountable for what it is and is not is a mistake. In this sense, the problem is not that religion was made by man, the problem is that the Biblical lessons do not transcend no matter how much theologians attempt to change meaning or how much they ignore the growing mountain of valid critique, forever binding the practitioner to the fear and the anxiety-inspired notions of ages past. How surprising is it that, according to John Cacioppo of the University of Chicago religious affiliation actually negatively affects African Americans today, or that almost all countries that modernize leave religion? The U.S. is the last bastion of modernized Christian stronghold, but this is due to the number of people from other countries and their Christian/Catholic influence. This also does not speak for most of the 1 percent class or most elite scientists. The masses are the ones who believe, and unfortunately are limited in potential because of this influence.

Chapter Four

82%

An interesting look at the mentality of the upper class in Dana Thomas' *Deluxe: How Luxury Lost Its Luster* reveals the mindset concerning valuable possession among the Roman citizens near the time of Jesus in 1st Century Rome. Historian Jonathan Stamp explains the Roman thinking of the time when he noted, "wealth itself didn't confer status. You needed something else, like objects." Interesting to note is the mindset of the Roman upper class, and what they would do to attain material possessions, or at least the impression of having material possession. Thomas went on to describe the social behavior of the Roman rich:

> "The politician and philosopher Cicero, for example, was an outsider who wanted desperately to be accepted by the establishment, so he spent a staggering one million sesterii on a citron wood table

at a time when the average annual salary was a thousand sesterii. Suddenly Rome's neavau riches had to have tables just like it, and since they couldn't afford the real thing, they had carpenters copy it in lower quality wood. Sculptors reproduced the great statues of the period in cheaper materials for the new moderately rich masses to use in decorating their homes and gardens."[1]

That this reflected the state of affairs among the elite social class during that period of time is telling: since the alleged life and death of Jesus, little has changed regarding materialistic points of view, especially among the religious masses. Whether it is the Christian, Jew, or Muslim, the vanity, along with the desire for social status, wealth and power, luxury and pleasure is as pervasive as ever, regardless of the "influence" of the holy spirit and other religious claims throughout the centuries.[2]

A unifying limited paradigm of awareness, all three religions display an indifference to, and even promote unhealthy behavior individually as well as collectively due to their lack of awareness, compassion and overall brutish authorship. It is to be expected that the shallow and materialistic perceptive views of long ago will remain today. This chapter will focus on these human tendencies and their relation to the scriptures as well as the effects such religious influence has on society. It will definitely look at more vacancy and locality of scripture as well as the lack of proper guidance the scriptures and lessons have had on its practitioners. Encouragement of basic human traits such as anxiety-ridden material attainment and greed is not only in the Bible, the behavior attributed to this mindset is still active today.

Such traits are indicative of the followers of all three major religions as they share a commonality with other systems. In the same way C. S. Lewis meant when he wrote regarding a similarity of different religions who all revert to something that speaks the same voice[3], the three religions all appear to echo the same identifiable tone when it comes to hedonism. Just like alcohol consumption and other behavior which is openly encouraged by religion, hedonism is promoted wittingly and unwittingly in the Bible. It is used as temptation to lure practitioners to behave a certain way as well as to tell tales encouraging a hedonistic outcome. Never mind the consequences of uncivilized business practice like exploitation found in the Bible, that the books of the Bible encourage a perceptive viewpoint towards something basic like hedonism shows how remedial and irresponsible it is. The effects of economic corruption are examples of such by-products in religion.

This is why it is important to examine the role in society that religion plays, the unhealthy behavior it promotes, and, in many cases, actively encourages. While the three main religions may not have a direct role in the victimizing treatment of others, their influence does not provide even a foundation for which to begin building what offsets such behavior. The basic worldview that religion encourages doesn't exactly help in formulating any cohesive and advanced society, but rather presents a world where the basic in humanity flourishes regardless of consequence. This influence is not just restricted to believers, but the non-faithful in religious societies who are indirectly influenced by religion and adhere to its notions.

The importance of economics in human affairs cannot be overstated. Malthus centuries ago exemplified this when he wrote that population and civilization are entirely reliant upon substance. So important is economics in human lives, that even the practice of religion is economically based. John Torpey explains this relationship between religion and economics in the periodical *Social Research*, "One does not engage in religious practice without some set of beliefs in a higher power or powers capable of bestowing sought-after rewards, even if one may also be doing other things—such as displaying wealth and prosperity—at the same time. Otherwise, why call them 'religious' at all?"[4] Professor of religion Carol Zalesky also noted of this resource-religion relationship, "In their classical forms, all great religions have considered it perfectly fine to pray for goods".[5]

Religious influence on the masses throughout the centuries[6] is related to this praise/request relationship with humans and a claimed higher power, and it has been ongoing for millennia in the hopes that needs will be heard and attended to by a god. The question proposed is this: Why would Biblical verses be riddled with stunning lack of awareness concerning economics and socioeconomics? Haven't those subjects played a major part in human affairs regardless of whether the masses were aware of their specific details? The question is brought up because, although its influence is enormous, mainstream religion's limited notions regarding these subjects are noticeable.

We can start with what would account for the foundation of any religious critique: that the subject being referred to is man-made. This is why religion has had no influence over actual micro and macro-economics. Something so local, trivial and vacant as the Bible is void of any complex economic notions or theories. As *New Encyclopedia Britannica* notes, "Economics and political science... have not made extensive use of religion as a factor in their studies".[7] Religious vacancy is once again the reason. What in religion or the Bible can be applied to such economic complexity? This question can be asked regarding the NT as well as the OT. A void that accompanies many religious notions assures this. One can also count out the Bible when dealing with the socio-political strata, as religious proponent Theo Hobson admits this in *Christian Century*, "The New Testament obviously has no conception of modern political liberty."

This is ironic, considering the important role socioeconomics plays in daily life, and yet religion has no effectual bearing regarding the subject. Not even its history provides a framework from which to decipher a possible political and economic link to any claimed religious effect.[8] That a God would not care to address such an important subject as socioeconomics seems odd, considering it is a matter of life and death for entire societies. If the authors of the Bible wanted to discuss anything regarding an introduction to humans, it would be nice if they regarded the more important facets of what would be a somewhat appropriate introduction.

Apologists assert the notion of a purposeful 'disconnect' taken by God to human affairs, such as Theo Hobson's contention that the Bible "detaches God from any form of state power", and "rejects" theocracy.[9] This would be like if Jesus never mentioned unhealthy disorders or germ disease because he "rejected" their effects. This is a convenient apology, but based on false assumptions. Were Yaweh, Jesus, and Muhammad all simply detached from basic human survival that could have saved countless lives?

With a more coherent, humane and deeper understanding missing in Biblical reference regarding socio-political economics, it is easy to see the disconnect in religion that allows victimizing to permeate human history. Exploitation and other unsavory business practices fill the religious world: whether it is Muslim, Jew or Christian, there seems little wisdom from the Bible or Koran to effectively address such issues in society. Many throughout the centuries have written about these unhealthy tendencies that Sharon Salzberg calls "obstacles to our happiness",[10] and it is no surprise that religion takes little active part in preventing them. That the Bible doesn't explain this natural exploitive tendency or even prevent practitioners from displaying such behavior is telling. Religious notions ignore the complicated nature of humans, dismissing everyday adversity as just one of the many circumstances of difficulty that life presents to the individual. Anything that requires a more complicated answer to life questions has the default setting notion of trusting a god to solve the difficulty.

The manifestation of unhealthy behavior such as violent conflicts is an example of this failure of religion to address such hazardous tendencies. While a small amount of wars waged globally have been for religious reasons, by far the majority have been for economic reasons, Analysis of 3,500 years of wars concluded that of the 1763 wars during world history, 123 were religious, and greater than 60% were not religiously influenced.[11,12] Clearly religion has had little peaceful or even preventive effect. War is so prevalent among humanity that it has been reported that there have been only a few days to a few years of peace on the planet since societies have existed. Even conflicts officially claimed by academia to be directly influenced by religion are questionable in their religious inspiration, with the religion is being used an excuse to conquer, as Graham Fuller notes in *Foreign Policy*, "After all, what were the Crusades if not a Western adventure driven primarily by political, social, and economic needs?"

Almost every single war the U.S. has engaged in was for economic reasons. The fact that it is a largely Christian nation (82%Christian according to Dr. Harold Koenig) and how much of an influence Christianity has on the populace shows religion does not prevent these wars or address war in any way deeper than shallow viewpoints. In fact, just as they are ignorant to anything relating to social sciences, the ancient works also display a primitive and irresponsible worldview. There are those like Rabbi David Wolpe who claim that wars are from tribalism and not religion itself, but it is clear that religion is powerless to prevent these wars, expected of such vacancy. This is not surprising, as all three major monotheist religions of the world do not even show respect for the religion of others or the society of others in the Bible and Koran (Psalms 10:16).

A verse which can best symbolize this childish, war-like nature of the Bible is in the book of Revelation. While in a war-ravaged existence where pretty much every single person in the world dies (again), chapter 19 verse 16 tells of a rider on a white horse who wears a robe dipped in blood and followed by the armies of heaven. On his thigh and robe the words "King of kings and Lord of the lords" are written. Today we see this as infantile and oafish. But for the times it must have been a real hook for the masses because this encouragement of primitive aggression -for whatever fear-based reason- has resonated for a species that is very drawn to such urges.

Conflict is just one of the many ways in which humans victimize others for economic reasons -what the Bible is ignorant of. Even the basics of social policy require an understanding of socioeconomics which is eerily absent in the Old and New Testament (as well as the Koran). A healthy operative social structure is even needed to maintain a society as well as show consistent progress in one. Consider the following quote regarding such basic requirements met for a society and how complex it all is to implement. Consider the following before analyzing scripture next time for any in-depth explanation of existence.

"Social policy involves more than the development of the welfare state or social programs. It encompasses a larger debate on the responsibilities of citizens and governments to meet basic human needs and promote equality and justice. The study of social policy requires thoughtful consideration of the following fundamental questions: What are basic human needs? How can individuals, organizations, and governments best meet those needs? Who, if anyone, is responsible for the welfare of others? What social ills can be addressed through policy?"[13]

The Bible does not represent such notions, or even indicate an inception to any future prototype of such ideas. No recommendations of what later would be social and economic systems, or government and civic action, but merely the prolonged details of vengeance against those who economically victimized set in a back drop that included a dictator who constantly tempts man with abundance as a reward for good behavior. Even NT events happen centuries after Aristotle wrote about social theory.

Proverbs 3:13-16 attempts to describe the nature of wisdom and understanding, but cannot seem to grasp them beyond the material. The verse does not go into any in-depth analysis of human nature, but merely keeps in line with the lowest common denominator:

> "Happy is the man that findeth wisdom, and the man that getteth understanding. For the merchandise of it is better than the merchandise of silver, and the gain thereof than fine gold. She is more precious than rubies: and all the things thou canst desire are not to be compared unto her. Length of days is in her right hand; and in her left-hand riches and honour."

That was ridiculous. The insinuation of a long life, "riches" and glory is what is described in this claimed realm rather than anything more complex.

That the many references of money amount to not much more than cannon fodder for fear-based rule is another example that the Biblical lessons were not beyond encouraging the superficial of perceptions. The references are not without using money as a parent uses candy to entice the child to behave a certain way. It is an important factor in considering the awareness level of Biblical authors, as the tone between the Old and New Testaments did not change concerning the basic hedonistic mindset. Even in the NT Jesus spoke of money in 11 out of 39 parables, and while he might have possessed a basic understanding of its socioeconomic importance, he did not display it. Not only is there no awareness of the unhealthy effects of hedonism in the scriptures, the lifestyle of hedonism is promoted in these religions with notions permissive of such superficial materialism to this day, rather than exposing practitioners to an ultimate reality.

A few examples of Biblical analogies to wealth and its relation to joy or empowerment includes Revelation 21:15 where an angel measures heaven with a gold rod, or in Revelation 21:21 where heaven's gates are made of pearls, and its "street" is gold. Psalms 3:9-10 reads "Honour the LORD with thy substance, and with the firstfruits of all thine increase: So shall thy barns be filled with plenty, and thy presses shall burst out with new wine." Psalm 9:18 reads, "For the needy shall not always be forgotten: the expectation of the poor shall not perish forever." Psalm 37:21 states, "The wicked borroweth, and payeth not again: but the righteous sheweth mercy, and giveth." Proverbs 27:24-27 reads, "For riches are not for ever: and doth the crown endure to every generation? After the hay is harvested, the new crop appears, and the mountain grasses are gathered in, your sheep will provide wool for clothing, and your goats will be sold for the price of a field. And you will have enough goats' milk for you, your family, and your servants." 2 Corinthians 9:8 reads, "And God will generously provide all you need."

Luke 6:38 reads, "Give, and it will be given to you: good measure, pressed down, shaken together, and running over will be put into your bosom. For with the same measure that you use, it will be measured back to you." 2 Corinthians 9:6-8 reads, "Remember this—a farmer who plants only a few seeds will get a small crop. But the one who plants generously will get a generous crop. You must each decide in your heart how much to give. And don't give reluctantly or in response to pressure. 'For God loves a person who gives cheerfully.' And God will generously provide all you need. Then you will always have everything you need and plenty left over to share with others." Wouldn't such painfully local verses call for apologists thousands of years later?

Not only is there not any awareness of the realties and theories concerning socioeconomics throughout the scriptures, but little more than a comforting tone for those unfortunate in the monetary system of the times is found regarding fairness or any type of socioeconomic equality, along with a sense of "punishment" for the rich and those who engage in unsavory business practices. Examples of such Biblical verses include Psalm 37:7; "Rest in the LORD, and wait patiently for him: fret not thyself because of him who prospereth in his way, because of the man who bringeth wicked devices to pass", Psalm 37:16; "A little that a righteous man hath is better than the riches of many wicked", and Proverbs 28:20; "A faithful man shall abound with blessings: but he that maketh haste to be rich shall not be innocent." Psalm 92:7 also insists; "Although the wicked flourish like weeds, and evil doers blossom with success, there is only eternal destruction ahead of them." This tone is throughout the OT and exists despite the best attempts by the authors to invoke a deeper meaning.

There are those who claim that the referencing of money was not as trivial as we might think, and those verses are metaphorical for something else. For example, in his article for *Catholic Biblical Quarterly*, theologian Nathan Eubank claims that the term "treasures" was meant to read as a body of righteousness. Theologian Gary A. Anderson contends that "financial language provided the conceptual framework for speaking of good and bad deeds beginning in the later strata of the Hebrew Bible."[14] However, these verses clearly not only indicate material wealth and abundance, but do not provide us with any deeper meaning. If the transaction analogy was used to indicate righteousness, what is the righteousness? Where is the understanding and general awareness so desperately needed for the economic times once the Christ is accepted according to tradition? Why didn't the authors give a simpler message rather than hidden codes to be unraveled at some point? Centuries of ludicrous Church explanations along with the more independent western theology from universities concerning religious notions (causing a strain between the two institutions), yet of all the time since the inception of Christianity, all the analysis by church figures and theologians cannot answer for what exactly "righteousness" is, what proven examples there are, or why some instant form of magic makes a person righteous. If righteousness is wisdom, are these secrets of magic words and rituals combined with faith included in some metaphysical process to make a human possess instant wisdom?

Not that the actual path of attaining such a trait isn't a gradual one, but if the claimed righteousness were to permeate the individual, would he or she even be aware of why they were incorrect in previous assumptions? Why not just promote critical thought? Although it is not known whether the authors of the Bible purposely left out socioeconomics, there are those who claim that a reason for no concepts on the subject as well as in depth analysis of other subjects. There are scholars who maintain that religion this was done for a reason, including Richard Dawkins who maintains religion is a tool used by the elite class to "subjugate the masses". Either way, any display of something other than the day-to-day understanding of the times is absent from scriptures, and the populace is left ignorant as a result.

The overall tone that is so limiting in the OT continues in the New regarding shallow and materialistic themes. While envy and greed are among the claimed sins to be avoided, Jesus ignores these human conditions with respect to their association to money, or *how* to control unhealthy tendencies later claimed to be "evil thoughts" by the Church. Effects of unethical business practices are entirely left alone, he also does not display knowledge of the social effects of economics throughout his teachings. No parallels with what would later become Malthusian theories, no talk about human instinct as a set of inherent necessary traits, but rather sins and what will be the consequence as a result.

Regardless of the economic beliefs and lack of praise for the wealthy that he displayed, nowhere does Jesus talk about the need to attain wealth or substance. Nowhere does he mention how primitive a social structure is to have empires, slavery and other victimizing practices of the time. He doesn't explain the mental make-up of economic exploitation. He doesn't even regard these economic realities or display any type of awareness which would bring about a transcending effect for followers to carefully analyze and follow throughout the ages in what could eventually be a liberating governmental prototype. Just think of what the Roman Empire would have been after Rome converted to Christianity and the significant cultural, political and economic changes the doctrines would propose based on such Biblical lessons were they to be accepted into the books of the

Bible. This would also indicate that Jesus had an inkling of knowledge as to just how important economics is to human beings and the collective society. Indeed, Jesus merely claiming that he came to Earth in order to restore Jewish sovereignty and save humans from their own sins is a tragic example of what has been ignored throughout the centuries regarding any deeper meaning or impact of such matters that Christianity, Judaism and Islam all ignore.

An example of the local references to hedonism and the same tired mindset in the NT carrying over from the OT is the blatant Mark 9:43-50:

> "If your hand causes you to sin cut it off. It is better to enter heaven with only one hand than go into the unquenchable fires of hell with two hands. If your foot causes you to sin cut it off. It is better to enter heaven with only one foot than to be thrown in hell with two feet. And if your eye causes you to sin, gouge it out. It is better to enter the kingdom of God half blind than to have two eyes and be thrown into hell, where the worm never dies, and the fire never goes out. For everyone will be purified with fire. Salt is good for seasoning, but if it loses its flavor, how do you make it salty again? You must have the qualities of salt among yourselves and live in peace with each other."

This and many other passages are splashed on to what are claimed purposely written lessons, tales concerning the divine. But the trivial nature of these lessons have yet to be disproved as just that. Even the passage in I Timothy 6:10 which reads, "For the love of money is the root of all evil" is not only wrong (with the popular *New Living Translation* reading "all kinds of evil". One can only wonder what the ancient Greek translation for "all kinds of" is) but doesn't even explain its argument. How exactly is a populace to grow with such lack of knowledge in scripture?

Since religion is so influential, we can only imagine the encouragement of hedonism and other notions popular of the times the two other Abrahamic religions produced. Islam especially exemplifies this. Mohammad retreating to solitude in order to escape the worldly came out just as worldly, not separating himself from the shallow perceptive views from the OT and NT at all. By the time Muhammad settled in as a prophet among the local people, his actions are as typically indicative of someone in that area and times. His life and words were what any common man of the time would have been given the situation he was put in. There was no hidden depth from the messenger Muhammad that humans weren't ready for in the previous "messages".

If one were to put someone else as the receptor of the claimed divine message at that time and place, would they not generally behave the same? What exactly is enlightening about taking a child as a wife? Because that shows something other than the wise actions of a prophet relaying the divine. We can see the insignificant growth in awareness within the Islamic world more than a century after Muhammad's death when, Abu Nuwas, while consoling Harun al-Rashid the ruler of what is now Iraq, said the following

"By God, I never saw a man so unfair to himself as the Prince of True Believers is. The pleasures of this world and the Other are in your hand: why not enjoy them both? The pleasures of the world to come are yours for the sake of your charity to the poor and the orphans, your performance of the Pilgrimage, your repairing of mosques... As for the pleasures of this world, what are there but these: delicious food, delicious drink, delicious girls."[15]

This describes a world where nothing was learned from Mohammed's intention to liberate himself from the worldly - if that was even his goal. It is curious to see what Islamic rule in nations would be had Muhammed actually received any meaningful notions about such things as economic equality or hedonism in general.

Centuries after the time of the NT, modern religious scholars display the same limited undertones as the religious texts in their writings regarding the religious economic dynamic. Little has changed when referencing economic hardship or basic needs being met centuries after Islam. Despite attempts from religious scholarship at linking religion with economic reality, the attempts come up flat. Examples of this include Terrence Penelhum and others in their book, *"Christianity" in Life After Death in World Religions*. Discussing the needs of humans in relation to faith, they write the following:

> "If you really believe you are a child of god, then you will be completely confident that God will see to it that your needs will be satisfied, and you will then not be anxious. If you do not believe this, love toward your neighbor is foolish and hazardous. But if you believe it (if you trust God), then you will be able to put your anxieties aside and act from love."[16]

This same tone of a see-God default setting is indicative of the lack of explanation regarding important subjects addressed in the scriptures centuries previous. In this sense, faith represents all that is needed in hardship, as the result will be a gift from the practice. How does the author know that showing kindness to neighbors under circumstances mentioned would be foolish? Is it a divine revelation?

Reflecting mainstream Christian thought, Penelhum's book makes a claim to link religion with society's plight in the sense that the understanding of the human condition is that the condition is something we need saving from, rather than awareness of. According to the authors, the saving from ourselves is in Jesus, someone "whose life and death are accorded a cosmic significance that holds the key to the cure of the deepest ills of the human condition".[17] This understanding, while well-intentioned, does not address anything real and simply cannot be referred to in any serious vein. How exactly does the Christ cure human ills? How is Christ's force noticeable for economic change? What is the metric used to even analyze something like that?

Another example of attempting to provide a religious understanding of our socioeconomic reality, religion and culture professor Marcus Borg blames economic exploitation on "evil" and links it to human suffering in his book, *The God We Never Knew*. "Systematic evil is an important notion; it refers to the injustice built into the structures of the system itself. Embedded in oppressive and exploitative social structures, systemic evil is a major (perhaps the single greatest) cause of human suffering."[18] This is dangerous territory to be assuming things. The system is only flawed because it is a stagnant, man-made concept that allows exploitation and promotes the adherence to basic urges. What Borg calls "evil" built into a system is of thin air, the exploitation vanishing once the economic system is different. The system -just like the concept of religious evil- is of man's imagination, and not a very good representative of that imagination either.

In contrast to Borg's notion of evil regarding economics and society, Cambridge University Professor of Developmental Psychopathology Simon Cohen has a slightly different take on the two subjects. His book, *The Science of Evil*, explains circumstances involving the human condition that is lacking in theology. Instead of referring to a vague and inhuman "evil", Cohen refers to a more scientific description of what he terms "empathy erosion" when he writes the following:

> "Empathy erosion can arise because of corrosive emotions, such as bitter resentment, or desire for revenge, or blind hatred, or a desire to protect. In theory, these are transient emotions, the empathy erosion reversible. Equally, empathy erosion can occur as a result of the beliefs we hold (such as the belief that a class of person is unworthy of human rights), or our intentions (for example, to make an employee redundant)"[19]

The preceding differs from theological works in that it can be verified. It is also man-made instead of from a claimed mythical origin that is detached from us. It is not an unrelated answer from a god to human dilemmas from which humans have no power in. Such scientific notions regarding society are better than the ones thought up by supposed gods too important for a conscious wakening for humans. In fact, anyone with a few semesters of philosophy can muster up something on their own which would be deeper than religious notions on society. It would have been only a matter of time when science discovered the role of economics and society, only a matter of time when the works of social theorists would build a platform of discovered insights into socioeconomics and inspire research in political science and sociology.[20] Still, concepts even hinting at foundations for inquiry which result in these kinds of findings are entirely missing from the Old and New Testament. Again, this is curious considering the importance of economics and socioeconomics in society.

Another example of advanced modern scientific analysis of society from experts in the field is from sociology professor Eduardo Terren, as he explains the fundamentals of what is required for a healthy and growing society in a paper for the *Journal for the Study of Religions and Ideologies*. Notice how the specifics of information differ from the vague verses of scripture:

"In the transition from the 20th to the 21st century a series of phenomena tied to economic globalization and population movements (Sassen, 1996) as well as the identity demands of very diverse (Castells, 1997) are opening a new horizon for citizenship. Among these phenomena, the growing multiculturality of resident populations in the same national territory is perhaps one of the elements which most clearly obliges us to reflect on the necessity of forging a new concept of citizenship capable of providing a new project of rights, participation and belonging to a civil society which is becoming increasingly more complex and heterogeneous."[21]

Nothing like this was even mentioned by Jesus. This is odd, considering Jesus was sent to return the economically displaced Jews to their desired status.

If corporations and governments have formed a new class model of corporatocracy, then wouldn't the divine reveal the intricacies of and how to liberate from the devastating side of something now commonly known in any social science class? Because the details of the reality in our daily lives outside of the superficial are nowhere to be found in the Bible, because the religious writings are so embarrassingly wrong about the most basic of humanity, what our generation has been left with is the viewpoint that allows for acts of gaining wealth at almost any cost, and the attainment of power and pleasure at an almost celebratory encouragement from many in modern society. In the same way that the pursuit of glory was considered noble among the Greeks in the time of Alexander the Great but seem trivial now as a goal, our own society will be seen as uncivilized to future generations in many ways, socioeconomics will be one of them and it is unfortunate that religion is so useless on the subject.

We can clearly see in today's society that hedonism and the pursuit of the basic and the material never left the religious realm of any three Abrahamic religions. Of course, the exploitative business practices of today's modern society are not under the scope of religious writings because Jesus never mentioned such complicated issues in the scripture like loopholes, monopolies, mass layoffs for share increase, defense contracting or corporatocracy. There is nothing in religious law about cronyism, the explanation of "wickedness" going only shallow deep in the scriptures. Not surprisingly, all three major religions lack an awareness beyond the anxiety-fueled daily existence where believers are "rewarded" for obeying, punished for not adhering to scripture. This is evident in the U.S. where the victimization must occur in order to profit in a free market economy and a world of scarcity. "Caring is the enemy of profit" is a phrase frequently used in a nation with the largest gap between the top and bottom class among developed nations. The consequences of such limited messages as the scriptures regarding economic exploitation are only self-evident today, the far majority of Americans are Christian, but the U.S. has been called a terrorist state by Professor Noam Chomsky.

As for the unhealthy human tendencies described by Salzberg, nothing has changed concerning the awareness or understanding of the human condition or the results of thousands of years of analysis. If there is any doubt as to the same shallow and uncivilized mindset of a society regarding daily life centuries after Christianity and Islam were first rooted, Zachary Karabell describes comparisons of the culture climate in the West and ancient mid-East in *Peace Be Upon You*: "While there are considerable differences between now and then, the similarity to the contemporary West is hard to deny... Western society has been a mix of the holy and the profane for some time."[22] The hedonism that exists in the modern believer is just as rampant at the time the scriptures were written.

While it has been discovered in multiple psychological studies that wealth does not bring happiness,[23,24] the pursuit of wealth comes at a high price with victimization. Hedonism promotes not just a love or obsession with increased finances and luxury, but detachment to the consequences of business practices. The book, *Social Problems*, documents that since the initial meteoric rise of the American capitalist, the poor or common were left out, and if there was profit to be made from the expense of the common worker, competitor or even the environment, the profit would be made.[25] The book notes the transformation of early American society into modern one through such a mindset:

> "The industrial revolution which spurned on egalitarianism also promoted individualism, separate from the aristocratic notions and ideals, and also birthed highly self-centered and intensely competitive individualism, which in turn made it difficult for successful Americans to feel responsible for others who lost out in the race for success."[26]

This was in a nation of businessmen that consisted almost entirely of Christians. The modern world of business reflects the influence religion has on our society. In a nation that claims 82% Christianity *and* the free market system, 5% of the world consumes 25% of its resource output. In Washington, there are 25,000 lobbyists for a House and Senate that consists of 535 members total. 400 Americans own 50% of the nation's wealth, and according to the July 2012 Cato Institute report on corporate welfare, 100 billion per year is spent on Corporate welfare per year which does not have to be paid back, an amount that consists of the largest portion of congressional aide to recipients, which also questions the legality of the U.S. government meddling in private industry.

Religious influence on such uncivil behavior is easy to notice. Prosperity preachers will encourage one to pursue their economic desires but ignore something like the nature of scarcity. While religion is not a direct cause of such exploitation, it certainly provides a tolerant and enabling tone in its lessons without a way out. 1st Peter 2:18 advises slaves to be good to their masters. Examples of today's understanding of the hedonistic tendencies and effects are evident in the teaching of those who maintain and encourage the same perceptive reality that refuses to break from its dome of obliviousness. Prosperity preachers like Joseph Prince and Joel Osteen instruct practitioners on how to obtain material wealth and Prince in particular, while in a televised broadcast and in front of his congregation, instructed the audience to ask God for money and "good things", as it was a better alternative than committing a sin for them. That this ignores the basic urges in his sermon is accompanied by the notion that happiness lies in pleasure, leisure, and wealth. Is there no other alternative to committing what is assumed to be unethical acts in many cases for "good things"? Mr. Prince then prayed that his congregation become free from the h1n1 virus and financial troubles.

Similarly, Joel Osteen in his book, *Your Best Life Now* tells his readers to never mind the poverty that they came from, and to imagine an abundant life. "Don't let your past determine your destiny or influence your self-image. See yourself the way God sees you. Picture yourself experiencing the wonderful things God has in store for you."[27] Assuming that he is referring to the same worldly subjects Joseph Prince referred to, attempts at meeting self-gratification-based goals are by nature limited in scope, unknowingly sacrificing the larger sense of self for temporary gratification. The drug–like effect hedonism has on the individual is not without its illusion of tangible effects and transcending promises, but clearly awareness of such concepts has not resonated with many super rich arch bishops worldwide, with over 40 million to renovate a home spent by one arch bishop alone, and with several others living in extravagance.[28] What this encouragement and even open promotion of monetary possession by religion and modern religious figures prevent are notions of a possible joy outside that restricted realm of thought or enforced ignorance as Daniel Dennett put it in a Cal Tech lecture.

The data is in concerning Americans and economic circumstances. Here is how *Atlantic Monthly* columnist Ken Stern explains the flippant nature of individuals concerning the economic plight of others:

"Lower-income Americans are presumably no more intrinsically generous (or "pro-social," as the sociologists say) than anyone else. However, some experts have speculated that the wealthy may be less generous -- that the personal drive to accumulate wealth may be inconsistent with the idea of communal support."[29]

This would certainly not be the first report of the innate self-regard displayed. Another example of increased self-regard in society comes from a survey conducted of 83 of Chicago's wealthy by political scientists Benjamin Page, Larry Bartels and Jason Seawright. Their survey revealed vast differences in general public responses versus the responses from the wealthy as well as their views on how economic woes of the country should be handled. Not surprisingly, only 8% of the wealthy surveyed felt that the government should find jobs for those who couldn't find work, versus half of the general public (Not free money, but work). According to the authors, "fifty-nine percent of those surveyed wanted more money for Social Security and federal health-care programs. Given a list of 12 areas, the rich favored cutting back funds in nine areas including job programs, Social Security, health care, and even defense. They, too, wanted to cut foreign aid."[30] This is not very Christian. Not that Christian lessons can answer for such complicated concerns in society anyway. What in scripture teaches or even provides a basic understanding of modern dilemmas, or what would amount to some framework from which to derive something that offsets them? What in scripture provides for real answers outside of the local and trivial accompanying tales which go on and on and on?

The increased self-regard can definitely be counted on when it comes to many of the rich concerning the plight of others. This is why modern era tobacco giants make and sell products that kill 5,000,000 globally, 600,000 in second hand smoke and take a life per minute in the United States alone (no nation is a larger consumer of drugs than the U.S.). This is what occurs when the void of reality permeates scripture and what the vague and empty lessons do not prepare people for. Mike Lofgren provides another example of the economic disconnect in the opinionated *American Conservative* in what he called 'secession of the rich', or the disconnect of one class from another:

> "What I mean by secession is a withdrawal into enclaves, an internal immigration, whereby the rich disconnect themselves from the civic life of the nation and from any concern about its well-being except as a place to extract loot. Our plutocracy now lives like the British in colonial India: in the place and ruling it, but not of it. If one can afford private security, public safety is of no concern; if one owns a Gulfstream jet, crumbling bridges cause less apprehension—and viable public transportation doesn't even show up on the radar screen. With private doctors on call and a chartered plane to get to the Mayo Clinic, why worry about Medicare?"[31]

The disconnect that the elite and even the masses themselves have with the class perceived as beneath a certain status is not surprising given the vacancy of such subjects in a religious society. That Jesus was almost flippant about slavery or economic exploitation should join one of the many warning signs he is accompanied with. Why didn't he mention that wealth doesn't even need to exist in an equal and free society? Why didn't he also mention the exploitation that wealth brings in many cases? Why did he not mention one single time that the Earth would be plundered for its resources, then polluted beyond our imagination? What in all of his lectures was too important to not include such notions?

It is not as if greed is a new trait or one exhibited because of certain circumstances, but one seen in humanity throughout the ages. In Richard Conniff's article for *The Smithsonian* regarding selfishness of the rich and leaders of society throughout generations, he quotes archeologist Brian Hayden who focused his studies on historical human greed. Commenting specifically on the elite in traditional Mayan villages, Hayden said, "I was completely blown away by the results. Instead of helping the community, people in power took advantage to sell food at exorbitant prices, or they hoarded food and wouldn't share it, or they used food in trade to take over land." This is not an uncommon practice in the region, much less globally (Aztecs would set the prices of goods in trade that would benefit them because they controlled the trade of the goods as well as who would be sold what). Hayden's studies globally have led to discovery of what he called "frequent accounts of despots and psychopaths--leaders who took what they wanted even when it meant disaster for their neighbors."[32] This urge to survive has permeated cultures throughout the millennia regardless of religion.

For a closer look at the inner workings of an economic predator in today's modern times, an FBI publication authored by PhDs Paul Babiak and Mary Ellen O'Toole concerning corporate psychology revealed the mentality of the modern corporate individual turned sociopath. In their report, they explained that the corporate predators "seems to get perverted pleasure from hurting and abusing their victims."[33] Many would view this information as alarming, but these arc the traits of a surprisingly large number of individuals in that position. In modern times, what is seen as unethical business practices -knowingly laying off thousands of people for increased share value, selling tobacco dipped in deadly chemicals, approving less than quality drugs for the corporate sector, or other practices committed by executives- are not some vague "evil" caused by devil-possessed people, or by an unknown and detached force from a different realm, but are due to natural tendencies which have been seen too many times throughout history. The "wicked" man who gets rich from unsavory practices does not end up suffering in the end as the Old and New Testaments suggests, but survives along with generations of offspring to come: that was his plan the entire time. The actions rationalized, the success heralded.

Economic stats today reveal disturbing but expected information about the wealthy in a nation of what some claim are 95% Christian. They show that a religious influence does not bare weight when it comes to economic inequality, regardless of claim. Surprising numbers in a U.S. Census Bureau Population Poll survey reveals this when it reported that even the recent growing American economy affected the wealthy, not those in poverty. Sasha Abramsky wrote in the left-leaning periodical *The Nation* of the unequal outcome. "That our poverty numbers have risen to such a high level exposes the fact that as a society, we are *choosing* to ignore the needs of tens of millions of Americans—as we have done for much of the period since the War on Poverty went out of fashion and the harsher politics of Reaganism set in."[34]

This number is backed by economist and Nobel recipient Joseph Stiglitz: "Most Americans got none of the growth of the preceding dozen years. All the gains went to the top percentage points." Even the wages for labor produced saw a decrease in numbers for everyday workers. Commenting on a *New York Times* report (titled "A US Recovery But Only For The 1 Percent") reporting 93% of 2010 wealth was accrued only by the top 1 percent of Americans, Owen Jones noted in the *New Internationalist*, "Indeed, male median wages in the US are now lower than they were in 1973".[35] According to *The Economist*, we have a nation where the income gap is the largest of any advanced nation. When Alan Greenspan speaks of two economies -one for the rich and one for everyone else- in this regard we can understand how the world elite have seen their net worth sky rocket since the 1980s, while the rest of the globe has seen their worth diminish.

A look at the notion of the American dream shows that it ignores not only scarcity and victimization, but Christ's teaching regarding wealth. Jesus says that it is easier for a camel to enter the eye of a needle than for a rich man to enter the kingdom of Heaven. This seems like a direct warning, yet the opportunity for success is not only the American dream, but in the countless prayers inundated on a god daily regardless of which major religion is subscribed to. It is well known that religious influence concerns most social and personal aspects in the lives of most in the civilized globe and it appears that all three major religious systems share this same general influence (in what C.S. Lewis in the 1940's argued in *Mere Christianity* that the different sects of the religion do not matter in influence). In this sense regarding Christianity, Islam, or Judaism, the unhealthy cultural effects, singlehandedly or not, are associated with the direct influence of the major monotheistic scriptures and lessons and that influence is not exactly healthy. It is doubtful that they will ever be without some serious overhaul of their themes, which would also compromise the initial messages, further proving them false.

This section will conclude with a sobering and urgent voice on economic victimization and injustice written by a theologian in South Africa who witnessed first-hand desperate circumstances. Roman Catholic Priest and native South African, Nolan Albert writes in *Journal of Theology for Southern Africa* regarding exploitation in the region by unbridled capitalism and its consequences in an area that has been largely victimized for some time, an economic practice that Pope Francis considers straight from the devil. Albert writes, "The liberal or neo-liberal capitalist system is so powerful and so entrenched that most people including many poor people have come to believe that there is no alternative".[36] The paper describes a number of 'theologies' pertaining to the struggle of economic inequality in South Africa:

"The first would be the Theology or Worship of Mammon. It is not as such a State Theology. The worship of money is a worldwide form of idolatry, our unjust economic system. But the State in South Africa has become for the most part, despite all its protestations to the contrary, an instrument of the liberal capitalist system. So, let's call the first theology the Worship of Money or Mammon. Church Theology today could then be seen as the attempt to find a compromise between the worship of money and the worship of God.

"Even when the Church does not actually encourage its members to become rich, it nevertheless hesitates to condemn the worship of money and the system that promotes this worship of money. Prophetic Theology would then mean the outright condemnation of the worship of money in all its forms and a call to action, a call to participate in the struggle against economic injustice. In other words Prophetic Theology would challenge the Church to worship God and not Mammon by taking a clear option for the poor in the South Africa of today."[37]

As frustrating as the plight must be for Nolan, that which can be used to offset this injustice is not found in the Bible or in any major religion's teachings. Black theology[38] concerns the same tone as Nolan's work, containing a sense of liberation from an oppressive system, but these economic systems were set up independent of religious notions or theocracy, and such religious notions simply cannot be relied upon in real world cases (There are some, like Daniel Dennett, who accuse the concept of religion of being created by man for nefarious reasons, what he calls "a brilliantly designed product"). There will never be a perceptive view religiously influenced that provides notions concerning economic equality and justice because it was never suited to handle such complex matters for the people.

We can only assume that without the change of perception, the cycle of victimization disguised as "policy" or business practice will continue. More disconcerting is the influence (or lack of) religion will likely have on matters concerning future economics. We can forget about the religious masses addressing problems of such a nature due to the mishmash of words and locality that is the Bible. Exploitation will continue, and the religious inspired notions the practitioner will refer to will be a distant and faded set of one-liners in Biblical verses as Harvard and Berkeley religious teacher John Shelby Spong admits to this (in his book, *The Sins of the Scripture*, he writes, "I am now convinced that institutional Christianity has become so consumed by its quest for power and authority, most of which is rooted in the excessive claims for the Bible, that the authentic voice of God can no longer be heard in it."[39]) We can assume there never was a voice of God, but rather the voices of something inherent in us all, complex and way out of the league of religion.

Marcus Borg makes the contention that the certain members of the elite who exploit economically are not the issue and offers that they "can be good people".[40] His belief is that the social system itself and not the individual is to blame for the "evil" perpetrated. His view is that "wickedness" of the elite is not the cause of human suffering but rather the social structure itself.[41] But where are the lessons addressing this in scripture? If Jesus was the resister of the elite as claimed by the *Occupy Religion* authors, where is his alternative? Why is there no economic system based on his principles in a world of scarcity? What exactly about the economic system did he oppose?

What has been poured over for centuries in scripture by otherwise very intelligent people, its complications, its possible metaphors and even blinding contradictions will continue to stun, and religious scholarship will continue to examine possible interpretations. Jesus's word and actions will continue to be used to address economic circumstances. The disturbing truth is that corruption and tyranny are not distant behaviors once prevalent in our ancestors to be ignored in modern times. So prevalent is greed, corruption and victimization that government tyranny and predatory business practice continue today and are not simply practiced by a few "bad apples" generations ago. Even with the acknowledgement of past terrible behavior, the human race has not evolved beyond any gone predatory tendencies to exploit others. It is clear that this paradigm is not simply part of our history where the plundering and sacking was somehow an early and uncivilized human condition, separate from the current one. Religion not only fails us regarding such devastating traits, but blindly encourages them because of authors thousands of years ago who were too irresponsible to know any better.

After centuries of discussion and tens of millions of dollars funding studies which can provide links between positive human traits and Christian principles, there has yet to be any evidence presented of teachings more advanced than a basic tone in religious lessons. The notions remain as vacant as ever regarding these traits. The make-up of just what "wickedness" is, its nature, and specific steps to successfully employ a stable society are entirely lacking in both Testaments. Where in the religious influence is the instruction to ignore hedonism, or that luxury wears off with time? To follow such a blind road in a world of stark realities, to hide our heads in the ground that is blind faith in a world of constant catastrophe is to delude ourselves in a most fatal of ways. There is no religious understanding of civilization-ending socioeconomics because the authors of the religious texts weren't even aware of such a thing. If they were, they certainly made sure their followers would not be aware of them. The vague and shallow references to the superficial when describing real life circumstances involving behavior and claimed divine realms should be obvious signs that the subjects the Biblical authors discussed are no different from any other subject in the Bible in complexity.

Not that it matters if there was an awareness by the Biblical authors of such complicated subjects anyway, the scriptures are retold tales stemming from myths long ago which deluded an ignorant populace. They have no place in economics or any other subject for that matter, as its vacant and ignorant nature can only reveal to us the same amount of information as it was able to reveal on the deepest levels when man first conjured religion. This is why modernity kills religion in almost every country worldwide. If religion could address such complicated subjects as hedonism, it would. The fact that the Biblical worldview does not stray from a hedonistic tone not only shows the inadequacies of Biblical influence, but further proves that religion is man-made to begin with. It is not difficult to assess this, anyone can.

Chapter Five

Twists

-Child play

Influential 5th century theologian Augustine's position on the literal reading of the Bible, a stance the Church took as well, was that the reading should be accepted as literal, but when defeated by reasoning or facts presented, "then one changes."[1] A look at the growth of theology 800 years after Augustine's advice is evident in the works of the popular 13th century theologian Thomas Aquinas whose writing Michael Shermer described as "word play concerning somewhat confusing logical twists and turns".[2] This is not surprising regarding the advancements of theology. Centuries after Augustine and Aquinas we can see the same tone taken by religious philosophers regarding interpretation and religious thought.

Such play on words among theologians in their works resulted in a rift between the Church and what is now Western theology due to those differences beginning with the founding of the first universities. Academic theology and Church assertions would continue in their differences concerning explanation of existence and reality to this day. An example as to the state of affairs concerning the tension between the two institutions currently can be found in theology professor John W. O'Malley's conceding of the rift in the Catholic periodical *America*: "There are no easy answers to the question of reconciling issues arising from the confrontation, most especially not in the intellectually and technologically complicated 21st century."[3] The fact that the tension between the two schools of thought continues to this day concerning explanation of existence suggests the obvious: that there has yet to be any advancement in theology since the time of Thomas Aquinas and going back to Augustine. There exists not one discovery which 'proves' any claim, not any significant findings since the guesses of the Church in the Middle Ages.

Not that the tension between the Church and theology isn't interesting in itself, their differing stances should suggest that the other is wrong regarding explanation of existence and Biblical interpretation anyway. Although the seemingly complex notions in the work of current theologians has little to do with Old Testament absurdities or the cultural context of either Testament, their philosophical claims and personal beliefs are just as embracing of the localized scriptures. The customs practiced as well as notions affirmed to congregations by preachers every weekend are examples of this. The widespread identity and nature of ancient and outdated notions along with religious customs permeate the lives of the religious masses regardless of seemingly complex theological contentions.

Arguments made in defense of religion by theologians will be looked at in this chapter as well as tactics used by them. Attempts at changing the culture by powerful religious proponents like Phillip Johnson will also be discussed. The tone of theologians seems to be that of a superior attitude. According to theologians, one has to be schooled in theology to question them on their religious thought. If one doesn't have a PhD in some form of religious studies, then the excuse can always be used that the opponent doesn't fully understand the intricacies of what they are asserting. However, there are many flaws in their contentions, and for the influence they presume to have as an authority in religious thought, those flaws are too glaring and too easy of targets not to be discussed here.

Although this chapter will refer to theologians as they prefer to be known, there are some like Richard Dawkins who would not be so kind. He has referred to theology as a "haven for fakes and charlatans", refusing to mention theologians by name or debate them. Christopher Hitchens would not have been any less dismissive, referring to theological arguments as "feeble". Most of the people discussed in this chapter have earned their PhDs. They have powerful backers of religious notions for cultural purposes along with a field of colleagues and religious leaning scientists to support their claims with powerful but misleading stats. One stat, however, is that only 15% of the elite scientific community can be considered sympathetic to religion, the rest actively against religion or dismissive of it. Ultimately the scientific work asserted by religious factions are not worthy of being taken seriously, as we will see.

The majority of people throughout the world are not aware of the latest works of theologians worldwide, and most probably haven't heard of backers like Phillip Johnson or John Templeton. This is odd considering Christianity and the work of theologians involve a claimed truth or absolute truth. Due in large part because times have changed for Christianity since its golden age before the scientific revolution changed the way the world was perceived through advancements in various scientific fields, many have little to do with those notions on reality and existence in their modern daily lives. Theologian Howland Sanks admits this in the periodical *America*: "Many who are not professional theologians themselves have the impression that theology merely repeats or rehashes the theological debates of the early church -- the Christological or Trinitarian controversies or those that arose with the Reformation. Others think that theology merely passes on a rigid set of dogmas and doctrines: catechism with footnotes."[4] How-ever theology managed to keep isolated throughout the centuries, the insulation has been beneficial for them because there definitely is plenty to criticize.

It is not difficult to spot the work of a theologian or a Christian philosopher. Most of them are products of colleges with the word "trinity" or "divinity" in the title. They mainly specialize in religious history and the quotes they refer to give credence to their arguments are from other Christian "philosophers" as well as Christian leaning scientists. The peer-reviewed publications in theology from which they commonly reference in each other's "papers" have titles such as *Religious Studies Review, Theological Studies*, and *Journal of Ecumenical Studies*. Not exactly in lockstep with one another regarding beliefs and notions, one theologian might be a Calvinist while another may be of a different form of Protestantism. There are some theologians who preach religious pluralism, and others who preach exclusivism. They all in most part, however, tend to favor the faith argument over evolution and have plenty of points to make on the topic.

Their books are packed with impressive documentation of historical events pertaining to religion, but also infused with claiming the existence of God premised in scientific gaps, a well-placed argument that cannot be invalidated with current scientific knowledge. But as impressive as these arguments may initially seem -indeed even the style with which they write- they always reveal a message hidden in a shallow cup of evidence which can easily be kicked over, what Sam Harris referred to as "magician's patter."

Pick any random theologian off the street and it will be a forgone conclusion that their main argument will be based on some derivative of the Intelligent Design theory (ID). The notion that creation began with a designer, ID started as part of a campaign to convince non-believers of the existence of God and increase the validity of religious scholarship. Formed by former law professor Phillip Johnson, ID is supported by pro Christian scientists, and promoted in academic institutions globally. The current defensive stance of choice taken by theologians is not without its critics, especially in the scientific and academic communities. This is due to the fact that the "science" of ID is less than convincing and not conspicuous in narrative either.

Even a *Time* cover story referred to ID as not something to be taken seriously, "[a]scientifically worded attempt to show that blanks in the evolutionary narrative are more meaningful than its very convincing totality."[5] Proposed almost wholly by non-scientists, the arguments appear mere debate fodder in order for the religious explanation of existence to remain relevant. This is also despite the fact that intelligent design is not even original and is simply a less ridiculous version of creationism, or as Geoff Brumfiel referred to in the science journal *Nature* as "creationism in a cheap tuxedo."[6]

The reason for the change to ID by those seeking to detach from the less attractive creationism is obvious: since the scientific revolution, there has been little said from the religious community that coincides with any relevant discovery or notion. This is what Rosenhouse and Branch wrote regarding the attempted new narrative from creationism in *Bioscience*, "In the public consciousness, that term is laden with the sort of religious connotations ID supporters wish to abjure. They claim that there are scientifically rigorous methods by which the products of an intelligent agent can be identified..."[7] Although the concept of ID adheres to many of the same theories as creationism, the features of creationism are downplayed.[8] 6,000-year Earth age theory and literal interpretation of scripture are no longer encouraged. In its place is a designer too complicated for human comprehension,[9] something science cannot measure or scrutinize.

Criticism from the scientific community of ID range from the sensible to ridicule. Tactics of word-placing from religious scholars are also becoming a more frequent point of criticism from the scientific community, specifically regarding placing arguments in favor of theism in scientific gaps as in the ID argument. Bruce Alberts, a microbiologist and president of the National Academy of Sciences explained the presumptions held by ID supporters in *Nature*. "Its proponents say that scientific knowledge is incomplete and that there's no way to bridge the gap except for an intelligent designer, which is sort of saying that science should stop trying to find explanations for things."[10] An example of this accusation from religious proponents Alberts is talking about is Dinesh D'Souza's interview in *Publisher's Weekly*. "It makes no sense to discredit the arguments in the Bible because the Bible doesn't make any arguments... The Bible doesn't attempt to prove anything, it merely asserts things, such as, "In the beginning God made the heavens and the earth."[11] D'Souza cleverly takes the less than credible notions of the Bible and mixes them philosophically in a more credible tone, one where scripture is beyond possible criticism.

Most arguments used in theology that include the inarguable "gap" assertions are the cosmological argument, teleological argument, ontological argument, epistemology and the anthropic principle, notions where the religious proponent attempts to base claims on what is not yet known in science. Of the main arguments (the teleological argument calls for an intelligent designer in the natural order, the cosmological argument supports a first cause or universal cause, and the ontological argument deals with being, existence and reality), the assumption is that the creator is not of our understanding. None of these or any other like-arguments can be disproved due to claims of ignorance by the scientific community, theologians present them as absolute.

The notion is pressed that their assertions are to be considered above scientific skepticism, claiming they are proof to contend with megalith theories like that of evolution. An example of such an inarguable premise is in Patrick Glynn's book, *God: The Evidence,* where he calls for the cosmological, teleological, and anthropic arguments. "Modern science is not interested in the final cause. It looks rather for the efficient cause, the mechanism that actually brings things about. The anthropic principle harks back to the older style of thinking. In effect the anthropic principle says that humanity is (apparently) the final cause of the universe."[12] Not unlike the tone of uneducated guesses from the Church for centuries, Mr. Glynn discusses what clearly cannot be known with modern science, and he does it with a narrative that indicates confidence of his knowledge in the subject matter, as if what he is discussing is a given and obvious.

Another example of this type of argumentation from theology is in Gerald L. Shroeder's book, *The Hidden Face of God.* In it, he inserts a God-of-the-gaps premise into a world of scientific analysis. Notice the academic tone used in the long set up before the introduction of a creator notion:

> "The unifying cohesiveness we found in the laws of physics has come shining through in the workings of biology as well. But in both fields, we see it only when we seek it. A superficial reading of the world teaches of a reality built on entities as diverse and unrelated in

their composition as the steel of a gun barrel and the fragrance of a rose. Can they actually have anything in common? Indeed, they can and do. Surpassing the harmony of the laws of physics and the workings of biology lies the subtle truth that every bit of existence is composed of a single substrate-energy-created at the beginning."[13]

These arguments are nothing new in theology. The ontological argument alone was first introduced by archbishop of Canterbury St. Anselm in the eleventh century and the teleological and cosmological argument stem as far back as the ancient Greek philosophers. Although the notions concerning billions of years ago at first appear noteworthy, some of the notions are caught in their own web of designs. An example is Anselm of Canterbury's work *Proslogion*, in which he calls for the ontological argument. It is a target for *Stanford Encyclopedia of Philosophy*, which takes issue with such concepts.

"St. Anselm claims to derive the existence of God from the concept of a *being than which no greater can be conceived*. St. Anselm reasoned that, if such a being fails to exist, then a greater being—namely, a *being than which no greater can be conceived, and which exists*—can be conceived. But this would be absurd: nothing can be greater than a being than which no greater can be conceived. So a being than which no greater can be conceived—i.e., God—exists."[14]

Because it makes sense in theology, under theological grounds these notions of creation are valid. This is what is meant by credibility given the current faith/science debate. If one wants to give credence to such notions and enable this type of thinking, they are only fooling people and themselves. What guidance for the masses do such notions bring? The answer is they do not bring guidance. They cannot make sense of the localized scriptures in today's society, and they cannot bring about any relevance. When we as a society allow for such an institution to continue and flourish with their insulated fantasy world, we allow for an entity that is basically useless to the major part of society.

How exactly is theology useful in modern times? What break-through have they had which isn't considered a breakthrough only in their circle? With credibility like theirs, it is no wonder the halls of their colleges are filled with members who are aware of the logical flaws in their "philosophy", and silence of such exposure to theology is encouraged among the religious "academic". A goal of theology is to be taken seriously outside of theist opinions. Once that occurs, religion can be taken outside of the context it is currently at, and the thought paradigm attempted for so long by desperate theologians can be increased.

The number of books being published based on arguments popular in theology continues the wordplay in that arena. The cosmological argument, for example, will be the entire tone or undertone of a book that reads like a novel with a personal testimony or attempt to establish credibility to a religious notion. A typical book of a theologian reads like this: The author will have the high praise of multiple religious history PhD recipients and professors of religious studies written on the back cover. They may even have the nod from a religious-backing scientist. The title will present the notion of something akin to a scientific break-through. When the reader opens the book, however, he/she discovers quotes like "personal", and "theology" in it. The citations and quotes to back up arguments asserted will mostly be from other religious "philosophers". Yet aside from historical religious information, the arguments asserted in these books are not much more than that of the current religious main argument: the god-of-the-gaps. Easily arguable, easily beatable.

The book *God: A Brief History*, for example, by theologian John Bowker has an academic suggesting book title, like a gloss-over of perhaps previously unlit events in the history of human beings and their concept of a deity. In what reads more like a case for the evidence of a god (a Christian one specifically), the book explains its real purpose in the very preface: "It is not a comprehensive history of all that has been thought and believed about God, nor does it record all the stories that have been told about God. Instead, I have described ways in which people have made their own discoveries of God and have developed and changed our understanding of who and what God is, and how God became real to them."[15] A personal claim for the existence of a God through the testimony of the lay, the book becomes something other than a historical document or a search for truth. *Introduction to the Encyclopedia of Religious Phenomena* by religious scholar J. Gordon Melton is another example of wordplay. The book sounds like an in-depth objective analysis of what the word "phenomena" suggests in the title (given that the word "encyclopedia" is included in the title), but contains articles like the one on Noah's Ark which includes the rather biased description of a scientist's conclusion on possible Ark wood samples discovered. "Unfortunately, when subjected to scientific testing, the samples of wood proved to be of relatively recent origin."[16]

The quoting of other theologians is also rampant in theological books as well as their own reviewed published papers. For example, the very beginning of the introduction to PhDs Ralph and Valerie Carnes' book *The Road to Damascus* reads as follows:

> "Something vitally important is happening all around us. People of all ages are turning or re (italics, cell) turning in increasing numbers to churches and synagogues all across the country. In many countries, it takes the form of 'base communities'. As Harvey Cox has pointed out in *Religion in The Secular City*, atheistic parents are appalled that their children are slipping on Sundays to go church."[17]

Harvey Cox is a Professor of Divinity at Harvard whose books authored include, *When Jesus Came to Heaven, Fire from Heaven, Common Prayers, The Persistence of Religion* and *Lamentation and The Song of Songs.* This is just one example of the many attempts at credibility theologians make regarding their work, as if quoting each other will have any effect on the outside world.

The peer-reviewed work of theologians reads as no different. Papers published by religious philosophers for religious philosophers and in religious philosophy publications will have the same background as books written by that circle. They will be published in a theologian publication, with theologian citations, reviewed by theologians before print. They will contain the same history of religious documentation but will be riddled with wordplay and what cannot be argued by modern science. Vladan Perisic's paper in *St Vladimir's Theological Quarterly* is an example of such a work. His calling for "the liberation of theology from the shackles of contextualization" reads more like asking for an interpretation of the word of God to be taken to mean something other than the current one which is easy to criticize. Concerning this notion of liberation through another interpretation, he writes:

> "This would, in fact, be its liberation from worldliness and its reorientation to its proper 'object,' the transcendent yet immanent God, who is the same yesterday, today and forever. In other words, what we need is not reading the Gospel in light of its cultural

context but reading (and moreover transforming) the cultural context in the light of the Gospel."[18]

And in even other words than that, if the word of God was perceived as if in this other realm, it could be completely removed from critique. The arguments and notions presented by these individuals when really looked at hard are little more than veiled attempts to make religion hold on to what credibility it has among the masses. Making religious notions appear more important than they are, although some hearts may be in the right place, is simply lying for what one believes in. This is fine if people want to engage in such an ideology, but to call it a search for truth or to even take it seriously is something else. Theologians know this, so they lie.

If one questions the scholarly standards and philosophy of these papers, they are likely to be answered by theologians that it is indeed a real philosophy, a *Christian* philosophy. In this sense, it does not matter how the immanence and transcendent being referred to in the quote is what liberates theology, because it is claimed to be of a personal matter, one that is believed rather than analyzed. Such authors not only use this unseen realm as a premise for arguments asserted as if it were a tangible part of a formulaic method, but refer to this Christian realm and characters with the utmost of confidence in their work and do so often.

Gustavo Guttierez's work is another example of a "peer" reviewed published paper. One will notice a similar theme in religious thought in his piece for *Theological Studies*. With regard to the religious claimed metaphysical and explanation of reality, Guttierrez gives advice on daily life in relation to a god, but makes assumptions without metrics, claims without specifics. He writes:

> "Following Jesus is a response to the question about the meaning of human existence; it is a global vision of our life, but it also affects life's small and everyday aspects. Discipleship allows us to see our lives in relation to the will of God and sets goals for us to strive for and realize through a daily relationship with the Lord, which implies relationships with other persons. Spirituality comes into being on the terrain of Christian practice: thanksgiving, prayer, and a commitment in history to solidarity, especially with the poorest. Contemplation and solidarity are two sides of a practice inspired by a global sense of human existence that is a source of hope and joy."[19]

That this is taken as actual philosophy is stunning. What is this man talking about? How does he know about these subjects, and what to say on them? Is it through the same revelation that gave members of the Holy Roman Church such wrong answers regarding existence throughout the centuries? To mention spirituality with such casualness is insulting to the intelligent mind, much less linking it with Christian notions which are too limited to be linked with any advanced spiritual journey.

Another "peer" reviewed work, Karl Barth describes the works of Christ in relation to the person in *Anglican Theological Review*, but his definition of anything concrete is, of course, vague. "Giving the person and work of Christ each its proper due is no mean feat. To summarize the identity of the person who is present in the work of salvation is one of the most important and salutary tasks of Christology. This is because we are considering a person who even in his humiliation—in his assumption of 'adamic human nature'— never ceases 'to be who He is'."[20] This claimed science of the personal reads exactly like how an invalid book of trivial tales would be interpreted after thousands of years of analysis. Again, how does the author know what he is talking about in such an area? What is the metric used to measure or analyze any of this?

That the masses aren't openly hostile towards such 'philosophy' is puzzling. What does the Christ being who he is in humiliation have anything to do with? Certainly nothing when it comes to real humanity where any child can brush off humiliation today. To try and give complex meaning to the utterly local is to justify the trivial and meaningless. All those songs in Psalms, all those verses of dust and fire and salt, they had no meaning other than what daily life was then. To make that appear any more complex is to just kick a horse that has been dead for some time now.

In a final example of claimed peer-reviewed papers, *New Advent* is a grouping of Catholic Church-related works from religious authors. A self-proclaimed encyclopedia, the publication defines theology in the quote below, yet follows the same line of exactly zero proof as the works it collects:

> "To define dogmatic theology, it will be best to start from the general notion of theology. Considered etymologically, theology (Gr. *Theologia, i.e. periTheou logos*) means objectively the science treating of God, subjectively, the scientific knowledge of God and

Divine things. If defined as the science concerning God (*doctrina de Deo*), the name of theology applies as well to the philosophical knowledge of God, which is cast into scientific form in natural theology or theodicy. However, unless theodicy is free from errors, it cannot lay claim to the name of theology. For this reason, pagan mythology and pagan doctrines about the gods, must at once be set aside as false theology."[21]

What are we to make of such work in the 21st century? What is the current count of how many times the Church or others in religious scholarship have been wrong? That this is even considered valid, even in the ranks of theology is disappointing. First of all, there is no science concerning god because god is a man-made myth. So that pretty much kills that concept, as it is difficult to link science with an entity that has never existed. Secondly, thinking theology has anything to do with science is insulting to science. If the article would mention anti-science concerning theology then it would make more sense, as all these claims of modern religious thought conveniently involve what science cannot disprove. It is also no wonder that this type of perceptive view concerning existence has little to do with modern day life. If the masses were to be exposed to this type of literature often, what would their reaction be? If they were asked their opinion, would they think that this is applicable to something as important as a life guide? Would they even allow themselves to critically think outside of such notions proposed by the strict, ill-informed and delusional Church?

Though these tactics employed in such works appear ridiculous, this is taken seriously by the religious scholar establishment. It is no surprise that, while the premise for such argumentation seems biased, for theologians it is a requirement. This is what philosophy professors Paul Draper and Ryan Nichols tell us in *The Monist*: "The belief of some of the most influential philosophers of religion (e.g. Plantinga 1984) that philosophers who happen to be Christians should take the truth of Christian doctrines as a starting point *for philosophical* inquiry."[22] In other words, they are to believe that what they are discussing isn't nonsensical. But taking the 'truth' of Christianity as a starting point for something like philosophy is a large task. The book of Genesis alone contains so many contradictions that Augustine advised against its notions in order to not look foolish. He was wise in that respect.

The reason for this mystical and complex-appearing subject regarding religious explanation is that theologians know they have no bearing on such a platform. Arguments which are out of range of critics' sights are propped up instead. Theologians dance and dance on top of these arguments, daring scientists to disprove the inarguable. It is also the reason why they always change the subject to the inarguable when contradictions are brought up regarding their religious claims. Tell a theologian this, however, and they will be quick to point out how most religious skeptics are not aware of theological principles, and therefore cannot argue theological points. Religious authors can take confidence in the logic of their perceptive views and can appear credible because the work being done is that of a 'religious' scholar, and under such assumptions made in this institution they are applicable to explanation of reality. Under this notion, only those who attained the knowledge of their specific field (or a scientist sympathetic to Christianity) has the ability argue the points made. In other words, the vehicle that decides whether theologians are right or not consists of theologians. This exclusive school of thought can maintain this disposition all theologians want, but without proof, their opinions are just that. It does not matter if they refuse to have a perceptive view outside their encouraged notions. That outside world exists, and the inner realm of religious thought is forced to deal with such notions questioning their work.

Public debate is another area where theologians take a little too much liberty in points made. Although skilled with wordplay and eloquent sounding, these performances are riddled with debate tactics which can hardly be called fair. The arguments are cleverly worded but designed as a distraction from the premise of weaker arguments. In analyzing the argument, even narrowing it down to what it really is from -an inarguable premise- is made difficult by this wordplay from the religious proponent, mostly theologians. Instances of trick play in these debates are the cancelling out of certain topics to be discussed during the debate that will hurt the religious argument. Theologian William Lane Craig's argument in a debate against Christopher Hitchins is an example of this.

Craig first introduces his argument, then cancels out debate topics that he does not wish to discuss later in the debate: "There is no good argument that atheism is true, and second that there are good arguments that theism is true." He then expands on what was *meant* in his statement. "Notice carefully the circumscribed limits of those contentions. We're not here tonight to debate the social impact of religion, or Old Testament ethics, or Biblical inerrancy, all interesting and important topics no doubt, but not the subject of tonight's debate which is the existence of God."[23] In this one statement, he has canceled out Biblical criticism or limited social impact from being discussed while laying the foundation for what Craig wants allowed in the discussion –the inarguable.

Religious proponent Dinesh D'Souza employs the same practice of wordplay. In his first statement, D'Souza, in a debate with Christopher Hitchins asserts, "In this debate at no time will I make any arguments that appeal to Revelation, scripture or authority."[24] In what appears to not rely on the strength of a revered word of God, this essentially translates to 'instead of discussing this topic, let's discuss another.' These topics D'Souza attempted to cancel out from discussion were delicacies for someone of Hitchen's background and intelligence, yet were all attempted to be wiped from the debate in D'Souza's very first statement in order to shift focus on to his inarguable premise. D'Souza might as well have said that he will not discuss any weakness in the religious argument whatsoever, and instead discuss the weakness in the theory of scientific theory.

The fact that theologians will evade these topics harmful to the religious point of view is noteworthy; using the inarguable, the religious make the burden of proof on the debate opponent. Turning the tables rather than feeling compelled to prove his assertion, the burden of proof is put on the opposing side to *dis*prove the inarguable-based premise from which their entire main argument lies (and of which they have no proof). This is knowingly lying and one reason why Professor Dawkins refuses to debate theologians. The debate becomes about what cannot be disproved, referring to it multiple times. It does not matter that the debate opponent disagrees with the premise, the premise according to the theologian has been set and will be followed by the theologian regardless of what is said concerning the limitations of religion. Such practices define why theologians are not taken seriously in most science and academic circles.

It will also not be uncommon for religious proponents to suggest a truce between science and faith in debates, the appearance for cohesion and acceptance by the science community of religious works. Rabbi David Wolpe once said in a debate that religion and science should coexist, and religious proponent Ken Ham in a debate with Bill Nye suggested, "science and religion are linked".[25] Alvin Plantinga and John Wilson in addressing the rift between faith and science in *Christianity Today* asserted,

> "In certain areas, the right word would be *alleged* conflict. For example, I argue that there's no real conflict between evolutionary theory—that is, the scientific theory of evolution apart from any naturalistic spin—and what C. S. Lewis called 'mere Christianity.' There's no real conflict, even though conflict has been alleged by people on the Right as well as on the Left."[26]

Unfortunately, the practice of lying is coached from the very moment students undertake serious theological programs at religious universities. This is accompanied by outright attempts at sullying the credibility of science while maintaining a veiled contempt for scientific theory among many in theology. Debate tactics by the religious should not go unnoticed, as hiding and defending false claims by people of times long forgotten trivializes the discourse. Misleading arguments are not from a few bad apples in theology or the misunderstood work of a certain exclusive set that has an understanding of it. It is rampant, purposeful and obvious.

In a final note on wordplay by the religious, although there are many theologians who are well known in religious circles and the religious debate arena, one of the more interesting figures that kept surfacing during the research of this book was professor Alvin Plantinga. An influential figure among Western religious scholars, he is considered the greatest religious philosopher of his generation by his peers. William Lane Craig, for example, reflected on Plantinga's work for *Journal of the Evangelical Theological Society*: "By the sheer force of his intellect... he not only acquired national attention but has also almost singlehandedly changed the face of American philosophy with respect to religious thought."[27]

An essay written by Plantinga, an attempt at "solving the problem of evil", where he attempts to rid the problem religious scholars have with the claim of morality invokes times of creation and forever changed the landscape of religious scholarship. John Stackhouse Jr.'s piece on Plantinga for *Christianity Today* reveals a version of Plantiga's "free will defense" argument which would solve the philosophical problem: "It essentially was this: God desired to love and be loved by other beings. God created human beings with this end in view. To make us capable of such fellowship, God had to give us the freedom to choose, since love cannot be either automatic or coerced. This sort of free will, however, entailed the danger that we would use it to go our own way in defiance of both God and our own best interests."[28]

This type of work is not only taken seriously by theology, but is sad. Why don't they just come up with whatever they want to say and add that "philosophically" to something loosely tied to scripture? Why don't they just say whatever they feel like and assert that in under the name of a disprovable "personal" based realm of religious thought? Religion professor John Stackhouse shows his appreciation of a particular piece by Plantinga and his wordplay when he wrote the following:

> "It is important to remember that the original charge of inconsistency is an absolute one: there is no way for the theist consistently to hold belief in God's power, goodness, and the existence of evil. All Plantinga had to do in response was to show at least one way to hold all three together— regardless of whether each detail of the defense is true or even plausible. The consensus among philosophers of religion... is that Plantinga has done this successfully."[29]

This 3rd grade logic where anyone can simply move around certain notions as they please is not philosophy. There is nothing philosophical about referring to one-time Biblical occurrences and mixing or matching possibilities to present religion in a more respectable view. However, this is what is being done. This type of thinking is so ostracized from reality, so void of logic that one can easily counter these arguments by taking ridiculous liberties regarding the inarguable too. One can easily counter free will argument of Plantinga in this same fashion by referring to the invisible Flying Spaghetti Monster argument, in that when God made humans, the monster actually took the free will that God was going to use on humans and used it to salt its invisible sauce. The free will jar was then given back to God after its contents had been emptied. One can easily go beyond the boundaries of reason to make up concepts. Anyone can make arguments based on what hasn't been proved *yet*, then allow for the only critique to be from that same ridiculous school of thought.

Argument points by theologians are not serious discussion points but merely inarguable rubbish based on tales which were plagiarized from other tales told hundreds and hundreds of years ago. These are stories with no sense of a real community, no daily life that had anything to do with a real human sense, yet they are being poured over by men with a near fatal interest in proving their validity. Although it is obvious that these are weak arguments, the insulated theological work continues. If there were some type of mechanism to expose theology for what it really is, maybe more people will realize this and cease to give credence to such notions. Additionally, separating the locality of Biblical context with complex and inarguable premises is not keeping up with the science-versus-god debate. It is wordplay and it is not even intelligent at that. This is not so much an example of scholarly attempts at puzzling religious messages as it is a dime store philosophy the likes of which are opinion in nature. Of course the deciding theological opinion will be in favor of the religious proponent in their works. What else would it be in favor of? Theology does not play fair and it should be held accountable for it. If those in this field are looked at by the masses in this perspective, it would likely lead to a different understanding of theology.

As distracting as theology remains, it is also not without its backing. A powerful vehicle engineers the infusion of religion into the mainstream consciousness, or at least it tries. If it is not the theologian or religious philosopher, it is the scientist sympathetic to religion or a powerful billionaire who carries out a questionable agenda. As hard as religious scholarship works, sympathetic figures in academia, science and philanthropy work just as hard to promote a more religious view of reality. Neuroscientist Mario Beauregard and his work with journalist Denyse O'Leary along with the work of mathematician and biologist Martin Nowak are examples of published non-theologians in favor of arguments claimed by religious proponents. Although there have been many theologians asserting religious claims, their effect does not have the impact regarding the perception of the populace compared with those in the academic and science fields.

The tricks used by religious in academia and science may appear on a more credible platform, but the results of the works are just as weak. In his book, *God Is Not Great*, Christopher Hitchens suggests religion for the believer as a matter in which "we should not care, as long as they make no further attempt to inculcate religion by any form of coercion."[30] Unfortunately, those attempts have been made in increasing instances by many in the religious-leaning academia as well as religious-leaning philanthropy. The power and influence of a few wealthy men command a great deal of mobility concerning academic goals for religious proponents and will be discussed in this section.

An example of pro-religious academic personalities of today, Edmund Gettier is a Cornell educated philosopher and was mentored by the likes of Christian philosopher Norman Malcolm, and was at one time a colleague of Alvin Plantinga at Wayne State University. He once published a three-page paper (with just as many citations) in the 1960s examining the definition of the word knowledge. Gettier surmised that the defined valued prerequisites of knowledge being justified, true and believed (JTB) did not alone comprise knowledge, and that there existed another value, that of luck. The religious community hailed the paper as a landmark, and while many criticized the reshaping of JTB in the paper, it reshaped how some view knowledge and its properties today.

Scientist Martin Nowak's is another example of pro-Christian work. His game piece theory which attempted to supplant the theory of evolution with a design theory literally changed the path of a scientific field. Nowak's book, *SuperCooperators,*, which questions evolution, explains his notions. His criticism of natural selection, for example, includes the following explanation on why it prevents human progress. "At its heart natural selection undermines our ability to work together. Why is this? Because in what mathematicians call a well-mixed population, where any two individuals meet equally often, cooperators always have a lower fitness than defectors-they're always less likely to survive."[31] Asking the following question, Nowak provides his stance on his work and game piece model on the subject of cooperation to *Scientific American*. "Why, then, is selfless behavior such a pervasive phenomenon? Over the past two decades I have been using the tools of game theory to study this apparent paradox. My work indicates that instead of opposing competition, cooperation has operated alongside it from the get-go to shape the evolution of life on earth, from the first cells to Homo sapiens."[32]

Nowak along with Roger Highfield sound very confident about their work. They begin *SuperCooperators* with the book's declaration. Describing the importance of mathematics, they write, "The truth really is out there and it can be expressed in this extraordinary language…Some would go even further than this (here it comes). They regard the mathematics that describes our cosmos as a manifestation of the thoughts of a creator. Albert Einstein once remarked, 'I believe in Spinoza's God, Who reveals Himself in the lawful harmony in the world'."[33] One can only guess what the authors conclude at the end of the book based on an introduction of this sort. Nowak's game theory, which included math-based game pieces ultimately showed support, according to Nowak, of a designer influence on living things based on cohesive actions of the pieces. In a submission to the journal *Science*, he elaborated:

"Before reviewing the recent developments in evolutionary game theory, we sketch a few basic types of interactions that help to familiarize readers with terminology. A 'game' is an interaction between a set of individuals. These 'players' act according to their behavioral phenotypes, which are called 'strategies.' The players' payoffs, which translate into fitness, depend, in general, on their own strategy and on that of their co-players. A tree's height, a parent's sex ratio, a parasite's virulence, a female's choosiness, or a male's ornament are instances of strategies. This terminology is by now well established, but occasionally still induces reactions like 'animals don't play games'."[34]

A paper he co-authored for *Nature* warns of inclusive fitness arguments which lack models to support their evidence.[35]

When Nowak's paper published, it was hailed by the religious community and criticized harshly by the scientific community overall. Richard Dawkins, for one, wrote that the famous *Nature* paper "misses the whole point of kin selection" and called the science in *SuperCooperators* that addresses the topic "embarrassing". University of Chicago biology professor Jerry Coyne mocked the experiment, asserting that Nowak's work "shows that humans are genetically nice, ergo Jesus."[36] Nowak's work turned out to be an embarrassment, and Harvard's *Nature* received criticism for publishing the paper, and was for the first time ever in serious risk of losing its elite credibility. Although many question whether or not actual science was used in the study, the work of such religious proponents should not go unnoticed, as their actions indicate an attempt at a paradigm shift in culture and thought.

Powerful philanthropists also are included when discussing influential religious proponents outside of theology. The following individuals show that it is important to take notice of such activity. Although we want to live peacefully as a society, theocracy and its ugly tentacles are a very real threat by individuals who are dead serious about religion and aren't exactly docile as a collective whole. Their influence is to be considered, especially when religion is generational, and the next generation of the religious will also attempt such foolish acts. That those spawns will be armed with just as much power and influence will be all the more difficult to offset without proper exposure to their notions and work.

Nicholas Shunemann's three era break down of the anti-evolution movement, presents a good description of attempts by theists to insert a more religious perceptive view in the mainstream consciousness:

> "After Epperson halted creationist attempts to exclude the Theory of Evolution from public school curricula, creationists adopted a new strategy, supporting legislation that requires "equal treatment" for evolution and creationism in science courses. This tactic was quashed by the Supreme Court in Edwards v. Aguillard on the rationale that such legislation served no secular purpose; thus ended the era of balanced-treatment statutes.

"The third era, which continues to the current day, involves primarily subtle attacks designed to minimize the role of the Theory of Evolution in public education as well as to diminish its credibility in the eyes of students. These attacks have taken the form of attempts to eliminate evolutionary theory from state standardized tests, the use of disclaimers which marginalize the Theory of Evolution and suggest creationism as a viable alternative, and the presentation of scientific and philosophical "evidence" against evolution to either imply or directly support the hypothesis of creation by a supernatural agent."[37]

A couple major backers of religious-leaning educational material are briefly talked about here. One includes John Templeton. He is a religious proponent who attempts to advance religious notions (albeit notions which lean towards the religion typical of those in his geographical region), but his influence is far more powerful than that of someone like Martin Nowak. This is the description of the well-funded Templeton Foundation on its web site:

"The John Templeton Foundation funds independent research and public engagement, pursuing breakthrough discoveries to expand our current knowledge about the universe, the full potentials of humanity, and life's ultimate purpose." The Foundation's motto, 'How little we know, how eager to learn,' exemplifies its support for open-minded inquiry, commitment to rigorous scientific research and related scholarship, and encouraging civil, informed dialogue among scientists, scholars, theologians, and the public at large."[38]

The one word "theologians" in the entire paragraph, as hidden as it may seem, has a much, much bigger connotation than the authors of the page allow. Why on earth would one promote theology in a discussion that includes scientists and scholars except to encourage a more tolerant view of religion in such discussions? What other respectable foundation that considers the complex includes such a field as theology? The truth is that billionaire and religious proponent John Templeton has been funding pro Christian "studies" for decades to allow for the undermining of discrediting theology.

As far back as the 1980's Templeton thought scientific fields could be used to discover what might have been considered spiritual territory. Subjects like compassion and philosophy would be the focus. Since that time, the foundation has spent hundreds of millions on projects which he hoped would validate religion. Science journalist John Horgan when interviewed by Robert Carroll reported the money from the 1.1 billion-dollar Templeton Fund is spent "on prizes, academic programs, publications, broadcasts, lectures, conferences, and research on topics such as the neurobiology and genetics of religious belief; the evolutionary origins of altruism; and the medical benefits of prayer, church attendance, and forgiveness."[39] The reason the fund spends all this money on such subjects? As John Miller writes in *National Review*, "in order to discover links between religion and science."[40]

Millions have also been spent towards Oxford's Ian Ramsey Centre for Science and Religion as well as Centre for Anthropology and Mind to "determine scientifically why people believe in God."[41] 4.4 million was donated from the foundation for the study of "free will" to Florida State University's Alfred R. Mele in 2012.[42] Florida State University Chemist and Nobel Chemistry prize winner Harold Kroto told *Nature* Washington D.C. editor M. Mitchell Waldrop of the Templeton award, a prize worth significantly more than the one million-dollar Nobel, "there's a distinct feeling among the academic community that Templeton just gives the award to the most senior scientist they can find who's willing to say something nice about religion." "A lot of money wasted on nonsensical ideas" was how Kroto described the tens of millions given to study religious compassion, altruism and forgiveness by the foundation.[43] The Foundation has socio-political aims as well. It awarded $2 Million to Mercatus Center at George Mason University, known for its Koch brothers' association and its anti-regulation stances.[44]

The accusation of Templeton ties to Intelligent Design has come up many times throughout the years, forcing Senior Vice President of the organization Charles Harper to write that the foundation "vigorously disagrees" with the ID camp. But the obvious goals have been in plain print more than a few times. Defending giving Billy Graham the Templeton award in 1992, Templeton gave an interview with the *Saturday Evening Post*. "In the case of Billy Graham, the emphasis was on new methods for preaching spiritual ideas. He was wise in how he used electronic methods to preach to a wider audience than previous evangelists. He set a new standard, a new ambition, for other people to follow about how much a single preacher can do".[45] As if evangelists get serious recognition for their "work" outside of religious circles.

This veiled association with religious concepts is why goals of the organization have been scrutinized by many in science. For example, in response to the award being given to royal astronomer Sir Martin Rees of Cambridge's Trinity College in 2011, biology professor Jerry Coyne noted that the foundation "plies its enormous wealth with a single aim: to give credibility to religion by blurring its well-demarcated border with science"[46] and Templeton prize winner physicist Paul Davies was criticized by Richard Dawkins in *The God Delusion*, claiming Davies's *The Mind of God* "seems to hover somewhere between Einsteinian pantheism and an obscure form of deism", asserting this the reason for the Templeton prize awarded to him.

Another power player in the ID movement is Phillip Johnson. A former UC Berkley law professor and born-again Christian, his views on theism led him to co-found Discovery Institute, an organization dedicated to changing public opinion as well as the opinions in the scientific community. Johnson's scope is a little less subtle than Templeton and made no secret of the institute's agenda when he declared in 1997, "If we understand our own times, we will know that we should affirm the reality of God by challenging the domination of materialism and naturalism in the world of the mind. With the assistance of many friends I have developed a strategy for doing this... We call our strategy the 'wedge'."[47]

The institute has been accused of creationist code language in state legislature, the cleverly worded bills calling for the teaching of creationism and other notions which challenge scientific status quo.[48] Johnson is the most influential figure of the current ID movement. The Wedge, a document later leaked on the internet[49] includes a 20-year goal of reshaping American views and the lexicon concerning intelligent design along with openly questioning the Constitutional ideology of separation of church and state. In a 1999 speech, Johnson commented on this "intellectual movement in the universities and churches" that he helped to create. The movement, he claimed, "is devoted to scholarship and writing that furthers this program of questioning the materialistic basis of science."[50] That same year the first Intelligent Design and Evolution Awareness club was formed at the University of California at San Diego in 1999 with strong Johnson backing. The club has since formed in chapters worldwide including American high schools.

It looks as though Johnson's design will move full speed ahead in the future and warning signs are already coming in about it. Mark Terry gives us such a warning in *Education Digest* regarding the Wedge and its sphere of influence on schools in the coming years. "Before you dismiss this as of no interest to you as a history, English, or social studies teacher, watch out for the Wedge. For it's looking for you, too. Evolution is simply the initial target, and if the first dangerous weed, modern science, can be removed from the garden, your area will be ripe for replanting as well."[51]

These were just a couple examples of religious influence on society today. Skeptics are asked why debate whether God exists if they doubt him. It is for reasons like these, arguments which muddy larger debates and have the potential to destroy what society has worked for. What they ultimately represent is a bump in the road of human progress. Religious proponents no doubt continue their efforts to spread religiously influenced notions and policy, but the façade is apparent with every attempt. The effects are not as immediate a concern compared to, say, Islamic fundamentalism, but this does not mean that attempts to dispel science are not at least questionable. Even aside from attempts at making religion appear credible, what theology essentially boils down to, if we look at it in their own words, is a study of wishful thinking in the interpretation of religious writings. The problem with wishful thinking is that it does not explain anything, regardless of the determination behind the work. It is merely the hopeful explanation of some notion.

Theology can interpret scripture anyway they like and can come up with thought-provoking notions based on modern thinking regarding religion, but at the end of the day they are stuck with what they started with, a vacant nothing from which they can also look forward to accepting further false interpretations of reality. The arguments may seem impressive at first and may seem legitimate, but involve the same roots, the same school of thought that produced the widely-accepted notion that the Earth was created at a time nowhere near the actual event and viewed women in exactly the time period of such prevalent ignorance. What a coincidence that all these local Bible attributes criticized showed the same local thinking regarding every single subject, yet theology insists on maintaining a paradigm where the lessons aren't endlessly local.

John Derbyshire describes exactly the disposition Christian-leaning religious proponents are in today when he wrote the following in *American Spectator*:

> "They have been plowing their lonely furrow for 20 years now, insisting on their right to a seat at science's banquet and promising that their ideas will bring about a revolutionary overthrow of orthodox biology (which they call "Darwinism" for propagandistic reasons) Any Day Now...They drop heavy hints that biologists are in a panic about the instability of their foundational theories, but are anxious to hide their doubts from public gaze. Really? One would naturally like to see some illustrative examples. Twenty years on from the inception of ID, the revolution seems as far away as ever. The ID-ers are still shut outside the banquet with their noses pressed forlornly to the window, and the ancient régime looks to be as firmly established as ever. What's the problem here?"[52]

But that theological revolution will never occur, the value of the root in their religion is still nothing, as myths have that tendency. When all the variables equal nothing, the result will still be zero regardless of how much make-up is applied and regardless of how high the number is used to multiply zero with. It is, and always will be zero.

The overall tone of daily existence in Biblical times did not change from the OT to the NT, yet theologians tell us not to look at the OT for what they are asserting, but the New. Treatment of women and animals along with utter ignorance of alcohol effects are a stark contrast to the impressive and claimed other-worldly theologian logic and analysis. They should just interpret the scriptures any way they want, it's not like the myth will appear and punish them for being wrong. Although notions presented by modern theology regarding interpretation can be complex and unlike the local times of scripture, a large part of the religious masses form their opinions of the world from a literal interpretation of the Bible. This means that modern Western theology has a rift not just between Church notions, but the views of the practitioners as well. This is a problem that should be dealt with by the masses. But of course, religious proponents aren't interested in promoting that. The truth is, the stuff of theology is mere theory based on texts which aren't even authentic or known in authorship. The more people know this the better. What is at stake is worse than some people might know now.

They aren't even honest about their work. They know there is no science in Nowak's work or real philosophy in Plantinga's theories. If they didn't, they would be fooling themselves. Even they are not that blind. Of course, this is all made possible by the fact that anyone can make any claim they want regarding other realms because there is simply not enough proof to disprove it as of yet. William Lane Craig dances on top of these types of arguments, daring someone to disprove their inarguable assertions. This is not a smart move, and religious proponents should be the last ones celebrating notions based on what science has yet to claim. It is why the Department of Biological Sciences at Lehigh University wrote, "It is our collective position that intelligent design has no basis in science, has not been tested experimentally, and should not be regarded as scientific."[53] It is also why theology will never fall into an important school of thought, never matching the rigors of philosophy, never resembling analytical philosophy requiring what philosophy professor Jonathan Jacobs describes in *Society* as "conceptual clarity, high standards of argumentative rigor, the articulation of principles and their implications, and often, the explication of relations between philosophical claims and theorizing on the one hand, and other types of claims and theorizing (scientific, commonsense, ethical, psychological, aesthetic, moral, etc.) on the other."[54] This is almost all missing in theology, a field which claims to be above science.

If it appears cruel to criticize theology in such a way, it is important to keep in mind their willingness to discredit and/or muddy the scientific method while claiming to be Christian the whole time (lying for Jesus?). It says something about theologians. It says that they don't care what the truth is, forcing their version to be followed by others is priority. This is not a respectable field but a contemptable one, and Richard Dawkins is right about them. This is added to the fact that theology also enjoys a great backing by the powerful and the wealthy, and that factions are actively trying to create a paradigm shift in thought, a cultural environment suitable to an opinion. In this fashion, they are attempting a paradigm shift, a church state, a revolution. If this is the way they wish to choose course, then they are also inviting others to act accordingly.

Being that science and philosophy cooperate, why doesn't theism and science cooperate? Why aren't scientists accused of fumbling around with their work the way theologians are and at the rate they are? It appears every time a theologian presents a paper for study, it devalues the field. Nonetheless, they will continue weaving a web of lies, a reminder of Augustine's plea to offset the notions that would make religion look lame. (Ex-chief religion writer at *Time* David Van Biema and others admit in *Time International*,

"Augustine explicitly warns against a very narrow perspective that will put our faith at risk of looking ridiculous."[55])

Chapter Six

"Happiness"

As we know by now, the power of a person's viewpoint is either a formidable tool or weapon. Someone's mere worldview impacts their beliefs, expectations, desires, the choosing of partners, friends or careers, essentially their entire existence so much as they can control. So important and influential are perceptions in human existence that health is directly affected by our perception of daily life. As Troy Adams and Janet Bezner assert in *Journal of American College Health*, perceptions are "at the core of several health theories."[1] Our viewpoint is to be impacted by outside influences, unfortunately the religious influence is a limiting example of a system promoting any enlightenment. Often called the lowest common denominator, mainstream religion ignores spirituality and the practitioner is left stranded in a world where limited help is at one's disposal when confronted with life's adversity due to limitations of the religious texts.

The purpose of this chapter is to counter the position taken by religious proponents regarding their claim of spirituality. The system discussed here which will be presented to counter ones by religion will be non-theistic and its concepts -unlike religion- adhere to objective inquiry. It will also be an Eastern philosophy-oriented one. While there remains many questions concerning Eastern philosophy, the amount of literature being written and scientific studies being conducted on the field grows along with recognition. Although there certainly have been critics of Eastern philosophy (Christopher Hitchens dedicated an entire chapter in his book, *God Is Not Great* to criticize Eastern thought), the truth is slightly more complicated, and the science-validated sections of material and metaphysical claims are difficult to ignore as numerous credible figures are now writing about it.

The Latin expression "experiential docet" -or experience teaches-[2] has given rise to numerous proverbs related to the notion. The experiences and wisdom gained in Eastern philosophy have for some years been the focus of much serious scientific inquiry. It is important to include Eastern philosophy in this discussion since, like Western philosophy, it indulges the curious, with notions based on objective reasoning. In this sense, Western and Eastern philosophy are two forms of thought that differ from religious scholarship. According to *Columbia Encyclopedia*, "philosophy rejects dogma and deals with speculation rather than faith."[3] We will look at such a personal philosophy in this chapter.

While Western philosophy provided the foundation for modern science, Eastern philosophy has provided a foundation for something modern science is just now beginning to discover. Eastern philosophy reminds us that training the mind produces positive and healthy results that are effective personally and collectively. It also presents in-depth personal insights, none of which are found in religion due to strict rules to not go outside of the religious teaching. If scientific progress itself is according to a secular mind as anthropologist Peter van der Veer notes in *Social Research*[4], it only makes sense to include philosophies which are secular in nature.

When regarding spirituality, it is important that we do not confuse the topic with religion. Religious proponents often claim the spiritual, the metaphysical effects and its associations which directly influence the individual. This claim is misguided, however, as spirituality has been described as distinct or separate from religion multiple times,[5,6] and USC Keck School of Medicine as well as University of Maryland Medical agree that spirituality is *not* religion.[7] Although religious proponents claim spirituality and the metaphysical, the experiences which occur in the religious cannot have effectiveness with regards to a religious influence that is simply vacant at its very core spiritually as no steps to follow in order to gain wisdom and clarity and inner peace is anywhere in texts like the Bible or the Koran. Instead, what the practitioner is actually going through is a medically explained phenomena, something that is universal, and which occurs in spite of whether or not the person is religious.

Nevertheless, it is interesting to note a Christian understanding regarding general spirituality, considering how many Christians claim spirituality. Writing of a connection the religious have with an outside realm for instance, a religious author contends in *American Catholic,* "rather than a sense of oneness with the whole globe, the Christian experience is a claimed sense of oneness with Jesus, filled with his spirit."[8] It is only obvious what results in a personal experience with a deity that has throughout history been called a myth: not much. The spiritual experiences claimed by the religious practitioner are simply misunderstood as a Christian experience for the Christian, or an Islamic experience for the Muslim, but no "experience" occurs, at least not in a true religious sense. In what way does Christianity relate to spirituality? The truth is the author couldn't possibly know what the supposed experience is, much less know how to relate to it in a religious context.

How fitting that the Bible should be ignorant to subjects like spirituality, objective critical thinking and empowerment? Doesn't the Bible even discourage critical thought? The apostle Paul perfectly displayed this spiritual ignorance when he allegedly wrote regarding empowerment, "we are able to recognize that we are sinful and may well want to reform ourselves by turning back to God, alone we do not have the inner power to make this change."[9] The naiveté of the fact that the human mind can actually be trained for betterment and empowerment is not only further indication that the scriptures lack such sense of empowerment, but the limitations placed on the religious concerning personal development is inevitable with such vacancy.

Of course one can gain inner strength through man-made concepts and mental training. We alone do have this power and we have been using it long before the apostle Paul. Empowerment is exactly what is needed to escape the chains of a limited existence, yet the main monotheistic systems do not encourage this. Instead, instructions of leaving it all to God are given along with following the vague scriptures. Rather than encouraging a sense of knowledge-gathering and sense of self, the scriptures call for an outdated version of relying on a deity and his command as deeper guidelines are nowhere to be found.

It is not as if the religious are encouraged to even consider Eastern notions and practices outside their own religious law. The church alone instructs its clergy to warn individuals of Eastern thought and alternative "methods of prayer", and have encouraged the faithful fully to understand Catholic doctrine before taking on such "New Age themes."[10] It is easy to see the threat Eastern thought poses to a vacant-natured religion. Such empowered thinking causes the individual to leave, the hold that religion has on the individual decreases. Christian lessons and concepts obviously do not hold weight spiritually, a oneness with Jesus or faith in a creator to solve human dilemmas is once again reminiscent of all other vacant concepts of the Christian tradition, and in no way resembles the deep personal commitment to real spirituality, try as the practitioner might. Although his/her heart may be in the right place, the expectations placed on a religious system is unfair to the highly outdated system and meaning is lost in the centuries of time regarding everyday personal adversity.

If religion was spiritual it, would embody something transcendent in its practices. It would have some kind of guidance where a step by step practice yields personal results, something that can be felt other than hope, comfort and sense of community. Just one way in which religion is not spirituality is its material-based concepts and viewpoints. Rather than inner awareness and *how* to be compassionate, local and trivial hedonistic desires are fulfilled and promised throughout the OT. This worldview carries on to the NT where even concepts of material gain is used as a backdrop for a shallow setting, if not directly used to motivate certain actions as if leading a herd. We will not even get into

Muhammed, whose spiritual level was probably in the negative when taking on a 6-year-old bride or the spirituality of the Torah encouraging child sex to get away with adultery.

The almost exclusively materialistic and shallow viewpoint of the Bible, when it isn't obscurely referencing a vague otherworldly holiness, riddles the document as if the authors were not even aware of the nature of hedonism. Even an awareness of what the material is on a deeper level seems to elude scripture. The Bible, for instance, clearly does not contain something resembling the following by Gerald Lampolsky: "When we have a desire to *get* something from another person or the world and we are not successful, the result is stress expressed in the form of frustration, depression, perceptions of pain, illness and death. Most of us seriously want to get rid of the pain, the illness, and frustrations, but we still want to maintain our old self-concept. Perhaps that is why we are going in circles, because we rigidly hold on to our old belief system."[11]

Of course it would not include something this complicating and transcending. Even Proverbs consist of not much more than one-liners without explanation regarding any personal development or betterment. In a basic material-based perspective where daily tasks become molded to include a material price tag, favors are worth transaction material and score is always kept. Life becomes a shell of the material. The wants and desires of the global population occur despite the religion practiced. The sense of discipline in any deeper level of awareness other than daily behavior is not there. This world of materialism is not only practiced in Biblical times, but there clearly is no indication of any mindset above the superficial in scripture, much less an indication that the authors were aware of how basic that mindset was.

The personal systems discussed in this chapter present an entirely different picture of spirituality than religion. Although many in science and academia share the same misnomer of spirituality, and often refer to it in the same context as religion[12,13,14,15,16,17,18], spirituality is distinct and separate from religion. For one thing, spirituality works, and its practices can be verified. It can also be properly addressed in the philosophical sense, unlike trying to philosophize one-time Biblical events. Although there are some who come close to a notion of spirituality and its relationship to religion such as Dr. Larry Culliford who asserted in *Psychology Today*, "Spirituality can be thought of as the 'active ingredient' of major world religions (and some humanistic ideologies too),"[19] there are others like those at University of Maryland Medical who come closer to the nature of spirituality: "Although spirituality is often associated with religious life, many believe that personal spirituality can be developed outside of religion."[20]

The initial spread of spirituality is noteworthy. When first conceptualized, it naturally led to an emergence that guided individuals outside the boundaries of religious thought with its premise of objective reasoning. According to professor Van der Veer in *Social Research*, "The emergence of spirituality as a concept enabled the inclusion of a variety of traditions under the umbric of universal morality without the baggage of competing religious institutions and their authoritative boundary maintenance."[21] Many somehow knew or felt that the true components of such a metaphysical relationship lie outside the cycle of a religious-fed thought paradigm. Even if the events of the Bible were real, even if people did not commit horrible acts in the name of religion throughout the centuries, the paradigm of its worldview was so limited that it became obvious to those exposed to Eastern thought.

Spirituality has been called notorious in its difficulty to be defined,[22] mainly because it encompasses a reality that is not material and cannot be sensed.[23] However, many can agree on David Hodge's definition of spirituality: "One way to conceptualize spirituality is in terms of connectedness with what is perceived to be sacred or transcendent. As such, spirituality can be seen as a fundamental human drive for transcendent meaning and purpose that involves connectedness with oneself, others, and ultimate reality."[24] As far as its medical benefits, spirituality is often cited as "the core of health",[25] and regarding spirituality linked to an overall well-being, doctors and psychologists have reported on the positive effects from the understanding that comes with spirituality, including inner peace and a nurturing sense of wholeness.[26,27] The effect of spirituality is evident among those in the science fields as well, as sociology professor Elaine Howard Ecklund admits in *Social Science Research Council*, "for some scientists, rather than science replacing religion, spirituality may be replacing religion."[28]

With regard to spirituality, it is important that Eastern thought be given the attention it deserves, especially when compared to any of the three major religions in terms of personal results. An Eastern thought system is an example of a worldview that can be non-theistic, helpful for the individual and the collective, and all without the dogmatic and limited themes of religion. When it comes to spirituality, Eastern thought is unparalleled, and is a good area to get in to when comparing systems with the helpful effects of mainstream religion. The following will discuss a system that seriously considers avenues to spirituality which religion strictly forbids. It will attempt to show a real human system that works on deeper levels than mainstream religion. The spirituality claimed in this system is real and with evidence of transcendence as well as greater sense of meaning in the vast literature written on it.

Although our focus will be on a non-theistic Eastern system, some of the techniques presented briefly are also examples of transcending-associated Eastern practices which are not concerned with Christianity, Islam or Judaism. These are man-made systems which provide incredible insight and produce significant, transcendent changes in multiple areas of personal development. They are systems that include philosophical concepts which have complied with the boundaries of logic and reason and have developed remarkably throughout the millennia, improving not only peace and well-being, but also providing astounding explanations of reality and existence which have yet to be questioned by science. While the practices in various systems of Eastern philosophy are surrounded by mythology and a haze of claims that clearly cannot be taken seriously in modern times, a wide number of metaphysical aspects of Eastern traditions remain impressive in their teachings and effectiveness.

Introduction of Eastern thought to Westerners went about as awkward as can be expected. Early British discovery of Eastern philosophy can be considered laughable as their initial take on the Indian Vedas were misunderstood, fumbled with and deemed savage. Centuries later, however, a more developed view of these and other writings have been taking place. As more scientific analysis is being applied to the rigidity of Eastern systems, they are finding striking discoveries. For example, in writing of the effective practices and lessons of Eastern philosophy, Joan Atwood and Lawrence Maltin write in *American Journal of Psychotherapies*, "For several thousand years there has existed a body of experience, teachings, and techniques that have addressed issues of the nature of human beings' awareness and suffering, the interrelatedness of the universe around them, and pathways to peacefulness and harmony."[29] The pathways mentioned contain personal journeys of self-reflection, objective reasoning, open minded honesty, discipline and experiences that ultimately result in enlightened wisdom, sense of wholeness, sense of community and an inner calm.

Initially dating back to 5,500 BCE, theistic Eastern philosophy introduced globally the results of personal objective reasoning. Many of these systems are riddled with what can be seen as non-credible: Vedic texts in Hinduism, for example, entail hundreds of hymns to a fire god and thunder god. Hinduism remains the oldest existing religion, though, and implored respectable techniques and values on the practitioner. The four Vedas, which are a central theme in Hinduism dating back to 5000 BCE,[30] were initially emphasized in the religion. The Upanishad texts were then written by learned men who acquired their information through gained knowledge rather than ritual, information rather than prayer. The viewpoint of sacrifice-based notions of the age inspired by the Vedas saw a transition, a shift in focus in Hinduism which would lead to questioning through philosophy and discussion of the Aranyakas and Upanishads.[31]

Rather than fulfilling personality, Hinduism teaches to escape the personality by removing ignorance.[32] The Savitri mantra of high caste Hindus, for example, is associated with its reach for enlightenment.[33] Meditation, yoga and chanting can also be found in Hinduism, along with the Hindu traditional medicine Ayurveda and the origin of mantras and meditation. The 200 Upanishads make up the theoretical basis for Hinduism involving intellectual and philosophical analysis and points of view. Although Buddhism would later reject Hindu scripture, Hinduism remains a highly influential theistic system in many ways. It was Eastern thought from India that inspired Emerson's 1836 essay *Nature*, quoted in his famous Divinity School address where he proclaims the limitations of Christianity. "Historical Christianity has fallen into error," and that it "destroys the power of preaching."[34] By the time Eastern philosophy was introduced to mainstream popular America again during the 20th century, the audience was almost waiting for its message as the affluent without need for basic necessity began to breed hunger for spirituality in suburbs across the U.S.[35] This was the backdrop of American sub-culture when the 1960's arrived -the most documented decade ever- where transcendental thought was introduced to mainstream society in a fashion not seen since a century earlier. This Hindu influence resulted in a major awakening among the affluent and middle class, who in turn responded to domestic and international injustice, particularly focusing on U.S. foreign policy.

Similar Indian systems based on knowledge arose out of Hinduism. Krishna Consciousness, for one, is based on the Hindu scriptures Bhagavad-gita. Although Krishna Consciousness is focused on the Hindu god Krishna, in his book, *The Science of Self Realization*, popular spiritual teacher Swami Prabhupahd wrote regarding the group's strive for enlightenment and inner peace, "Krsna consciousness enables us to reach highest perfectible form among current human form". The sense of oneness also is present in Krsna Consciousness,[36] and according to Bhagavad-gita, all earth species are part of a whole and are separate parts meant to serve the whole. Notice the difference in conceptual views compared to the notions of the three major Abrahamic religions. One is a model of future human relations, the other is a set of tales and vague instructions. Health effects of Krishna Consciousness are also noticeable, as a study on 3 groups of 62 people in each group chanting the Hare Krishna mantra for 25-minute daily sessions and clinically monitored showed reduced signs of stress and depression. It was also reported to help with bad habits and addictions. The results of the study formed a PhD thesis at Florida State University.

The practices brought on by these Eastern systems also implore the curiosity of many in science. Eastern practices like meditation have been discovered to provide strengthened mental health among other things. Such practices are found in many Eastern systems throughout the world. The most widely practiced and researched form of meditation globally is transcendental meditation (TM). TM techniques bring about relaxation, stress reduction and self-improvement through sustained periods of insight. Started by Maharishi Mahesh yogi, this spiritual practice is also promoted by Dr. Deepak Chopra and is the focus of several studies involving positive health aspects. Psychiatrist Norman Rosenthal, when challenged as to whether or not other forms of meditation are equally as effective, pointed out two reasons in favor of TM. "First, approximately 340 peer-reviewed published studies have demonstrated TM's positive effects on various medical conditions, including PTSD, attention deficit disorder, depression, addiction and cardiovascular disease. Second, different forms of meditation (such as focusing on the breath or an image) affect other parts of the brain and affect people in different ways, which may or may not be as helpful in healing emotional pain."[37]

Another Eastern practice is Traditional Chinese Medicine. Beginning as a spiritual form of practice thousands of years ago, it is currently showing results of improved attention as well as self-control through its short-term meditation practices.[38] Texas Tech University Chair of Nueroscience Yi Yuan Tang and University of Oregon professor Michael Posner, who had subjects practice Integrated Body-Mind Training (IBMT) taken from Traditional Chinese Medicine, discovered significant increases in intelligence and problem solving along with a significant decrease in stress as well as a strengthened immune system.[39] The practice of IBMT also stresses a balanced state of relaxation while focusing attention.[40]

A focal point of many Eastern traditions, meditation and mental training can be found throughout different Eastern systems. In recent years, a number of articles have demonstrated the benefits of various forms of meditation and mindfulness training. Psychologist Marsha Lucas described mindfulness as "paying attention in a particular way: on purpose, in the present moment, non-judgmentally."[41] Not going unnoticed by many, the U.S. Department of Defense has recently donated 1.7 million in a grant to Amishi Jha of University of Miami to study mindfulness and how it improves attention, a reported major component of intelligence.[42] As expected, mindfulness meditation also helps with health, such as preventing relapse in drug and alcohol addiction.[43] Mental training has also been found to boost altruism,[44] and, according to author Ed Halliwell, the most effective way to create mindfulness in daily life is to train in a formal way the concepts of meditation (as stated to Margarita Tartakovski).[45] Harvard Medical School's John Denninger alone has released multiple findings of scientific studies on meditation, including a government funded one concluding that meditation improves health in numerous areas, decreases stress, increases awareness and compassion, and builds the immune system. Meditation is also associated with a deeper happiness, sense of purpose, meaning, as well as fulfillment, and, according to psychology professor Matt J. Rossano, meditation may have been employed by humans to fully develop into our current evolved forms.[46]

Such benefits offered by Eastern philosophy overshadows the metaphysical explanation of the 3 major monotheistic religions. Where in the Bible do we find a narrative even close to the complexity of Eastern philosophy? A typical response from religious proponents might be in some variation of Jaroslav Pelikan's quote: "For if it is profoundly true that there are truths in the Bible that only the eyes of faith can see, it is also true that the eyes of unfaith have sometimes spotted what conventional believers have been too preoccupied or too bemused to acknowledge."[47] In other words, those who do not believe can perceive messages the religious might not. However, what is spotted by the 'unfaithful' is a lot more than what is presented to the faithful.

To make matters worse for this religious response, what the religious claim to see is not what is going on, but their subjective view of it. Are they positive that a message from the universe occurred in the form of their deity? Is this deity the exact same one typical of that region? What exactly do the religious see that those who do not have faith don't see? Is this this wise and otherworldly source of those perceptions from the same religion that taught how to treat slaves? The lack of sight in Pelikan's contention and in those who subscribe to this notion is not in the claimed distraction or the claimed bemusing of joyous events, as Pelikan describes, but lies instead in the very shell that does not permit seeing the effects of a broader view, which is why a metanalysis of 63 studies concluded that religion and intelligence are inversely related due to factors like lack of being openminded and relying on faith over facts. Lack of open mindedness is why Eastern practices are foreign to a Christian, Islamic and Jewish worldview.

Not only is there no insight, but no foresight in life when it comes to religious practices. There is no wisdom brought on by guided steps and proven practices that promotes advancement. The initial misunderstanding and fumbling of Eastern philosophical texts is not a one-time occurrence, and if religion were spiritual as claimed, the Biblical texts would have been understood by now in some transcendent way in comparison to Eastern texts, they would have some relation to a deeper personal dialogue (although there are claims that the Bible indirectly mentions meditation, these claims clearly cannot be taken seriously due to the historical nature of theology along with its theologians. No steps guiding the practitioner on the meditation, or what to focus on. They are forms of practice known as Christian meditation which focus on God and Bible passages versus specific and effectual steps taken in Eastern philosophy).

It is only fair for this discussion that we include an atheistic, non-dogmatized and non-subjective system that is also perspective-based to compare with religion as another major example of what is meant by vacancy in a religious sense regarding spirituality. This section is meant to provide solidly backed counters to arguments from religious proponents regarding the claimed personal experience and effects of religious claimed spirituality. Spirituality is something widely talked about but understood by few, it seems. While many may lay claim to be spiritual, what it is and what many religious believe it is are two different things.

Albert Einstein once wrote nearly a century ago regarding the ancient practice of Buddhism, "The religion of the future will be a cosmic religion. The religion which based on experience, which refuses the dogmatic. If there's any religion that would cope the scientific needs it will be Buddhism."[48] This prediction is proving to be prophetic. With Western discovery of Buddhism which led to significant growth in comparative studies, Buddhism has slowly become the fourth largest religion in the world. Though Buddhism is not theistic, it implores the practitioner to discover ultimate truth. It is still largely classified as a religion. The system itself has been practiced for thousands of years, evolving into Zen, or Chan Buddhism.

Buddhism claims its roots 2500 years-ago when prince Siddartha Guatama was born in what is now

Nepal. Swearing off the worldly, Siddartha left his wife, child and princely throne to seek a life without suffering through contemplation. He became the Buddha, or "enlightened one" while meditating one day underneath a tree. His teachings grew in practice and popularity well after his death, with a wide spread of Buddhism in China beginning near 200 AD[49] and eventually all of Asia. Europe was to follow beginning mainly in the 1800s, and Americans would be introduced to the practice by Chinese miners and Japanese harvesters.[50] It did not take very long for Indologists to discover links to psychology in Buddhism, and by the early 1900s works by Caroline Rhys Davids were introducing terms like "Buddhist psychology" to the world.[51] Currently Buddhism is enjoying a period of worldwide attention, and analysis as well as Buddhist philosophies are now being implemented in therapy for those who suffer from poor physical and mental health.[52]

Scientists who write about the effects of Buddhism include Donald Lopez and Howard C. Cutler, while Theologian L. Stafford Betty once admitted, "I still can't quite figure out whether the Buddhist or theist is on the truer track." This is due to the many insights discovered in the system. It is also a system where notions are in line with modern scientific discovery, something religious scripture is not. Commenting on this linear path with Buddhism and science, Buddhist and 14th Dalai Lama Tenzin Gyatso once proclaimed at a Life Science conference, "If science proves some belief of Buddhism wrong, then Buddhism will have to change. In my view, science and Buddhism share a search for the truth and for understanding reality." It goes without saying that this objective search for truth is different from the dogmatic sphere of religion. Also, the personal results of this philosophy are beneficial and tangible, unlike that of religion.

The positive benefits discovered in Buddhist philosophy are also praised by science and implemented in different scientific fields. Specifically regarding mental health in relation to Buddhist philosophical concepts, Perry Garfinkel reported in *National Geographic*, "(they) are being applied to mental and physical health therapies and to political and environmental reforms. Athletes use it to sharpen their game. It helps corporate executives handle stress better. Police arm themselves with it to defuse volatile situations. Chronic pain sufferers apply it as a coping salve."[53] As far as mental health aspects of Buddhism, an *American Scientist* editor Michael Spzir wrote the following in the periodical:

"Perhaps no other religion or spiritual practice has explored the structure of the mind so carefully as Buddhism. With a precision that approaches the rigor of the best scientific taxonomies, Buddhists have dissected and redissected the mind, generating a catalogue of "mental afflictions" (figuratively citing as many as 84,000) that lead to inner transformation as afflictions are overcome. The top five—hatred, desire, confusion, pride and jealousy—are comparable, though certainly not identical, to the destructive mental states identified in the West. The thoroughness of the Buddhist approach to understanding the mind, and the apparent peace of mind enjoyed by Buddhist monks, has attracted Western scientists hoping to shed further light on the neurobiology of emotions and new pathways to mental health."[54]

Despite the praise it has received, categorization of what Buddhism is cannot be explained simply. Its concepts and practices are difficult enough to comprehend and carry out, but the themes are even more elusive to the eye without at least an introduction to its basic concepts. Buddhism is not theistic. However, as Diane Morgan noted, "Buddha knew that people put accountability for their actions on to a deity. He also knew that deities create dogma, dogma eventually following with his own religion any way in spite of his beliefs."[55] Regarding spirituality, not only were the effects of enlightenment known long before the Christ, but the power of those effects was known. It can be claimed that Buddhism searches for ultimate truth without a subjective viewpoint but with objective reasoning. Solitude, practice and elevated states of consciousness surround Buddhist concepts. The analysis of self and the nature of reality is among many practices within the system that lead to understanding and enlightenment, a path that is not encouraged in major religions, and actually forbidden in such insular and narrow systems.

Although many Buddhist concepts lead to an increased well-being, this section will focus on the concept of attachment and its relation to personal inner suffering. Concepts of aversion and delusion are also associated with suffering in Buddhist thought, but it is important to discuss attachment in particular due to its consequences socially. This attachment viewpoint (according to Buddhism is a hedonistic desire for the materialistic and the worldly) is something that is not addressed properly in religious texts as this book has so often accused, the religious texts are at least ignorant even to its effects, much less the worldview such concepts present.

While it is true that many great minds have throughout the centuries contemplated humanity's ills and their overwhelming effect on the human psyche, very few have come close to the insights that Buddhist notions have. An important concept in Buddhism, suffering -or specifically ending suffering- uniquely is something that is to be found at the core of Buddhism.[56] Inner human suffering has devastating effects and is responsible for diseases and suicides worldwide along with strained relationships and many personal growth obstacles. David Brazier, commenting on the universality of inner human suffering illustrates the point that many share towards suffering when describing our world when he asserted that the intensity of suffering was, "a place of such suffering that any intelligent person who really understood the situation would ardently wish to be free of it."[57] Emotional suffering has long been the catalyst for a need to escape the inner turmoil.

While being liberated from suffering has eluded so many humans regardless of religious practice involved, the Buddhist teachings seek to end the suffering as well as the ignorance attributed to it, something else that escapes religious practice. A cause of suffering (along with delusion and aversion) according to Buddhism, is desire, or attachment to the worldly and the materialistic.[58] An important subject in Buddhism, some of the Buddha's first lessons were about the damages created by pleasure. There is no doubt that desire permeates us all: Beckett once referred to human desire as "insatiable" in *Proust*. Many have tried to end suffering by overspending, overusing energy or overthinking worldly problems containing worldly solutions that don't fit. The Buddhist view on suffering is different from many systems in that they perceive desire or attachment to the worldly as the cause of suffering as those goals become a significant part of the individual's perceptive view daily.

Desiring and in many ways expecting to reach pleasure along with luxury-oriented goals becomes an anxiety-filled burden: one becomes frustrated when they do not attain what he or she seeks, their world appears to crumble before their eyes in despair as they are not living the lives they desired yet. However, studies show that once the pleasure is attained, the nature of the pleasure is temporary, unfulfilling, non-transcendent, illusory. The nature of the worldly, according to Buddhism, lures a promise of what appears to be tangible, but the illusory nature of the pleasure sought is repeated in an endless cycle of a perceptive reality that simply does not relent in its open encouragement of ignorance from an exclusively trivial standpoint. The pleasure does not better the person or represent any step toward enlightenment.

The dichotomy of desire and daily life is an especially complicated issue regarding personal well-being. Buddhist monks to this day find it difficult to discover which is the right and ethical path, considering desire is wired into us. Desire is sought by most people, but the health aspects are complicated. Writing of desire according to Tibetan Buddhism, Judith Brown notes in her book, *Dakini's Warm Breath*, "Desire in human life is, at its root, an expression of the yearning for wholeness and is fundamentally healthy. Yet working with this desire in harmony with practice is a great challenge for the Vajrayana practitioner. It is difficult to honor passion without being overwhelmed by a self-centered desire for gratification."[59] Once again, this philosophy would have been useful in Biblical times as the devastating and self-destructive path hedonism lies out for humanity could have been at least clarified in some sort of agreeable concept such as the Vajrayana model. If it is only a matter of perceiving the world in such a way, that perceptive worldview can be changed for the better.

It is not just the hedonistic lifestyle that causes human suffering. Taking joy through pleasure is seen by Buddhists to be a misleading view of a whole perceived reality. Emphasizing the attainment of success, while a healthy tool for survival, is not without its limitations. According to Buddhist notions, those who think fulfillment will be met in a hedonistic pursuit is not without anxiety and disappointment for the individual. This is similar to a study called "Does Great Wealth Bring Fulfillment?" from Boston College on people whose fortunes were beyond 25 million and the psychological effects associated with wealth and success. The study found, "a surprising litany of anxieties: their sense of isolation, their worries about work and love, and most of all, their fears for their children."[60] Although an outer appearance of security and constant reward is appealing, the experience is not what it seems, and the burden of financial instability is replaced with other fears, just as repetitive, just as haunting. The happiness does not increase with financial stability.

In addition, the fulfillment of desire becomes a temporary lure for a lifetime. Those caught will forever attempt to fulfill desires, but the gratification it leaves is temporary in nature.

Journalist Greame Wood explains such a reaction to luxury from studies on the subject in his *Atlantic Monthly* piece:

> "Just as the human body didn't evolve to deal well with today's easy access to abundant fat and sugars, and will crave an extra cheeseburger when it shouldn't, the human mind, apparently, didn't evolve to deal with excess money, and will desire more long after wealth has become a burden rather than a comfort. A vast body of psychological evidence shows that the pleasures of consumption wear off through time and depend heavily on one's frame of reference. Most of us, for instance, occasionally spoil ourselves with outbursts of deliberate and perhaps excessive consumption: a fancy spa treatment, dinner at an expensive restaurant, a shopping spree. In the case of the very wealthy, such forms of consumption can become so commonplace as to lose all psychological benefit: constant luxury is, in a sense, no luxury at all."[61]

Left with an illusory perception of reality, the fleeting and mindless gratification that accompanies a hedonistic life even appears a pursuit of happiness but, is a temporary sensation in a biological network that constantly urges man to survive, reproduce, eat, etc. These temporary desires, as basic as they are, appear to be pretty important for most humans, even surpassing religious practice in priority. Good luck convincing someone today to not get married to a divorced person which is forbidden in supposed more modern lessons of the NT. One will quickly see where that advice will go with the person it is being said to. That stuff no longer applies in most of humanity. It simply doesn't compare to the biological urges of humans.

Arianna Huffington explains the unhealthy dichotomy between desire and attainment of success in an interview promoting her bestseller, *Thrive*, which includes 55 pages dedicated to science confirming Eastern philosophy:

> "We've reached this tipping point partly because the value of the practice is pretty incontrovertible and partly because the old way of doing things has so demonstrably not worked for people. We are seeing the side effects of stress on our health-care system. When we have the CDC saying that 75 percent of health-care costs are for chronic, preventable diseases, and how many people on Wall Street and in finance committing suicide? There's something wrong with our values if we are basing our entire life on these two metrics of money and power and success defined in those terms and we see the impact they're having."[62]

The negative effects of wealth are also easy to disguise in a hedonistic perspective. Because of this, it seems odd that pleasure, the desired state of being for so many around the world for so many centuries and encapsulated dreams and aspirations are illusory, temporary and spiritually unfulfilling. It is difficult to gauge this aspect of luxury and pleasure as being unhealthy for the individual, but that is exactly what Buddhism contends.

Regarding the effects of hedonism being temporary and fleeting, more research is being conducted on this along with its non-transcendent nature. Shirley Wang reported on the studies of researchers for *Wall Street Journal* regarding happiness and its effects. She noted, "The pleasure that comes with, say, a good meal, an entertaining movie or an important win for one's sports team—a feeling called 'hedonic well-being'—tends to be short-term and fleeting. Raising children, volunteering or going to medical school may be less pleasurable day to day. But these pursuits give a sense of fulfillment, of being the best one can be, particularly in the long run."[63]

There are many studies that appear to suggest this same conclusion. For over a decade studies have shown the differences between the two forms of happiness, the opinions of researchers favoring the eudaimonic state of being. This includes a more recent Harvard study published in *PNAS* that asserts, "the physical benefits of happiness come not from a happy life, but from a meaningful life."[64,65] The study also found that the hedonic incur more stress and do not attain fulfillment, meaning or transcendence with the pleasure sought. Eudaimonia, however, not only transcends and fulfills, but also encourages compassion, an emphasis on others and a "greater", more meaningful sense of purpose. This also gives light to the notion that our happiness is designed to be community oriented, rather than self-serving.

Columbia University professor and Buddhist Robert Thurmond wrote regarding wealth and happiness in his book, *Infinite Life*. In it, he explains the relationship between the self and society regarding a self-oriented concern for wealth. "The feeling of wealth is enhanced when you give, not when you take, since, subliminally, giving means you have enough to share, while taking means you may not be getting enough. Giving is a relief. Taking is a burden. This is a breakthrough discovery for American psychologists, though it is rather commonsensical for Tibetans, supporting the teaching that the cause of all unhappiness is self-concern, just as the cause of all happiness is other-concern."[66] Hedonism becomes a fool's gold, and the seemingly natural stance to take becomes a compassionate one. Equally accessible to the human and equally natural as the hedonic perceptive view, eudemonia is not only transcending, more meaningful personally and collectively and with more healthy results, it involves the infinite rather than rules, inquiry rather than dogma.

Taoists have a saying regarding the pursuit of wealth that has a similar theme: "Chase after money and security and your heart will never unclench. Care about people's approval and you will be their prisoner."[67] Social status, financial security and image become fear-based, no longer considered a wise motive for decisions. Additionally, a study by Australia's Deakon University which was published in *Journal of Happiness Studies* indicates that acceptance of what cannot be controlled predicts satisfaction. This is also a Buddhist notion, yet its meaning is somehow missing in all three major religions. States of mind lacking in religious texts, these Eastern philosophical notions tell us something profound about ourselves. Concepts regarding eudaimonia are more examples that disprove the religious proponent claim that science cannot define happiness. Not only can it define happiness, but the result of these findings indicates yet another weakness in religion. The eudaimonic form of happiness brings what hedonism cannot: fulfillment, meaning.

The encouraged lifestyle and point of view in the Bible is clearly and unsurprisingly of the lowest common denominator. Where is transcendent meaning in sacred lessons located in the Bible? Where is the emphasis on happiness in its truest sense? No sense of transcendence or empowerment, but instead dogma and ritual. Even the NT has Jesus and others going on about physical pain for bad behavior and an apparent relaxed sense of being in a jewel encrusted kingdom in the sky. What spirituality could possibly come from seeing lots of rare metals in the afterlife? This mindset encouraged at around the time of the Christ occurred 500 years after the time of the Buddha and after the path to enlightenment was known.

Although Buddhist spiritual practice and insight-based enlightenment breaks through the "web of ignorance" associated with the aversive, the deluded and materially attached, diligence is expected of the practicing Buddhist. In order for results to occur, the hours of training are necessary. As Diane Morgan noted with regards to Buddhism, "it is not enough to take refuge in the dharma (phenomenon), some work must be done on the part of the practitioner."[68] Solitude or silence, for example, is recommended for meditation. Putting in the hours to achieve results is necessary. Such practices and lessons focus on destroying ego and desire, ignoring pride and jealousy to reach an intended goal of becoming a compassionate and understanding, enlightened human. The illusions of social status, vanity and ego become apparent and disregarded. The study of the nature of reality, the nature of delusion comes with such practice.

Ultimately what results in the Buddhist answer for suffering or the liberation from the effects of desire, is detachment from it. According to Buddhism, extinguishing one's desire or detaching from the worldly results in a true happiness, not one that is fleeting from short term pleasure. International relations professor Rosita Dellios explains this Buddhist detachment from the worldly in *Social Alternatives*, "The aim of Buddhism is to develop compassion for all living beings and to realize that suffering arises from desire. To overcome suffering one must not be too attached to anything."[69] David Brazier also notes the spiritual transformation in the Buddhist practitioner once the detachment takes place: "desire can be abolished by following a prescribed programme of spiritual training. The implication is, therefore, that it is desire that both creates the suffering in this world and that keeps one anchored to this world. If one follows the instructions, then one will eventually be free from all desire. This will be the cause of immediate happiness."[70] The realized goal of the practicing Buddhist is surrounded in awareness, an enlightened understanding. Nirvana, which means to extinguish, or blow-out, is sought by the practitioner.[71]

Rather than looking to outer sources for an escape from the personal inner suffering like luxury or other worldly sensations, the chaotic and overwhelming emotions become calm and at peace, a self-reliance develops for a sustainable self-empowered future, free from the suffering as a peaceful inner being lacking turmoil has no need for the hedonic happiness, no more need to escape. Through an open mind and ignoring hedonistic notions (along with aversion), awareness and compassion is revealed in a liberation from the depths of ignorance, which so many religious suffer from.

The religious cannot claim spirituality to compare with such a practice because one-time Biblical events in the Bible do not contain such enlightened paths. Let us face the fact that the three major religions do not have this philosophical system which leads ultimately to empowerment and compassion. If they did, religious scholars would flaunt the results. This is what separates theology from actual philosophy. Since philosophy is the foundation for science, is it any surprise that Eastern philosophy is backed by scientific analysis? This system is what was missing from Jesus's endless speeches that included lakes of fire. This is what the OT doesn't even come close to regarding personal development. Century after century passed before the time of Christ with many individuals attaining enlightenment and many, many Centuries passed after the death of Christ with more enlightened ones, and yet not one comparison on a deeper personal level when it comes to Christian, Jewish or Muslim inspired notions in the Bible or Koran. The fact that Muhammed was more local and worldly after his encounter with an angel is depressing enough, as it took place hundreds of years after the Christ.

What is more depressing is the notion that all those Biblical lessons throughout the centuries have been so limiting in comparison to Eastern notions. What potential the practitioners of those religions had through the years. Even if something close to this system existed in these religions, it would provide some insight in to the personal and into reality, but it doesn't. General statement commands of "loving" a neighbor is given without the slightest notion of how, or even how to not get hijacked by one's emotions with basic reactions. Such a system is simply not enough.

Other spiritual notions are drawn from the Buddhist practice which have also been honed for thousands of years and which focus on the human being. There are different forms of the Buddhist system, including Zen Buddhism and Tibetan Buddhism, each effectively producing results.

Taoists introduction to Buddhism led to Chan Buddhism or Zen Buddhism. Zen Buddhism in particular focuses on silence and reflection in response to human suffering. According to *Oxford Companion to World Mythology*, "For the Zen Buddhist, the wisdom to be gained from meditation or from a master who has achieved enlightenment is more important than anything that can be gained from ritual or scripture. Therefore, mythology plays a minimal role in this form of Buddhism."[72] Translated as "absorption" or "meditative state", Zen is a school of thought from Mahayana Buddhism in China which also emphasizes attainment of enlightenment through direct insight into existence via the Buddhist teachings. Zazen, called the core of Buddhist sects, is emphasized, or a meditative practice of calming the body and mind in order to concentrate on the nature of existence, gaining enlightenment in the process.

Regarding Tibetan Buddhism specifically, analysis done on this system indicates unsurprising results as the concepts reveal an objective-based inquiry at its heart. A study published by *Social Cognitive and Affective Neuroscience* describes Tibetan Buddhism's Cognitive Based Compassion Training (CBCT). "Compassion Meditation Enhances Empathetic Accuracy and Related Neural Activity", the title of a published Emory University study by Jennifer S. Mascaro and others explains: "When most people think of meditation, they think of a style known as 'mindfulness', in which practitioners seek to improve their ability to concentrate and to be non-judgmentally aware of their thoughts and feelings. While CBCT includes these mindfulness elements, the practice focuses more specifically on training people to analyze and reinterpret their relationships with others."[73] An *American Psychological Association* cover story on the similarities between Tibetan Buddhism and research psychology also covers many of the advancements of the system, including their monks' mastering of fear, a concept not previously thought of as possible in Westerners.[74]

Other nontheistic systems in Eastern philosophy include the ethics leaning Confucianism (Confucianism is not a religion, although it is very spiritual and is an updated version of the aristocratic codes of behaviors and moral qualities of the fadding period of 50-256 B.C.),[75,76] and the artistic leaning Taoism. Each in their own way provide insight, involve reasoning and a goal towards harmony. Clinical psychologist Frank MacHovec reported as early as 1984 on the importance of these systems in the *American Journal of Psychotherapy* when he wrote, "Gestalt, existential, psychoanalytic, transactional-analysis, cognitive, and family therapy concepts are traced to ancient Taoist, Zen, Confucian, and Buddhist source materials."[77] The works of Carl Jung have also been used to analyze Taoist notions,[78] showing a cross reference in concepts. As we can see, there are many systems which people can turn to for an answer to their personal suffering and concern. Not only does Eastern philosophy provide deeper answers that Christianity, Judaism and Islam simply cannot provide, but theistic notions can-not even come close to those of Eastern philosophy, and it is glaringly obvious.

A final note on Buddhism, growing in size and influence, Buddhist philosophies are also being applied to reforms both politically and environmentally, something else that will challenge traditional religion in its influence on politics.[79] A quote from Sulak Sivaraksa on society from a Buddhist perspective gives some insight on what might be expected in future society leadership with Buddhist influence. It would later be published in *Social Policy*. He asserts that without meditation or Buddhism, "those trying to transform society will be more likely to be greedy, wanting to be big shots, or full of hate, wanting power, or deluded, wanting an impossibly ideal society or being a naïve do-gooder. Meditation or critical self-awareness help one to see those questionable motivations, or at least ask oneself, 'Am I doing that stuff out of greed or hatred?' even if there is no clear answer."[80] Either the individual can free their mind, or they can stay in the same paradigm. Either way, the choice is there, and the results are obvious regardless of what is believed.

In their entirety, the Abrahamic religions do not contain any of the deeper and more meaningful lessons found in Eastern philosophy. As discussed earlier, training the mind to ignore the worldly results in a transcendence, it changes the personality of the practitioner for the wiser and more compassionate. The lessons experienced differ from the impersonal religious lessons and literal one-liner commandments on behavior of religious doctrine. The preceding Eastern practices all contain information which deal with the nature of reality as well as relieving of human suffering that the three Abrahamic religions cannot come close to. This is complimented with the philosophical principle of objective inquiry found in most of these systems which is also missing in the Abrahamic religions where bias, dogma, and belief are a must. Such Eastern thought overshadows the religious lessons with an understanding of the personal that is beyond any of those religions, despite claims of the personal and claims of spirituality from the religious.

The three major Abrahamic religions differ from spirituality in that they do not include search for truth so much as a continued search for what is claimed to be true, already set and unchanged. Alleged non-recurring events interpreted as divinely influenced and laws set by entities believed to be divine simply do not offer transcendence, and while it is acceptable to be considered religious, let these people not confuse being religious with being spiritual, because as we have seen, they are not the same thing at all. Religion demands, spirituality sets free. That freedom is something the religious do not get to enjoy. They don't get to enjoy critical thought, self-reflection, and philosophy because those were all omitted in mainstream religion.

The maze of dead ends in analysis of the scriptures does not speak to anything in the human deeper than the limited. Spirituality differs from religion in the awareness gained, the emotional and mental health it directly influences and the lack of anything transcendent or empowering that permeates scripture. The training of Eastern philosophy leads somewhere, results are produced, enlightenment is reported. Obvious behavior indicating an awareness, or a different perceptive view of life is noticeable, emotional stability is felt. This is evident among spiritual practitioners not because it is religious law, or because of what they are told will happen, but because of what does happen through guided experience and practice. If an alternative to religious practice and ritual is suggested, the notions are rejected by the strict religious observer according to his/her individual belief system's exclusivity. The vicious circle is of vacuous notions and practices ensures limited spiritual growth that might be empowering.

The self-autonomous tone of what is spiritual is not "revealed" but experienced, not from faith or a miracle, but objective observation involving consciousness and critical thought. What might be a magical effect on an individual may not be the next time the religious practice is undertaken in either Christianity, Judaism or Islam. There is no interest in the perfection of the human being. The stifling cycle psychiatrist Jerald Lamposky referred to earlier, whether purposely designed or not, is a big reason for the unenlightened in religious masses. These masses can either empower themselves through critical thought with systems outside their own, or continue suffering this limiting cycle along with their children. As long as the believer stays with such notions, they will continue to experience needless adversity.

As for the future of Eastern thought, it is being reported at universities that numerous scholars are in the process of researching early Taoist, Buddhist, Confucianist and Neo-Confucianist material, "with an increasing interest in a comparative approach that covers Western philosophy, psychology, sociology, ethics, and aesthetics."[81] Other studies are being carried out which will also shed new light on Eastern thought, and it is only a matter of time before more is discovered through scientific scrutiny. We can count on mainstream religion having nothing directly to do with it, however, as there is not much about humanity that religious texts emphasize deeper than basic themes and behavior admonishment. If accountability or any other rule that is more difficult to follow than the religious doctrines were emphasized such as critical thinking or the illusory nature of perceptive reality, we can only wonder what societies would have become. That is not the reality though. The reality is a much bleaker existence filled with questions religion has not been able to answer for a long time now.

Chapter Seven

Service

Today we live in a society that stands on the brink of a different era technologically, culturally and socially. What that era will be depends on our actions today as our intentions decide our survival. It is no surprise that today that the human race faces several concerns, and one can take their pick of which concern is a priority because they are all very real and very immediate. Nuclear annihilation and ecological havoc are a part of that possibility.[1] Add a mixture of draining resources and economic instability[2] and we have what many are calling the end of civilization as we know it.[3] We can also add onto that what finance professor Stephen Nagel asserted as humanity's inability to see change until confronted with it up close. If we also take into account Stephen Hawking and Bill Gate's warning about the dangers of artificial intelligence, we have a perfect recipe for catastrophic events we might not be prepared for.[4] Unfortunately, religion is nowhere to be found concerning these dilemmas, regardless of how the book of Revelation verses concerning end-times are "interpreted" today. The plights humanity faces are real. As usual, religion is simply outmatched in such complex adversity. Specifically regarding economic instability, the dire situations that await us are only decades away according to experts, and are also imminent. The answers provided by religious notions to our dilemmas are striking as we will see, and should not hold such credibility in the mainstream consciousness.

To rely on religion for answers to real modern-day problems in society is to rely on something without capability of relating to humanity. Warning signs coming from science and other fields suggest a reality far different than imaginable by humans previously, much less by Biblical notions. Although religion has run its course, that course is obviously finished in many ways; as expected, religious explanation provides no insight into what might actually bring on something catastrophic to our civilization. Christians claim that we may be able to progress in humanity if we understand God's message, yet as we have seen, even different interpretation is pointless. The truth is it is impossible to follow religious scripture and progress in modern society. Obviously the problems our society faces today are complicated compared to tales of a deity destroying the enemies of Israel. Whether it is religious fundamentalism or other obstacles in our way, these problems linger in our future and can no longer be ignored. As we will see, following a religious path will not get us any closer to our desired goals as a society. They are worn, not for humanity and pretty disreputable.

If religion were somehow stripped of its power among the masses today, would the reaction to difficulties presented to humanity be different? Would there be a more critical thinking, mobile and less divided result? Or would there instead exist a docile, dumbed down, immobile and divided society unprepared for threats? Interestingly enough, if an elite class wanted to increase or maintain a thought paradigm over a society, the latter would read like a blueprint on how to do so. Regardless, it is society's obligation to heal itself, as it is clear from centuries of religious influence that no one from a heavenly realm will help us.

Considering the horrible acts humans have engaged in, the question of when we will destroy ourselves is unavoidable. No longer can this impending dilemma be brushed off as insignificant or contemplated by religious proponents as part of a larger plan, unless the death of the whole world and start of a new Earth in the book of Revelation are to be taken seriously along with other religious notions regarding end-times. If this other Earth exists, it would be nice if a celestial dictator were to make such an event occur -if we ignore the part containing the death of everyone- but as we have seen with other religious-based predictions, this will not occur. The reason is because this entity thought up by man is not *real*! It is not capable of anything whatsoever regarding these realities because it doesn't exist.

The point of this chapter is to detail why religious-based notions on circumstances involving the socioeconomically complex -such as the compromising of an entire civilization due to greed- fall short when considering them seriously, unless the practitioner wants to follow instructions on loving thy neighbor in the jungle that is the business world, which will ensure they have a difficult time relating any of this mess we are currently in to any of the notions in scriptures. The general naiveté on display from religious-based notions regarding economics is alarming enough, let alone their recommendations for economic action concerning society's economic-based plights. The indifferent and uninformed reverence towards economic reality and the general notion of circumstances being just "the way it is" is rampant among the lay, as if there were no better choice. If religious proponents wish to argue this, they might consider that such ignorant perceptive view is common in church sermons every week, as if stuck in the bubble of an economic thought the Bible speaks to.

Religious proponents may point out economic notions stemming from a religious foundation based on scripture and other teachings, but the reality of human economics is far different from the notions given to us by religion. Competition flourishes in unchecked free trade leaving the consequences to someone else, something else. Exploitation the likes of which humanity has never seen before goes uninterrupted due to factors like deregulation. We deal with corruption and unprecedented pollution rates, telling us pretty much all we need to know about how civilized the religious influence has been for society after thousands of years.

We can begin our look at religious notions regarding our economic reality with socioeconomics and the role religion plays in possible end of civilization scenarios. Isn't economics claimed as the most important link to our survival? Does our society not need some sort of stable and complex social structure? Misguided and misunderstood, some examples of religious inspired economic notions and their relation to every-day reality show how ineffective religion is when it comes to answers for adversity outside of praying for the destruction of those who exploit economically as in the Bible. Though their hearts are in the right places, it is important to point out the understanding of something as crucial as economics claimed by the religious, especially concerning the scriptural roots of many such notions.

Religious authors Joerg Rieger and Kwok Pui-lan are examples of this religious understanding concerning economics. Their book, *Occupy Religion,* calls for a religious reflection in solving economic dilemmas such as the predatory practices of the global 1 percent class, which they refer to as the "transnational capitalist class". Regarding the difficulties of modern society and socioeconomics, the authors call for a religious solution: "The Occupy movement calls for serious reflection on the social and economic teachings of the church, its images of God and other topics, and a public theology that speaks to the challenges of our time."[5] We can stop right there, as the religious answers for the challenges of our time are limited at best. As many theologians know well, there is little to gain from the empty message that is the Bible. Plaguing the philosophies of Kant, Emerson and

C.S. Lewis, the lightweight of theistic notions is as present in notions of religious proponents in other fields like economic philosophy. The scripture's "principles" regarding economics have not yet proved to be anything but inconsequential. The values presented in it are not even of the basic, so how can those principles be the basis of a way to understanding our modern dilemma? We are talking about tales which have been called meaningless by modern intelligent minds, these are ancient notions without merit. Plato's Rebublic was more impressive in its notions regarding society. What can be gained regarding today's survival in what has been deemed even by theology as a book stuck in its own time? As much as one may think the Bible has answers, as much as one might believe it has the answers, the cruel truth is otherwise. It is also pointless to detach from the Bible in such modern thinking on the part of religious proponents when it comes to religious-inspired solutions to socioeconomics, as the scriptures make up the foundation for all this modern theorizing by them. Try as they may in separating from the triviality of the Bible, they are stuck with verses like Revelation's Satan being thrown "down" along with angels joining him.

In another section, the *Occupy* authors claim political harmlessness of religious themes, but is this claim realistic regarding what we know? In discussing political aims of religion, they write, "Religion does not seek to dominate: instead, it becomes a part of the larger quest for liberation. As such, it can find its own voice and contribute its distinct insights without falling into the trap of exercising control like the 1 percent."[6] This argument is problematic. Not only does religion seek to dominate our entire existence with very specific instructions of how to live and perceive reality in the Old and New Testament along with the Koran, but the figures of each text demand and enforce these rules. In fact, a main theme of religion is to not just dominate the actions of its followers, but also the mindset of the individual practitioner. That is one of the very problems with theocracy. Social engineering done in Islamic dominated countries alone are an indication of this, not including the problem of a way to exist without religious exclusivism and with religious extremism. If one doesn't think this type of social engineering is done in the U.S. already in a comparable type model, Professor Noam Chomsky might have something to say about it.

Not even self-reliance or critical thought which strays from the limiting doctrines of each religion is allowed regardless of the effectiveness. Activist and author David Swanson wrote regarding religion's flaw in this respect: "The problem is that theism is anti-democratic at its core. It moves us away from relying on ourselves. It teaches us to rely on someone supposedly better than us."[7] This is the wrong move. Why can't there be critical thought or self-reliance in these religions? Why are they so demanding of total obedience to their stupid notions? The concept of putting faith into this supreme being certainly is available, but just as our ancestors slammed their heads into the ground that is religious notions of thunder gods and lightning gods before the knowledge of what storms were, the value or basis for this type of concept is unreliable at best and oppressive at worst. The *Occupy* authors also noticeably fail to mention current attempts of religious proponents at exerting control in academics, sciences, the public consciousness, medicine, and government. It is ignored like so many other realities when pondering religious explanation, religious scripture, and current theological work.

Reiger and Pui-lan list in their book George Soros and Warren Buffett among billionaires who support policies which promote economic equality, quoting Soros in that if there exists more equal income distribution, "the average American will be better off." The sad reality the authors appear to overlook in their book is that for every George Soros there is a Charles Koch, a proponent of the other economic viewpoint of anything to gain profit no matter how exploitive it may seem. Koch is so powerful that he is known for simply overspending on campaigns to ensure election results even when the opposition victory appears almost obvious. According to a *Wall Street Journal* article on Koch in 2006, "he thinks billionaires Warren Buffett and George Soros, who fund organizations with different ideologies, 'simply haven't been sufficiently exposed to the ideas of liberty.'"[8] Koch is not alone: a swarm of self-interested billionaires in America alone share his economic ideas.

We can also forget about talking sense into people like the Koch brothers. According to *Forbes,* "Ironically, the Koch brothers believe they're fighting against power, at least in the political realm. For the Kochs the real power is central government, which can tax entire industries into oblivion, force a citizen to buy health insurance and bring mighty corporations like Koch Industries to heel." To get an idea of how much power the Kochs wield, this is what executive director of Green Peace Phil Radford reported:

> "Recent Greenpeace analysis of lobbying disclosure records reveals that since 2005, Koch Industries hired more lobbyists than Dow and Dupont to fight legislation that could protect over 100 million Americans from what national security experts say is a catastrophic risk from the bulk storage of poison gasses at dangerous chemical facilities such as oil refineries, chemical manufacturing facilities, and water treatment plants. Koch lobbyists even outnumber those at trade associations including the

Chamber of Commerce and American Petroleum Institute. Only the American Chemistry Council deployed more."

The same thwarted ideology is believed by many in the Koch brothers' economic class, and, although men like Soros and Buffet are to be commended, they are but a drop in the bucket when it comes to what many wealthy support in terms of economics. To think otherwise is to be naïve.

Charles Koch is known to "disdain" government and has donated millions to organizations dedicated to promoting unregulated industry.[9] Koch's description of liberty is far different from that of Reiger and Pui-lanis, and his power is shared with a conglomerate of an elite who agree with his economic point of view as well. Steve Forbes likewise will have clear and well-polished arguments in favor of economic policies which favor the top 1 percent, and, like the Koch brothers, holds as much conviction for his economic views. There are so many individuals who think like the Kochs that it is unrealistic to think that someone like Buffet or Soros can advance economic equality in the endless ocean of individuals who are essentially economic predators.

Another attempt at linking scripture with problems society faces is in Marcus Borg's book, *The Heart of Christianity*. In it he attempts to make some recent sense of end-times in the book of Revelation. "Revelation not only discloses what John thought would happen soon, but also discloses the nature of empire... The Beast from the Abyss: John speaks of the Roman Empire as 'the beast from the abyss', the ancient serpent who threatens the creation itself with chaos, as the incarnation and embodiment of Satan."[10] Even if the "beast" empire represents modern dilemmas, what is the remedy? What on earth does any of that gibberish have to do with what causes major problems for society? There is definitely an abyss alright, but not one described by Borg. It is one where humanity is faced with a very stark existence and this rhetoric of the religious is not helping anyone.

It isn't as if this attempt at a modern viewpoint is a new concept for theology: As early as 1600 years-ago theologian Augustine was accusing man of hedonism and materialism, while presenting heavenly possessions in a light above the material. A satisfactory description of the heavenly possessions is of course not given beyond notions of vague "joy". The continuous attempt by religious proponents to find a relevant position for the scriptures inside subjects like economics not only takes on the Christian theme of general 'heavenly' possessions like in those in scripture, but falls short of an actual picture of just what to expect from the possessions, not just economically, but emotionally (Is fortune really what the human psyche of thousands of years ago really needed?). This is because the authors do not know and therefore cannot claim to, and what we get from all the vacant and local themes of scripture is of not much use when it comes to harsh reality.

Even in remote religious areas where religion is currently claimed to be the driving force behind an economic boost, it is actually factors like education or more trust encouraged in a society that is the contributing factor.[11] Those who claim religion a driving force to such growth are not taking into account so many factors that can either increase or offset these driving forces in the masses.[12,13,14,15] What we need is more than is offered by the trivial tone of endless babble in scripture to motivate human beings toward a common society goal. How-ever theologians spin it, the notions remain from nothing but shallow myths and tales from the past. Something like the Weberian hypothesis/three class system does not apply to something as limited as notions from scripture, and religious proponents are running out of ways to credit the verses. How frightening it must be for them to know that people who are on to this stuff are harder to fool than the congregation and that time reveals nothing to them divine in relation to our existence.

What they don't understand is the negative role religion plays in what is not being said and not so much in what is being said. Yes, religion is directly related to horrible acts in humanity and at the same time it does play a part in socioeconomics, but the overall tone of the scriptures allows for and encourages the barbaric economic system we currently have (not to mention the system of Biblical times including legalized slavery), unless there are those who can come up with proof of anything otherwise. That is to say, unless someone can find some metaphor we just were not aware of previously that has to do with reality. The truth is that religion allows for the exploitation globally in the name of profit, the effects rationalized by the economic predator. It also allows for the destruction of the Earth and our ecosystem. All of the major economic dilemmas we currently face is in a world containing billions who claim a religion, yet we have what society is facing today society globally.

What part of the modern economic model is Christian in the U.S.? How can religious pundits or political pundits on either side speak so naïvely when they suggest which party Jesus would belong to, or what president he would side with, or how much wealth he would want his followers to enjoy? How can this be seen as serious when spoken by grown men and women? As if the president is not merely a figurehead who can't even make laws. As if both major political parties have not been corrupted to shocking levels today. As if 95% of the media in the U.S. is not owned by a conglomerate of a whopping 6 companies who commit social engineering. The reality that exists in the economic world of today alone is enough to justify a worldwide analysis of every religion to see why the all-knowing scriptures are so ignorant to the horrible reality of many worldwide.

Imagine a society if religious scriptures discussed anything like what one expert termed "ruinously self-concerned," or had any equivalent to the understanding of a Babiak and O'Tooles report for the FBI on what goes through the mind of a corporate predator. The Bible wouldn't have anything like this because it was loaded with the inconsequential. Aside from dominating the individual and society, religious explanation also demands the world and everything in it to be seen through its point of view. Religious and political author Carl Schmitt writes in *Political Theology*, "all significant concepts of the modern theory of the state are secularized theological concepts..."[16] but the religion he refers to is dictatorial and ridiculous to begin with, the reason for the need for liberation in the first place. At what point will we leave such an archaic influence behind? If Schmitt is right, then the failure of those concepts thus far implicates the religious leadership throughout history to today of not changing, if not maintaining underdeveloped, ignorant societies. What would these concepts be if mainstream religion were not so ignorant to nature? What could we have been had our societies not been so oppressed and repressed for generations?

Even in end-times scenarios which do not involve economics, such notions have a real effect on the religious masses. In addition to an overall lack of awareness concerning society conditions and survival, an almost empathetic aura permeates the pro-religious concerning end-times, specifically Christians and Muslims, as their religions emphasize such a scenario. The end-times notion is a popular one among the masses of Christians and Muslims worldwide. The notion of leaving one's entire fate to the divine and suggesting this end-times notion to the entire world is prevalent today. There is even a very thin line between extremist and moderate views when interpreting religious scripture correctly anyway, unless God giving instructions to Moses on how to sell his daughter is to be taken metaphorically as well. A religious view of our current circumstances is offered by religious proponents, the notion that more religious influence and guidance is needed to "speak the language" of the extremists has been proposed by them. This dialogue has occurred already for many centuries now between the extremists and the moderates with the position taken by those deemed extremist actually verified and vindicated by scripture.

The Christian who takes the Bible too seriously in his/her extreme actions applies the same toxic concept Islamic fundamentalists do in their actions. They are simply going by what their religions promote. The idea of God's anger towards certain people provides a foundation of intolerance and hate among the Catholic and Christian traditions (and the Koran). How can it not throughout the years? The same 1 Timothy 1:10 that abdicates slavery is the same verse that renounces homosexuality, liars and those who perjure. Even with the fact that we live in a world today mostly void of awful and prevalent events among the moderate masses encouraged in the Old and even New Testament, it remains for many a luxury that most who live in staunchly Islamic societies do not enjoy. The fact is that religious extremism is actually a literal interpretation of scripture. Have theology explain that when citing metaphors. The fundamentalists are doing in many cases what their religion claims in scripture.

Religion *is* extreme, and if the U.S. Christian population were to carry out instructions from the Bible, the ramifications from a literal reading of the Bible would be unimaginable. We are not talking about OT, but New Testament lessons. The limitations in essentially every subject attempted by religious tradition and scriptural authors are evident in the understanding of even the moderately religious who gladly throw aside strict religious rules in a world that demands more understanding than what the Bible can provide. End-times scenarios in the Bible obviously seem unlikely in modern times and many have noted this stark contrast publicly. Author Ian McEwan echoes this when he told a crowd at Stanford University in 2007, "If we do destroy ourselves, we can assume that the general reaction will be terror and grief at the pointlessness of it all, rather than rapture."[17] This detachment from religion concerning realistic end-times by many is mostly due to the fact that Biblical times did not have the awareness of anything like the current societal model, much less the awareness of any threats to its stability back then.

Regardless, the economic aspect specifically is enough when regarding religious influence over a doomed civilization. If anything can be blamed on religion regarding the awareness of certain economic practice by-products, it is the lack addressing greed: A lot of the economics of many believers seem to be entirely separate from their religious convictions- namely morals. Gone are the ethics he/she must adhere to in certain professions in order to survive, much less be flourish. If a corporate CEO discovers that laying off thousands will reap large short-term profits for shareholders and he does not lay off those workers, the board is likely to ask for his resignation. In a society where exploitation is extreme, it is difficult to claim a positive religious influence over society. Where is the influence in how people treat each other?

The modern world of business is a reminder of how ineffective this religious influence is over predatory business actions. If anyone 20 years-ago expected the business-as-usual notion that the elite class has adopted in the face of draining resources and economic collapse, they would not have been disappointed. In global pollution, the U.S. alone comprises 5 percent of the world's population but contributes 25 percent of global CO_2 emission. It is estimated that 300 billion tons of CO_2 alone will be emitted into the atmosphere with the expected opening of new power plants. The depletion of quality water globally can also be described as dire (ignoring scarcity is also prevalent in the Bible). In 1970 (peak oil), America produced 10 million barrels of oil per day, now we produce 5 million and consume 20 million barrels per day. The Hirsh Report says we are facing a peak oil predicament globally that is going to change every-day life and change many comforts. Global peak oil, according to the report, will either arrive this decade or certainly by 2030. What does scripture recommend on account of the lack of these resources?

This is what happens when knowledge of economics in a system includes Jesus telling followers to simply pay the authorities the taxes that are owed. Modern examples of today's economic stats show how basic greed has taken over human potential in our society. In terms of wealth, currently in America the richest 1 percent alone owns fifty percent of the nation's wealth, and the U.S. now is a nation that claims the highest gap in the world of developed nations between the rich and poor, and while the U.S. government collects a hefty sum per year in taxes, large amounts are literally seized in what is deemed legal if looked at in a certain "perspective" according to bills passed by congress. Tens of trillions have been set aside in tax havens, and up until a few years-ago, those clients did not even have to pay taxes for money deposited in certain offshore accounts.

Rather than the people benefitting from tax money for things like education, the rich benefit from the corporations not paying taxes and receiving tax incentives. The populace is limited while the rich are wealthier with taxpayer money. Put these stats in perspective with FAO stats of over a billion or 1 out of 6 humans hungry in the world today. This is an interesting stat, considering the world now produces enough food to feed well over global demand, but lack of access to the needy and lack of profit is why the people go hungry. With record profits made by the corporate sector each year, that there still exists hunger with the technology and surplus of food is another trait of this generation for the ages to look at, especially when 45% of child deaths in Sub Saharan Africa alone are due to undernutrition, 3.1 million per year.[18]

It is not only the singular business practice of one corporation or even a multi-national conglomerate. The exploitative actions by those in the name of profit is likely to be found essentially in any field that involves profit, just like one can point to any single country in the world and find corruption in its government. This can have a devastating effect on an economy and is essentially why our current economic course in the U.S. is not sustainable. Greed is such a potent element in a destructive course of society that it is capable of more that we know. While social scientists find that greed can be healthy, it is a trait that University of Chicago's Jean Bethke Elshtain calls a "recipe that destroys other values and kills a sense of community."[19] Of course a market economy that promotes such unregulated behavior is expected to have horrendous effects, not just locally but globally. It can be seen as a guarantee when considering how some opportunistic individuals manipulate the market. Fareed Zakaria in a *Newsweek* cover story on greed explains how the trait can do so much market damage. "In calm times, political stability, economic growth and technological innovation all encourage an atmosphere of easy money and new forms of credit. Cheap credit causes greed, miscalculation and eventually ruin."[20]

That something like this is not in the immensely influential mainstream religions, that this is not addressed in religious scholarship should signify the need to look elsewhere for some type of economic guidance from the spiritual sense. If basic survival was thought too inconsequential for Biblical authors, what exactly is so important about a message from God that supersedes survival? What would scripture advise for those engaging in planned obsolescence in a 70% consumer-based economy outside of what is in store for the "wicked"? What would he think of a system where the CEOs who don't even want to but are required by their shareholders to economically victimize others for increased share value? Most of these people don't even want to ruin someone's life for short-term profit but must do so in a system that forces exploitation in order to secure job safety. This and other actions exist on a global scale on the part of corporations regardless of religious practice, regardless of their "personal relationship" with a god. The overall acceptance of this type of blatant oligarchy where 25,000 lobbyists write bills for 535 members of Congress to pass, where most of the media in the U.S. is owned by a corporate consortium is not surprising considering the little amount of actual real knowledge dispersed by scripture on anything like this.

These stats show a world where babies are brought in to, but, with little to arm them from what is to come in their adult life. The stats also show little indication that the business actions discussed in this chapter will stop any time soon. One would think that exploitation for profit would be the extent of modern greed, but destruction of the environment and the draining of natural resources indicate that there is no limit to the desire for more, and mainstream religion is without the awareness to provide any guidance to limit the behavior that continues to threaten civilization. Although this is no surprise, we are stuck with problems that we ourselves still must find adequate solutions to. If theologians themselves admit to the irrelevance the Bible has on life outside the Biblical times, what in that book will help us with our dilemmas? What guiding notion can be extracted that addresses war for profit? Doesn't the Bible indirectly encourage that type of behavior with so many of the stupid tales involving conquering?

What Dangruneisen Areily and John Alineritter called the "disastrous effects of allowing competition to run free"[21] occurs again and again, the adverse effects of primal urges are simply not addressed in religious influence. Possible religious understanding of economic realities or their cause is not to be found in the scriptures to warn of unsustainability which is exactly what capitalism represents. The texts -just as riddled with the basic materialistic view of life that has been maintained to this day among the masses, instead encourage influence from a nonexistent savior rather than save themselves. Since attempts by religious proponents to link their religion to dilemmas we face only look ridiculous, we can count out their notions on the subject as well. The ancient mind frame and knowledge revealed in these texts to reference bear the minimum to satisfy the curious in what we have no choice but to leave behind on our quest to survive and progress.

Greed is just one of the many human traits that religion does not address properly. Just the mere complexity of a society allows for the smallest of events to cause catastrophe to civilization.[22] For example, even if society does not allow for the destruction of the environment for profit, the action sought to conserve does not exactly seem to be overwhelming in humans. In fact, humans seem to react insensitively to certain acts of horror (such as in times of war and crimes against humanity[23]). Are these traits a design of God as well? What about inhibitions among the populace towards killing being reduced on purpose in times of war? Did God also design this natural human trait? This could have been helpful throughout the centuries in preventing countless exploitation from an uncivilized human race. The fact is that religion is utterly clueless when it comes to these realities. Even if subjects like scarcity and unsustainability were purposely ignored in the Bible, out of all the thousands upon thousands of verses, there could have been some awareness that those realities were ahead, or that such plight even existed. A vague reference to the word 'greed' doesn't mean that the Bible even began to properly address the problem with it, much less a solution, and that is the case with every complex subject.

C.S. Lewis once wrote regarding lending money:

"Now there is another point. There is one bit of advice given to us by the ancient heathen Greeks, and by the Jews in the Old Testament, and by the great Christian teachers of the middle ages, which the modern economic system has completely disobeyed. All these people told us not to lend money at interest: and lending money at an interest -what we call investment- is the basis of our whole system. Now it may not absolutely follow that we are wrong. Some people may say that when Moses and Aristotle and the Christians agreed in forbidding interest (or usury as they called it), they could not forsee the joint stock company, and were only thinking of the private moneylender, and that, therefore, we need not bother about what they said. That is a question I cannot decide on. I am not an economist and I simply do not know whether the investment system is responsible for the state we are in or not. This is where we want the Christian economist. But I should not have been honest if I had not told you that three great civilizations agreed (or so it seems at first sight) in condemning the very thing on which we have based our whole life."[24]

If we are to survive, we must change our way of thinking about many things. Money and religion are two of them that we can reconsider.

Regarding the future of society and religion's role, physics professor Chet Raymo wrote in *Commonweal*:

"In coming years, biological science will present us with staggering moral dilemmas. Genetic engineering, cloning, reproductive technologies, consciousness-modifying drugs and surgeries: The possibilities for mischief are frightening. If the churches are to provide us with desperately-needed moral guidance, they must offer a vision of our "true selves" which is consistent with -- and relevant to -- the emerging biology of self. It will not be enough to simply assert the old dualism of body and spirit".[25]

Unfortunately, this is something that simply cannot be done. There is no mystery puzzle to unravel hidden lessons in the scriptures, no interpretation that will bring about the 'right' answers through revelation. This is precisely why we cannot rely on faith and dogma for answers so desperately needed for survival regarding our dilemmas. These dilemmas spell life or death consequences which religion does not equip us to deal with.

If theists were asked to find among "interpretation" any guidance for government, economic stability and social progression in the Bible, they would be lost. If there was any clarity regarding this in scripture, religious scholarship would have likely found it by now. It is not like theology did not have enough time to decipher certain messages in the ancient texts. Though sociological perspectives of religion have been championed by Durkheim, Weber and Marx before, religious notions of society and economics, despite the effort of many formidable minds, contain a vast emptiness concerning economic realities. If these notions ever did give way to any type of transcending guidance, the world would probably not be in such a state as it is today: the guidance would be adhered to, the knowledge implemented.

If it seems the U.S. economy will not suffer greatly due to the factors named in this chapter, consider the following: according to an article written by former International Monetary Fund chief economist and current MIT Sloan

School of Management Professor Simon Johnson in *Bloomberg News*, a possible decline of the American dominance of the globe is coming. The major factor he cited in ushering in this catastrophe is the American debt to foreign investors. Also, a recent report by the National Intelligence Council shows the United States will lose its superpower status by 2030 due to greed and other factors,[26] and Oswald Spengler maintained that the West itself is in decline. A good question to ask religious proponents is, when will the religious influence concerning circumstances such as basic survival be discovered? What Biblical quotes addressing economic catastrophe will be used? The disheartening reality is that religion provides for stagnant progress in a world where we are desperate for information in order to just survive. Information is the basic key element in any struggle, yet there is nothing to show for the scriptures and religious practice regarding any of what we discussed.

What will become of society in the coming times is a very real and imminent question. An eerie warning for the future regarding the need for life science by Joan Atwood and Lawrence Maltin in *American Journal of Psychotherapy* tells us what this current society has become and what we must do for the sake of survival:

> "Our supplies of water and food, and the very air that we breathe are threatened. Drug use, crime, distrust of authority figures, etc. have produced a socio-psychological environment containing individuals who are ridden with feelings of alienation, searching desperately for meaning and purpose. This world dilemma has been played out for centuries and reflects the multipotential capacity of the human mind for both self-transcendence and self-destruction. At this

time, we do not know enough psychology to find good solutions to these world problems. But if we do not build an adequate psychology, we will never build a good world".[27]

As human history has shown, our collective psychology can be referred to largely as less than adequate. Anyone can ignore the negative effects of crony or predatory capitalism. Our society does not require us to acknowledge those effects for an adherence to any moral or ethical standard. There's no law that says for-profit companies must feed the starving. As we have seen with Christianity, any horrific act can be made into an excuse. Tobacco companies can always maintain that a "service" is being offered to the people, and that jobs are created with such products. There is no obligation to have nightly panel programs on television promoting the awareness and understanding of other cultures or promoting tolerance. This economy has no law banning a doctor from going back and forth with positions in the Food and Drug Administration and the corporations it approves drugs from. These circumstances don't even require an explanation legally.

Describing the economic collapse of the 2000's, Fareed Zakaria suggested what occurred during the crises, and what must be done by society to ensure there will not be another collapse:

> "Most of what happened over the past decade across the world was legal. Bankers did what they were allowed to do under the law. Politicians did what they thought the system asked of them. Bureaucrats were not exchanging cash for favors. But very few people acted responsibly, honorably or nobly (the very word sounds odd today). This might sound like a small point, but it is not. No system--capitalism, socialism, whatever--can work without a sense of ethics and values at its core. No matter what reforms we put in place, without common sense, judgment and an ethical standard, they will prove inadequate. We will never know where the next bubble will form, what the next innovations will look like and where excesses will build up. But we can ask that people steer themselves and their institutions with a greater reliance on a moral compass."[28]

Unfortunately, religious notions do not provide avenues of guidance in such realities. Economically speaking, would Jesus, if he were with us today, agree with Peter Unger's words that a single dollar spent on anything but the absolute is money with the blood of children on it? Would he see the larger picture of environmental destruction and would he agree with Earth Policy Institute's Lester Brown that the circumstance is now about saving civilization and not the planet? It is a wonder what he would say concerning two collapses of the American economy in less than one hundred years, and the near dozen major economic road bumps in between the two collapses. These are notions which have nothing to do with the Bible, a document once claimed to reveal all the important information we need to know. This is odd, considering there is no more important issue for humanity's future than basic survival.

The tremendous influence religion has over society is impressive in magnitude, but it is also fantastically limited. The problem with such a society is that it fails completely to take into account actual human nature. What is said to explain why those who molest or rape in this ideal world do so? What conjured myth from the ignorance of pre-science will be assigned to this deviant human trait? Unless religious scholarship breaks further away from Bronze and Iron Age notions, there is no way to present such concepts in the real world. The notions of faith and dogma, no matter how complex religious scholars present them, are still blatant in their faults and limitation. Admitting to our humanity in a call to fellow Christians, Brian D. Mclaren admits in his book, *Naked Spirituality*, "We all can be seduced by the appeal of appearing more spiritual than we actually are... We're all pretenders, all religious broadcasters, all of us false prophets projecting an image by which we hope to rake in profits –financial, social, relational, spiritual... We all need to come out of the closet. We don't have to hide the real us, the insecure us, the doubtful us, the angry us, the complex, different, tempted, actual human us."[29]

This seems like such an honest look at the blatant and obvious in a religiously influenced society today. The possibility of civilization-ending events that are not yet in our capability to prevent such as natural catastrophe are beyond our control as of today (although new research suggests religion is to blame for stymieing scientific progress for centuries), but human affairs concerning civilization are not necessarily out of our control as draining resources and greed (along with religious zealotry), as destructive as they are, also can be tamed, the mind trained. Although the extreme fundamentalist is a dangerous spark to religious global war, the understanding influenced by teachings and enclosed boundaries of organized religion can be just as dangerous. It is what is not being discussed in churches and religious scholarship that proves ultimately to be encouraging what religion is and always has been unable to answer for. Realistically, our concerns may be addressable, but if we do not give ourselves a chance through a different way of viewing our reality, then we can expect a predictable outcome regarding our survival. The religious mindset concerning such matters, while well intentioned, is ridiculous.

Conclusion

Attempts to employ different metaphysical notions and emphasize reason in social platforms have occurred in the past. Incorporating philosophy in their views on society and a claimed religious spirituality was met with the same dead-end mazes as the phantom teaching of Christianity and other mainstream religious one-liners are known to lead the practitioner to at present. As we can see, religion does not account for basic survival in platforms such as economics and behavior. It ignores suffering emotionally and spiritually on any comprehensive level. Its basic themes and notions —no matter how religious proponents want to apply a pretty veil over them- are limiting at best. It doesn't matter what religion it is, and it doesn't matter if is claimed to be something other than traditionally touted to create more of a distance from ridicule. Notions from the old religious guard continue today and have a real effect on society. Its limitations are glaring and were clearly meant for a less knowledgeable populace centuries ago.

No matter how complicated religious proponents wish to make the argument appear, the value of the premise remains empty. Zero times a trillion is still zero no matter how complex the formula. There will never be more advanced notions finally revealed because the authorship was of a time where the knowledge of advancements in thought did not exist in the area. The Biblical authors wouldn't know what on earth modern theologians are talking about because such concepts were not even realized in Biblical literature. There will never be an answer because the foundation of religion was never adequate for humanity to begin with, the basis an unoriginal myth throughout time.

Almost as if built into our DNA by a faulty designer, the depth of religious influence on the masses is impressive in the size of its inadequacies which are seemingly endless. Swaths of practitioners appear unable or unwilling to surrender from religious concepts which have yet to be understood fully, much less prove fulfilling in any sense beyond hope, comfort and sense of community. This community setting, while its collective heart is in the right place, is severely overmatched in so many ways it is ignorant to. The truth is that most religious are too influenced by every day culture to realize that religion has been disproved over and over again, unless one would like to trust the same Church that was considered the highest authority in educational matters for hundreds of years that the Sun revolves around the Earth, taken from notions indicating so in Joshua and Ecclesiastes. The religious masses can either accept the concept of religion being vacant and be open to others and relate to a more modern setting, or continue on the path that they can see has not exactly brought them out of unenlightened and uncivilized ages yet. It isn't as if those lessons are going anywhere if the religious masses elect to seek real life guidance with other concepts.

Religion is claimed by its proponents to be mystical, from another world or force unreachable to us, but with numerous theologian omissions of religious vacancy and the result of the rampant behavior coming from modern practitioners due to such influence, we can see otherwise. Let the Biblical scriptures be a warning to us all to not take too seriously documents limited to its own time. The words in the Bible may be held as timeless, but the lessons certainly are not.

This would be as if Einstein's work was so loved that his work was preserved by extremists. The insistence that his work never be scrutinized or disproved would have a stagnant effect on society's progression. Religion is not the-be-all-end-all it claims to be. Just because we are wired to be attracted to certain things like religion doesn't mean it is healthy for society. We also tend to be angry, greedy, lustful, territorial and tribal. More than one-liner orders from scripture are needed to deal with such tendencies individually and socially.

Percy Bysshe Shelley once wrote regarding the propensity for religion in the masses:

> "That credulity should be gross in proportion to the ignorance of the mind that it enslaves, is in strict consistency with the principles. The idiot, the child and the savage, agree in attributing their own passions and propensities to the inanimate substances by which they are either benefited or injured. The former become Gods and the latter Demons; hence prayers and sacrifices, by the means of which the rude Theologian imagines that he may confirm the benevolence of the one or mitigate the malignity of the other."

This vacancy has lasted until today regarding religious-based notions. The examples are many when it comes to presenting an argument that religious proponents cannot stand on firm ground with religious-based philosophy. Theologians always ask how science accounts for the order of the Universe, but this is a question that is better asked to theologians. How *does* the order of the Universe work? Because the complex and inarguable theories presented by theology today are a far cry from concepts of Bronze Age authorship. Even if the new concepts make sense -which any scientist would be glad to challenge the quality of and any philosopher would be glad to challenge the reasoning used- the basis, the foundation of such notions are pretty much based on concepts of the near illiterate. This is why any educated guesses in religious theory include the default setting of "God" in their "equations".

Aside from its bigoted, violent and oppressive nature, a limited and critical theme in religion insists that a worldly mindset replaces notions like natural selection design, what we are, where we are in the universe and what our relationship to each other is. In the perpetual cycle of ignorance, based on greed or not, an entire civilization often finds itself inheriting realities complete with cultural influences and struggles. In that generation exists the flaws from the previous generation. The present generation is left to simply deal with the reality presented to them by its predecessor. The reason why we need to be cruel to religion is because of its vast influence which is limiting, discouraging of critical thought or empowerment and promoting of an overall unhealthy, unconcerned environment. This limited religious influence is only too obvious and the behavior which reflects this among the religious masses is too rampant to ignore. This added to the fact that religion prevents a shift in paradigm due its perceptive take on daily life, a false world-view where its very exclusivity of notions and exceptional-based nature prohibits outside perceptions that could help the individual or society.

Two fairly recent quotes which are interesting come from Bill Nye and Lawrence Krauss. Nye suggests, "science is the key to the future, and if you don't believe in science then you're holding everybody back"[1]. The second is where Krauss contends, "informed doubt is the essence of science."[2] If we are to survive, we will make it through years of increased modernity and objective inquiry, and this is regardless of what is believed. It is time to fulfill our potential as beings on this Earth and realize what we have before us and the unlimited possibility that this world will provide us with. The religious influence arguably served its purpose, but it is time for the modern world to take over along with the notions that develop. It can be a world of education, progression and community.

In such a world, religion will be left behind. just like all the other places where modernity increases. Secularization will increase and humans may no longer look to a higher power, as they will have everything they need, all without God, all without theologians. In fact, if critical thinking and accountability were among doctrines to be followed in religion and were both emphasized in the individual, we can only wonder what societies would have evolved to. Now that the sciences are our guide, we have the potential to grow beyond imagination. Theologians might contend that science is limited and cannot provide quality of life. We will see about this, because one day we'll know and be familiar with a lifestyle of an increased emphasis on health and adequate nurturing of children. We will know how to better educate and promote more harmonious and enriching societies. Vast amounts of empirical evidence will have existed by simply adhering to the scientific method. Psychology and other life sciences will merely be a few hundred years old, yet their results are expected to shatter current boundaries of awareness. This is all not only possible, but probable given time. Can anyone guess how many of these events will involve religion?

Introduction

1. Haynes, Charles. "What's Religion?" *Faces* 29.3. 2012.

2. Lewis, Bernard. "'I'm Right, You're Wrong, Go to Hell.'." *Atlantic Monthly*. 291.4 (2003): 36.

3. Fish, Jefferson M. "Science VS Religion Debate." *Humanist* 70.4 (2010): 27.

4. McGrath E. Alister, McGrath Collicut Joanna, *The Dawkins Delusion?* Pp 55. 2007. InterVarsity Press.

5. Joyce, R. 2012. What should an archaeology of religion look like to a blind archaeologist? *Beyond Belief: The Archaeology of Religion and Ritual*: Archaeological Papers of the American Anthropological Association 21(1): 180–88.

6. Hobson, Theo. "The Good Kind of Liberalism." *Christian Century* 130.19 2013.

7. Randerson, James. *The Guardian*. 12 May 2008. Childish superstition: "Einstein's letter makes view of religion relatively clear. Scientist's reply to sell for up to £8,000 and stoke debate over his beliefs."

Primates

1. Edwards, Paul. *The Encyclopedia of Philosophy*. C 107. 1972. Macmillan Publishing Co., Inc. & The Free Press. New York. Collier Macmillan Publishers. London.

2. Potter, David. "Middle East Exceptionalism," In Democratization, ed. (Cambridge: Polity,1997), 321–30.

3. No author given. "U.S. News and Beliefnet Prayer Survey Results." 2014. http://www.beliefnet.com/Faiths/Faith-Tools/Meditation/2004/12/U-S-News-Beliefnet-Prayer-Survey-Results.aspx.

4. Metaxas, Eric. *Miracles: What They Are, Why They Happen, and How They Can Change Your Life*. Pp. 68. 2014. Penguin Books.

5. Davies, Brian. Haught, John. "The Suffering of God." *Commonweal* 138.11 2011.

6. Van Beeck, Frans Jozef. "Divine Revelation: Intervention or Self-Communication?" *Theological Studies* 52.2 1991.

7. Pagels, Elaine. *Revelations: Visions, Prophesy, and Politics in the Book of Revelation*. Pp175. Penguin Books 2012.

8. Stafford, Tim. "A New Age of Miracles." *Christianity Today* 56.8. 2012.

9. Treece, Patricia. "Mysteries and Miracles." *Catholic Digest* 75.11. 2011.

10. Lugo, Luis. "International Obligations and The Morality of War." *Society* 44.6. 2007.

11. Chan, Francis. Sprinkle, Preston. *Erasing Hell: What God Said About Eternity, And the Things We've Made Up.* Pp135. Published by David C. Cook. 2000.

12. Harrison, Peter. "Miracles, early modern science, and irrational religion." Sept 1ˢᵗ, 2006. American Society of Church History. "Neither is there a consistent position on the evidentiary role of these events. In the synoptic Gospels--Matthew, Mark, and Luke--Jesus performs miracles on account of the faith of his audience. In John's Gospel, however, it is the performance of miracles that elicits faith."

13. Klein, Stefan. *The Science of Happiness: How Our Brains Make Us Happy-And What We Can Do to Get Happier.* Pp 73. Publisher's Group West 2006.

14. Breznitz, Shlomo. Collins, Hemingway. *Maximum Brainpower: Challenging the Brain for Health and Wisdom.* Random House. 2012.

15. Haught, John F. "Can Evolution Explain Morality?" *America* 203.17 2010.

16. Haidt, Jonathan. *The Righteous Mind: When Good People Are Divided by Politics and Religion.* Pp 4. 2013 Vintage Cooks.

17. Darwin C.R. 1871. *The Descent of Man, and Selection in Relation to Sex*, vol. 1. Hill.

18. Gorski, Philip. "Beyond the Fact/Value Distinction: Ethical Naturalism and the Social Sciences." *Society* Dec. 2013.

19. Luco A. The Definition of Morality: Threading the Needle. *Social Theory & Practice* [serial online]. July 2014.

20. Mironenko, Irina A. *Russian Social Science Review.* Nov/Dec 2013, Vol. 54 Issue 6, p88-100.

21. Sinnott-Armstrong, Walter Wheatley, Thalia. "The Disunity of Morality and Why It Matters to Philosophy." *Monist* 95.3 2012.

22. Davis, Joseph. "Social Science, Objectivity, and Moral Life." *Society* Dec. 2013.

23. Editorial board. *Christian Science Monitor.* "Women on The Front Lines of Faith vs. State" [serial online]. 12/28/11.

24. No author given. PBS Frontline. No date given. "The Gay Gene Debate.' http://www.pbs.org/wgbh/pages/frontline/shows/assault /genetics/

25. Mooney, Chris "Our planet may be on the verge of its sixth mass extinction". November 28th, 2014. *Washington Post.* http://www.washingtonpost.com/blogs/wonkblog/wp/20 14/11/28/we-may-be-on-the-verge-of-the-sixth-mass-extinction/

26. Kadlac, Adam. "Empiricism and Moral Status." *Social Theory & Practice* 39.3 2013.

27. Ohlson, Kristin. "The End of Morality." *Discover* 32.6 2011.

28. Bower, Bruce. "Morality Play" *Science News* 176.6 2009.

29. Anwar, Yasmin. *Science Daily*. University of California - Berkeley. "Highly religious people are less motivated by compassion than are non-believers." 4/30/12. www.sciencedaily.com/releases/2012/04/120430140035. htm

30. Farrington, Karen. *Historical Atlas of Religions*. Page 74. 2002. Thalamus Publishing.

31. Fish, Jefferson M. "Science VS Religion Debate." Humanist 70.4. 2010.

32. Jones, David Albert. *Angels*. A History. Pp 113. 2011.

33. Markham, Ian. "Hume Revisited: A Problem with The Free Will Defence." *Modern Theology*, 7.3. 1991.

34. Wenger, Jay L. Daniels, Amy L. Who Distinguishes Between Sinners and Sins at the Implicit Level of Awareness? *Journal of Social Psychology*. Dec2006, Vol. 146 Issue 6, p657-669.

35. Gasser, Luciano Malti, Tina Gutzwiller-Helfenfinger, Eveline. "Aggressive and Nonaggressive Children's Moral Judgments and Moral Emotion Attributions in Situations Involving Retaliation and Unprovoked Aggression." *Journal of Genetic Psychology* 173.4. 2012.

36. Teehan, John. "The Cognitive Bases of The Problem of Evil." *Monist* 96.3 2013.

37. Amato, Joseph. "Politics of Suffering." *International Social Science Review* 69.1/2. 1994.

38. Davies, Brian. Haught, John. "The Suffering of God." *Commonweal* 138.11. 2011.

39. Baxter, Mary K. Bloomer, George. *Divine Revelation of Deliverance: You Can Be Victorious in Spiritual Warfare.* Pp 9. 2008. Whitaker House.

40. Martens, John W. "The Witness of Suffering." *America* 210.15. 2014.

41. Teehan, John. "The Cognitive Bases of The Problem of Evil." *Monist* 96.3. 2013.

42. Prothero, Stephen. *Religious Literacy.* Harper Collins. 2009.

43. Geller, Jesse D. "Pity, Suffering, and Psychotherapy." *American Journal of Psychotherapy.* 60.2. 2006.

44. Baxter, Mary K. Bloomer, George *Divine Revelation of Deliverance. You Can Be Victorious in Spiritual Warfare.* 2008. Whitaker House. Pp 111.

45. Fehren, Henry. "Does God Give You More Suffering Than You Can Bear?" *U.S. Catholic* 61.2. 1996.

46. Geller, Jesse D. "Pity, Suffering, and Psychotherapy." *American Journal of Psychotherapy.* 60.2. 2006.

47. No author given. *Scientific American.* "Where We Come From." pp40-41. September 2014.

48. Bevere, John. Pp 83. *The Bait of Satan: Living Free from The Deadly Trap of Offense* Charisma House. 2014.

49. Feltman, Rachel. "Newly discovered fossil could prove a problem for creationists." November 5, 2014. Washington Post. http://www.washingtonpost.com/news/speaking-of-science/wp/2014/11/05/newly-discovered-fossil-could-prove-a-problem-for-creationists/

50. Raymo, Chet. "Science Vs. Religion (I)." *Commonweal* 121.16. 1994.

51. Gerber, Richard. "Newtonian Vs. Einsteinian Medicine." *Total Health.* Feb/Mar99. Vol. 21, Issue 1

52. Mlodinow, Leonard. Hawking, Stephen. *The Grand Design.* 2010. Bantam Books.

53. Makari, George. *Revolution in Mind: The Creation of Psychoanalysis.* Pp 406. 2008. Harper Collins.

54. Ingram, Chip. *Culture Shock: A Biblical Response to Today's Most Divisive Issues.* Pp 170. 2014.

55. No author given. *Psychology Today.* No date given. http://www.psychologytoday.com/basics/spirituality

The Unseen

1. *Webster's Dictionary* Fourth Edition. 2001. pp453. Random House.

2. Bellah, Robert. Religion in Human Evolution. From the Paleolithic to the Axial Age Pp 1. Harvard University Press.

3. Houmanfar, Romona. *Psychological Record.* 1972. According to Romona Houmanfar and her associates in *Psychological Record,* "Behavior analysts, like a majority of cultural anthropologists, draw no fundamental distinction between religious and nonreligious practices." (Houmanfar, Romona et al, 1972).

4. Harpur, Tom. *Toronto Star.* "Most Canadians see churches as mainly irrelevant, study says." *(Canada)* 11 Apr. 1986. The lack of metaphysical presence or effects in claimed religious influences has no doubt played a large role in diminishing opinions of religion among the masses. Specialized and inconsequential were the words sociologist Reginald Bibby of a sociological study conducted on the affairs of religion having on the importance of followers in Canada in a 1986 survey, along with the results finding that many Canadians saw churches as "irrelevant." Theologian Tom Harpur wrote of the study in the Toronto Star, "The survey, conducted ... for the Anglican Diocese of Toronto, has prompted Archbishop Lewis S. Garnsworthy to summon a special assembly of all 250 of his parish

clergy. In an interview, Garnsworthy said that while he was not surprised at the report's findings, he naturally was "disappointed."

5. *Leviathan*, Chapter XII. Thomas Hobbes. 1651.

6. Randerson, James. "Childish superstition: Einstein's letter makes view of religion relatively clear." *The Guardian*, Monday 12 May 2008.

7. Siniscalchi, Glenn B. "Alvin Plantinga On Religious Pluralism: A Catholic Appraisal." *Journal of Ecumenical Studies* 46.2. 2011.

8. Torpey, John. "A (Post-) Secular Age? Religion and The Two Exceptionalisms." *Social Research* 77.1 (2010).

9. Hirschfield, Brad. *You Don't Have to Be Wrong for Me to Be Right.* Pp 233-234. 2007. Crown Publishing Group.

10. Van Biema D. God vs. Science. (cover story). *Time International (Canada Edition)* [serial online].

11. Peterson, Dan. "What's the Big Deal About Intelligent Design?" *American Spectator* 38.10 2005.

12. Castelvecchi, Davide. "Hawking Vs. God." *Scientific American* 303.5 (2010).

13. Glynn, Patrick. *God: The Evidence: The Reconciliation of Faith and Reason in A Post Secular World.* Pp 77-78. 1997 Published by Patrick Glynn.

14. Beauregard, Mario. O'Leary, Denyse. *The Spiritual Brain:* A *Beuroscientists Case for the Existence of the Soul.* pp 212. 2007 Harper One.

15. Raymo, Chet. "Science Vs. Religion (I)." *Commonweal* 121.16. 1994.

16. Jones, David Albert. *Angels: A History*. 2010. Oxford University Press.

17. Binz, Stephen J. "All About Angles." *Catholic Digest* 76.3 2012.

18. Binz, Stephen J. "All About Angles." *Catholic Digest* 76.3 2012.

19. Iles Johnston, Sarah. *Religions of The Ancient World.* "Second century writers often stressed that the human soul is not naturally immortal but will receive the continuing life as a participant in God's immortality, through the gift of the Holy Spirit." Harvard University Press. Belknap Press. 2004.

20. Tibbs, Clint. "The Spirit (World) And The (Holy) Spirits Among the Earliest Christians: 1 Corinthians 12 And 14 As A Test Case." *Catholic Biblical Quarterly* 70.2. 2008.

21. Chan, Francis. Yankoski Danae. Pp 166. *Forgotten God. Reversing Our Tragic neglect of the Holy Spirit.* 2009 David C. Cook.

22. *World Book Encyclopedia* 2012.Volume 16. pp 215.

23. Aitken, Jonathan. "The Road to Heaven. (Cover Story)."*American Spectator* 45.5. 2012.

24. Eubank, Nathan. "Storing Up Treasure with God in The Heavens: Celestial Investments in Matthew 6:1-21." *Catholic Biblical Quarterly.* 76.1. 2014.

25. Boyett, Jason. *Pocket Guide to The Afterlife: Heaven, Hell and Other Ultimate Destinations.* Jossey Bass. 2009.

26. Pullella, Philip. "Catholic Church buries Limbo after centuries." *Reuters* | Fri Apr 20, 2007.

27. *Catholic News Service* International Theological Commission. April 2007.

28. No author given. *Time.* 1993 Nov. 15, 1993 "A Christian in Winter: Billy Graham." Page 74 of *Angels, Devils and Messages from God.*

29. Barrett, William. *Death Bed Visions* Pp1. 1926. The Aquarian Press. 1986 Edition.

30. White, John. *A Practical Guide to Death and Dying.* Pp17-18. 1982. The Theosophical Publishing House.

31. White, John. *A Practical Guide to Death and Dying.* Pp17-18. 1982. The Theosophical Publishing House.

32. Fox, Douglas. "Light at The End of The Tunnel." *New Scientist.* 192.2573 2006.

33. Williams, Daniel. "At the Hour of Our Death. Cover Story." *Time International* (South Pacific Edition) 35 2007.

34. Fenwick, Peter. *Truth in The Light.* pp29. 2012. White Crow Books.

35. Todd, Jude. "Corn Culture: A Story of Intelligent Design." *American Indian Quarterly* 32.4. 2008.

36. Pullella, Philip. "Catholic Church Buries Limbo After Centuries". *Reuters*. Fri Apr 20, 2007.

37. No author given. BBC article. No date given. http://www.bbc.co.uk/radio4/reith2003/

38. No author given. *New York Times* 2013 http://www.nytimes.com/2013/02/18/science/project-seeks-to-build-map-of-human-brain.html?pagewanted=1&_r=3&

39. No author given. BBC News. http://www.bbc.com/news/science-environment-29093700

Limitations

1. Callahan, Tim. *Secret Origins of The Bible* pp 19. Millenium Press. 2002.

2. Klemes, Vit. "Science Vs. Religion: An American Pastime?" *Physics Today* 56.11 2003.

3. Moller, Philip. "What Should They Be Saying About Biblical Inspiration? A Note on The State of The Question." *Theological Studies* 74.3.2013.

4. Christie, Douglas E. *The Pursuit of the Real.*

5. Young, Robin Darling. "An Imagined Unity." *Commonweal* 129.15. 2012.

6. Schniedewind, William M. *How the Bible Became a Book.* pp 14. 2004 Cambridge University Press.

7. Shelley, Marshall. "The Bible might not rule out the possibility that dinosaurs roamed the earth before humans". "Bible vs. Science." *Ignite Your Faith.* Serial online. March, 2006.

8. Hobson, Theo. "The Good Kind of Liberalism." *Christian Century* 130.19 2013.

9. Wills, Gary. Pp 15 *What the Gospels Meant.* 2008 Penguin Books.

10. Gmirkin, Russell, "Berossus and Genesis, Manetho and Exodus., *Continuum,* 2006, p. 103. See also

Blenkinsopp, Joseph, "Treasures old and new.." *Eerdmans, 2004, pp. 93–95.*₂ A. R. George (2003). *The Babylonian Gilgamesh Epic: Introduction, Critical Edition and Cuneiform Texts.* Oxford University Press.pp. 70–.ISBN 978-0-19-927841-1.Retrieved 8 November 2012.₃Rendsburg, Gary.) "The Biblical flood story in the light of the Gilgamesh flood account," in *Gilgamesh and the world of Assyria*, eds Azize, J & Weeks, N. Peters, 2007, p. 117   ₄ Robert Wexler, *Ancient Near Eastern Mythology*, 2001, and draw unmistakable parallels to Daniel and Ecclesiastes.

11. Barber, Elizabeth Wayland. *When They Severed Earth from Sky.* pp 124-125. 2002. Princeton University Press.

12. *New Living Translation.*

13. Shelley, M. "Bible vs Science". *Ignite Your Faith* [serial online]. March 2006.

14. Buehrens, John. *Understanding the Bible: An Introduction for Skeptics, Seekers, and Religious Liberals.* John A Buehrens. pp 31. 2003 Beacon Press.

15. Raymo, Chet. "Science VS. Religion" *Commonweal.* 9/23/94. Vol. 121, Issue 16.

16. Schniedewind, William M. *How the Bible Became a Book.* pp 14. 2004 Cambridge University Press.

17. Wangu, Madhu, Bazaz *World Religions Hinduism Revised.* Pp 21. 1991. Facts on File Inc.

18. Ehrman, Bart. *Jesus Interrupted: Revealing the Hidden Contradictions in the Bible (And Why We Don't Know About Them) Pp 89-90.* 2009. Harper Collins.

19. Tibbs, Clint. *Catholic Biblical Quarterly.* April 2008, Vol. 70 Issue 2, p313-330.

20. Santanachote, Perry. "10 Best Apps to Train Your Brain". CNN.com. Sept 9th, 2014. Updated 9/9/2014 http://www.cnn.com/2014/09/09/health/brain-training-apps/index.html

21. *The New Encyclopedia Britannica* volume 26.15th edition. Pp 539.

22. Witham, Larry. "Sociology allowed less room to see God's mysterious activity in society.") *The Measure of God: Our Century Long Struggle to Reconcile Science & Religion.* pp 147. 2005 Harper Collins.

23. Gerald Jampolsky *Love Is Letting Go of Fear.* 2010. Celestial Arts.

24. Rubio, Julie Hanlon. "Family Ethics: Beyond Sex and Controversy." *Theological Studies* 74.1 2013.

25. Dead Sea Scrolls 1.

26. Van Biema, David, Park, Alice, Cray, Dan, Israely, Jeff, Bjerklie, David "God vs. Science." *Time International* (Canada Edition), 11/13/2006, Vol. 168, Issue 20.

27. Armstrong, Karen. *A History of God: The 4000-Year-Old Quest For Judaism, Christianity and Islam.* pp 4. 2011. Ballantine Books.

1. Thomas, Dana. *How Luxury Lost Its Luster*. 2007. Penguin Books.

2. Salzberg, Sharon. *Real Happiness: The Power of Meditation*. pp 112. 2011 Workman Publishing

3. Lewis, C.S. *Mere Christainity*. 1952. Geoffery Bles. Harper Collins.

4. Torpey, John. "A (Post-) Secular Age? Religion and The Two Exceptionalisms." *Social Research* 77.1 (2010).

5. Szegedy-Maszak, Marianne Hsu, Caroline. "How We Talk To God. (Cover Story)." *U.S. News & World* Report 137.22. 2004.

6. Haynes, Charles. "What's Religion?" *Faces (07491387)* 29.3. 2012.

7. *The New Encyclopedia Britannica* Volume 26.15th Edition. Pp 539.

8. Hobson, Theo. "The Good Kind of Liberalism." *Christian Century* 130.19 2013.

9. Hobson, Theo. "But it already contains certain seeds of it: it detaches God from any form of state power, and it rejects theocracy" Hobson, Theo. "The Good Kind of Liberalism." *Christian Century* 130.19 2013.

10. Salzberg, Sharon. *Real Happiness: The Power of Meditation. A 28 Day Program*. 2011 Workman Publishing.

11. Austin Greg. Kranock, Todd. Oommen, Thom. "The Encyclopedia of Wars surveyed 1,763 violent conflicts across history; only 123 (7 percent) were religious. A BBC-sponsored "God and War" audit, which evaluated major conflicts over 3,500 years and rated them on a 0-to-5 scale for religious motivation (Punic Wars = 0, Crusades = 5)))))), found that more than 60 percent had no religious motivation. Less than 7 percent earned a rating greater than 3. There was little religious motivation for the internecine Russian and Chinese conflicts or the world wars responsible for history's most lethal century of international bloodshed."

12. No author given. "God and The Ivory Tower" *Foreign Policy* http://www.foreignpolicy.com/articles/2012/08/06/god_and_the_ivory_tower?page=0,2

13. Lerner, Ed Lee. Lerner, Brenda Wilmoth. Learner, Adrienne Wilmoth *Social Policy: Essential Primary Sources*. Detroit: Gale, 2006. p3.

14. Eubank, Nathan. "Storing Up Treasure with God In The Heavens: Celestial Investments In Matthew 6:1-21." *Catholic Biblical Quarterly* 76.1. 2014.

15. Karabell, Zachary. Peace *Be Upon You: The Story of Muslim, Christian and Jewish Coexistence*. 52. Alfred A. Knopf. 2007.

16. Penelhum, Terrence. *"Christianity" in Life After Death in World Religions*, ed Harold Coward Maryknoll: Orbis Books, 2001. Pp 31.

17. Penelhum, Terrence. *"Christianity" in Life After Death in World Religions*, ed Harold Coward Maryknoll: Orbis Books, 2001.

18. Borg, Marcus. *The God We Never Knew.* Pp 141. Harper Collins. 2009.

19. Cohen, Simon Baron. *The Science of Evil: On Empathy and the Origins of Cruelty.* Pp 7. 2011 Basic Books.

20. Stojanović Božo. "Economics and Sociology: Between cooperation and intolerance." *Economic Annals*: ISSN 0013-3264Volume: 52; Issue: 174-175; Start page: 131; Date: 2007.

21. Terrén, Eduardo. "Rethinking Ties that Bind. Religion and the Rhetoric of Othering." *Journal for the Study of Religions and Ideologies* ISSN 1583-0039 Issue: 8; Start page: 13; Date: 2004.

22. Karabell, Zachary. *Peace Be Upon You: The Story of Muslim, Christian and Jewish Coexistence.* 52-53. Alfred A. Knopf. 2007.

23. Quoidbach, Jordi. Dunn, Elizabeth W. Petrides, K.V. Mikolajczak, Moïra. "Association of the Psychology of Science. Money Giveth, Money Taketh Away: The Dual Effect of Wealth on Happiness." *Association of the Pschology of Science.* May 18th, 2010. http://www.cato.org/sites/cato.org/files/pubs/pdf/PA703. pdf

24. Lyubomirsky, Sonja. "Can Money Buy Happiness?" *Scientific American*. "New research reveals that reminders of wealth impair our capacity to savor life's little pleasures." Aug 10th. 2010. http://www.scientificamerican.com/article.cfm?id=can-money-buy-happiness

25. Stark, Rodney, Akers, L. Ronald, Atchley C. Robert, Blackwell E. James, Briar, Katharine, Briar, Scott, Brodsky, Archie, Erlanger, s. Howard, Hindelang, Michael J.,Kornblum, William, Peele, Stanton, Roberts, Lynn, Suelzle, Marijean, Turner, R. Jay, Weisbrod, Rita Roffers. *Social Problems*, pp 276. 1975 Random House.

26. Stark, Rodney, Akers, L. Ronald, Atchley C. Robert, Blackwell E. James, Briar, Katharine, Briar, Scott, Brodsky, Archie, Erlanger, s. Howard, Hindelang, Michael J.,Kornblum, William, Peele, Stanton, Roberts, Lynn, Suelzle, Marijean, Turner, R. Jay, Weisbrod, Rita Roffers. *Social Problems*, pp 276. 1975 Random House.

27. Osteen, Joel. *Your Best Life Now. 7 Steps to Living at Your Full Potential.* Pp 63. 2004. Warner Faith.

28. Burke, Daniel. "The Lavish Homes of American Archbishops". CNN. No date given. http://www.cnn.com/interactive/2014/08/us/american-archbishops-lavish-homes/?hpt=hp_c2

29. Stern, Ken. "Why the Rich Don't Give." *Atlantic Monthly* 311.3 2013.

30. No author given. "How the One Percenters Think."
    Wilson Quarterly 37.3. Summer2013, Vol. 37 Issue 3,
    p101-103.

31. Lofgren, Mike. "Revolt of The Rich." *American
    Conservative* 11.9. 2012.

32. Conniff, Richard. "Blame the Rich." *Smithsonian*, Dec
    2007.

33. Babiak, Paul. O'Toole, Mary Ellen. "The Corporate
    Psychopath". F.B.I. Law Enforcement Bulletin. 2012
    https://leb.fbi.gov/2012/november/the-corporate-
    psychopath

34. Abramsky, Sasha. "America's Shameful Poverty Stats."
    Nation 297.14 2013.

35. Jones, Owen. "Help the Rich, Hate the Poor." *New
    Internationalist* 459 2013.

36. Nolan, Albert. "A Luta Continua: The Struggle and
    Theology: Yesterday, Today and Tomorrow." *Journal
    of Theology for Southern Africa* 143. 2012.

37. Nolan, Albert. "A Luta Continua: The Struggle and
    Theology: Yesterday, Today and Tomorrow." *Journal
    of Theology for Southern Africa* 143. 2012.

38. Clardy, Brian K. "Deconstructing A Theology of Defiance:
    Black Preaching and The Politics of Racial Identity."
    Journal of Church & State 53.2 2011.

39. Spong, John Shelby. *The Sins of the Scripture.* P 25. 2005
    Harper Collins.

40. Borg, Marcus. *The God We Never Knew* pp 141. Pp 141.
    2009 Harper Collins.

41. Borg, Marcus. *The God We Never Knew*. Pp 141. Pp 141.
    2009 Harper Collins.

Twists

1. Ruse, Michael. "Natural Selection vs 'Intelligent Design.'" *USA Today*. Serial online. January 2004 "Traditionally, it was never the case that Christianity insisted on a completely literal reading of the Bible. St. Augustine (353-430A.D.), the most influential of the early Christian theologians, knew that there were all sorts of problems if the Bible was taken literally. St. Augustine's position, adopted by the Church, is that one accepts a literal reading, unless and until reason or empirical science shows otherwise. "Then one changes."

2. Shermer, Michael. *How We Believe*. Pp 93. 2000. W.H. Freeman and Company.

3. O'Malley, John W. "A Lesson for Today?" *America* 205.13 2011.

4. Sanks, T. Howland. "The Changing Face of Theology. (Cover Story)." *America* 205.12. 2011.

5. Van Biema, David. Park, Alice. Cray, Dan. Israely, Jeff. Bjerklie, David. "God Vs. Science. (Cover Story)." *Time* 168.20 2006.

6. Brumfiel, Geoff. "Intelligent Design: Who Has Designs on Your Students' Minds?" *Nature* 434.7037 2005.

7. Rosenhouse, Jason. Branch, Glenn. "Media Coverage Of 'Intelligent Design.'" *Bioscience* 56.3 2006.

8. Boston, Rob. "What "Intelligent Designers Are Really Designing." *Education Digest* 70.7 2005.

9. Boston, Rob. "What "Intelligent Design'Ers Are Really Designing." *Education Digest* 70.7 2005.

10. Brumfiel, Geoff. "Intelligent Design: Who Has Designs on Your Students' Minds?" *Nature* 434.7037 2005.

11. No author given."Dinesh D'Souza: A New Look at an Old Problem". *Publishers Weekly*. No date given.

12. Glynn, Patrick. *God the Evidence: The Reconciliation of Faith and Reason in a Postsecular World*. 1997. Prima Publishing. pp 32.

13. Shroeder, Gerald L. *The Hidden Face of God*. 2001. Pp 87. The Free Press. Simon and Shuster.

14. Oppy, Graham, "Ontological Arguments", *The Stanford Encyclopedia of Philosophy*. Edward N. Zalta (ed.) Winter 2012 Edition.

15. Bowker, John. *God: A Brief History*. pp 6. DK Publishing 2002.

16. Melton, J. Gordon. *Introduction to the Encyclopedia of Religious Phenomena*. 2007. Visible Ink Press.

17. Carnes, Ralph. Carnes, Valerie. *The Road to Damascus*. New York. St. Martins Press. 1986. (Quote used is from *Religion in The Secular City*. Harvey Cox. pp xiii 1986. First addition, St. Martin's Press).

18. Perišić, Vladan. "Can Orthodox Theology Be Contextual?" *St Vladimir's Theological Quarterly* 56.4 2013.

19. Gutiérrez, Gustavo. "The Option for The Poor Arises from Faith In Christ." *Theological Studies* 70.2 2009.

20. Holmes, Christopher R J. "The Person and Work Of Christ Revisited: In Conversation With Karl Barth." *Anglican Theological Review* 95.1 2013.

21. Pohle, Joseph. "Dogmatic Theology." *The Catholic Encyclopedia*. Vol. 14. New York: Robert Appleton Company, 1912. 11 Dec. 2014. http://www.newadvent.org/cathen/14580a.htm.

22. Draper, Paul. Nichols, Ryan. "Diagnosing Bias in Philosophy of Religion." *Monist* 96.3 2013.

23. Debate. "Does God Exist?" (2009-04-04) - Christopher Hitchens Vs William Lane Craig - Biola University.

24. "The God Debate." Hitchins vs. D'Souza. University of Notre Dame. 2010.

25. Ken Ham, Bill Nye debate. February 2014. Creation Museum. Petersburg, Kentuky. http://www.globalpost.com/dispatch/news/science/1402 05/bill-nye-science-guy-ken-ham-creation-evolution-debate

26. Wilson, John. Plantinga, Alvin. "Conflict Resolution: Alvin Plantinga Seeks to Disentangle Sound Science from Naturalistic Dogma." *Christianity Today* 55.12. 2011.

27. Craig, William Lane. "Alvin Plantinga." *Journal of The Evangelical Theological Society* 30.3. 1987.

28. Stackhouse, John Gordon. "Mind Over Skepticism: Philosopher Alvin Plantinga Has Defeated Two of The Greatest Challenges to The Christian Faith." *Christianity Today* 45.8 2001.

29. Stackhouse, John Gordon. "Mind Over Skepticism: Philosopher Alvin Plantinga Has Defeated Two of The Greatest Challenges to The Christian Faith." *Christianity Today* 45.8. 2001.

30. Hitchins, Christopher. *God Is Not Great: How Religion Poisons Everything.* Pp 96. 2007 Twelve.

31. Nowak, Martin. Highfield, Roger. *Super Cooperators: Altruism, Evolution, and Why We Need Each Other To Succeed.* Simon and Shuster Free Press. 2011. Pp11.

32. Nowak, Martin A. "Why We Help." *Scientific American* 307.1 2012.

33. Nowak, Martin. Highfield, Roger *SuperCooperators. Altruism, Evolution, and Why We Need Each Other To Succeed.* Free Press Simon and Shuster. Pp. 2. 2011 Martin Nowak, Roger Highfield.

34. Nowak, Martin A. Sigmund, Karl. "Evolutionary Dynamics of Biological Games." *Science* 303.5659. 2004.

35. Nowak, Martin. Tarnita Corina. Wilson, Edward. "The Evolution of Eusociality." *Nature* 466.7310 (2010) "Sometimes it is argued that inclusive fitness considerations provide an intuitive guidance for understanding empirical data in the absence of an actual model of population genetics. However, as we show in the online material, inclusive fitness

arguments without a fully specified model are misleading. It is possible to consider situations where all measures of relatedness are identical, yet cooperation is favoured in one case, but not in the other."

36. Barlett, Thomas. "Biologists Team Up to Quash New View of Cooperation." *Chronicle of Higher Education* 57.36 (2011).

37. Schuneman, Nicholas A. "One Nation, Under...The Watchmaker? Intelligent Design and The Establishment Clause. (Cover Story)." *BYU Journal of Public Law* 22.1 2008.

38. Templeton Foundation site http://www.templeton.org/

39. Carroll, Robert Todd. "The Templeton Fundies." *Humanist* 68.3 2008.

40. Miller, John. J. "Big Bucks, Big Minds, Big Hearts." *National Review* 59.6 (2007).

41. Carroll, Robert Todd. "The Templeton Fundies." *Humanist* 68.3. 2008.

42. Terry, Mark. "What's Design Got to Do with It?" *Independent School*, 01459635, Winter2007, Vol. 66, Issue 2.

43. No author given. Published online 16 February 2011. *Nature* 470, 323-325. 2011.

44. Ewing, Bob. 2/5/14
http://mercatus.org/expert_commentary/john-

templeton-foundation-awards-2-million-mercatus-
center-george-mason-university

45. Perry, Patrick. "Sir John Templeton---The Eternal
Optimist." *Saturday Evening Post* 275.2. 2003.

46. As quoted by Jaweed Kaleem of *Huffington Post*. April
4th, 2013.
.http://www.huffingtonpost.com/2013/04/04/desmond-
tutu-templeton-
award_n_3007612.html?utm_hp_ref=christianity

47. Johnson, Phillip. *Defeating Darwinism by Opening
Minds*. Pg. 91-92. InterVarsity Press. 1997.

48. Bathija, Sandhya. "Creationism's Evolving Strategy."
Church & State 64.1 (2011). "That's what has
happened in Louisiana. In 2008, Gov. Bobby Jindal
signed into law the "Science Education Act," which
allows teachers to introduce into the classroom
"supplemental textbooks and other instructional
materials" about evolution, the origins of life, global
warming and human cloning. The measure, which its
backers disingenuously call an "academic freedom"
law, was heavily pushed by the Discovery Institute, a
Seattle based think tank that promotes ID. The
institute had pushed similar bills throughout the
country that year in states including Florida,
Alabama, Missouri, Michigan and South Carolina. All
these measures contained creationist code language
seeking to sneak ID into the public-school science
curriculum."

49. Downey, Roger. "Discovery's Creation" *Seattle Weekly*,
February 1, 2006.

50. Johnson, Phillip. 1999 Speech. "How the Evolution Debate Can Be Won, in the conference." Reclaiming America for Christ.

51. Terry, Mark. "Intelligent Design" Wants God Across All the Curriculum." *Education Digest* 70.6 2005.

52. Derbyshire, John. "Occasionalism Isn't Science." *American Spectator* 47.1 (2014).

53. "Department Position on Evolution and 'Intelligent Design.'" http://www.lehigh.edu/~inbios/news/evolution.htm).

54. Jacobs, Jonathan. "The Fact/Value Distinction and the Social Sciences." *Society* Dec. 2013.

55. Van Biema, David, Park, Alice, Cray, Dan, Israely, Jeff, Bjerklie, David God vs. Science. *Time International* (Canada Edition), 03158446, 11/13/2006, Vol. 168, Issue 20.

"Happiness"

1. Adams, Troy B. Bezner, Janet R. "Conceptualization and Measurement Oo The Spiritual and Psychological Dimensions of Wellness in A.." *Journal of American College Health* 48.4. 2000.

2. Simpson, John. *The Concise Oxford Dictionary of Proverbs* pp 85. Second edition. Oxford University Press. 1992.

3. "Philosophy." *Columbia Electronic Encyclopedia, 6Th Edition.* 2013.

4. Van der Veer, Peter. "Spirituality in Modern Society." *Social Research* 76.4 2009.

5. Van der Veer, Peter. "Spirituality in Modern Society." *Social Research* 76.4 2009.

6. Ehrlich, Steven D. reviewed. NMD. No date given. http://www.keckhospitalofusc.org/condition/document/14285

7. Ehrlich, Steven D. Last reviewed 10/13/2011 http://www.umm.edu/altmed/articles/spirituality-000360.htm

8. No author given. *American Catholic.* No other information given.

9. Quote from the Apostle Paul.

10. Gary, Heather Grennan. "Spiritual Exercises. (Cover Story)." *U.S. Catholic* 78.5 2013.

11. Jampolsky, Gerald. *Love Is Letting Go of Fear.* 2010. Celestial Arts.

12. Abner, Allison. "The Miracle Cure." *Essence (Essence)* 28.1. 1997.

13. Ness, Erik. "Faith Healing." *Prevention* 57.12. 2005.

14. Hodge, David R. Horvath, Violet E. "Spiritual Needs in Health Care Settings: A Qualitative Meta-Synthesis of Clients' Perspectives." *Social Work* 56.4. 2011.

15. Hodge, David R. "Developing A Spiritual Assessment Toolbox: A Discussion of The Strengths and Limitations of Five Different Assessment Methods." *Health & Social Work* 30.4. 2005.

16. Cannister, Mark W. "Mentoring and The Spiritual Well-Being of Late Adolescents." *Adolescence* 34.136. 1999.

17. Hodge, David R. "Spiritual Lifemaps: A Client-Centered Pictorial Instrument for Spiritual Assessment, Planning, And Intervention." *Social Work* 50.1, 2005.

18. Van Zanten Gallagher, Susan. "Speaking of Vocation in An Age of Spirituality." *Change* 39.3. 2007.

19. Culliford, Larry. "Spiritual Wisdom for Secular Times." *Psychology Today.* March 5, 2011. http://www.psychologytoday.com/blog/spiritual-wisdom-secular-times

20. Ehrlich, Steven D. Last reviewed 10/13/2011
http://www.umm.edu/altmed/articles/spirituality-
000360.htm

21. Van der Veer, Peter. "Spirituality in Modern
Society." *Social Research* 76.4 (2009).

22. Van der Veer, Peter. "Spirituality in Modern
Society." *Social Research* 76.4 (2009).

23. Religion in "Philosophy". Last updated 8/19/2013.
Encyclopedia Britannica Online. Editors: Michael C.
Anderson, Michael J. Anderson, Adam Augustyn,
Marilyn L. Barton, Patricia Bauer, Linda Berris,
Naomi Blumberg, Henry Bolzon, Peter Bondarenko,
Steven Bosco, Lisa Bosco, Yvette Charboneau, Yamini
Chauhan, Laura Chaveriat, Kenneth Chmielewski,
Swati Chopra, Sandra Colmenares, Paul Cranmer,
John M. Cunningham, Darshana Das, Jeannine
Deubel, Nicole DiGiacomo, Letricia A. Dixon, Brian
Duignan, Promeet Dutta, Alison Eldridge, Annie
Feldmeier Adams, Andrea R. Field, Shirese Franklin,
Carol A. Gaines, William Gosner, Anthony L. Green,
Robert Green, Erik Gregersen, William Guerriero,
Anna Ha, Benedict Hane, Kurt Heintz, Carmen-Maria
Hetrea, Joan Hibler, John Higgins, Sherman Hollar,
Rosaline Jackson-Keys, Parul Jain, Steven N.
Kapusta, Thad King, Kathleen Kuiper, Joan
Lackowski, Melinda Leonard, Robert M. Lewis, Gloria
Lotha, Amethy Lu, J.E. Luebering, Marsha
Mackenzie, Lars Mahinske, Neha Mathur, Christine
McCabe, Mary Rose McCudden, Amy McKenna,
Michele Metych, E. Moragne, Ned Mulka, Lorraine
Murray Kimiyo Naka-Michaeli, Kathy Nakamura,
Richard Pallardy, Theodore Pappas, Neha Parwani

Renie Petropoulos, Melissa Petruzzello, Kenneth
Pletcher, John P. Rafferty, Michael Ray
Patrick Riley, Kara Rogers, Isabella Saccà, Marco
Sampaolo, Barbara Schreiber, Susan Schumer,
Stephen Seddon, Tatyana Sergeyeva, Veenu Setia,
Kathleen B. Sheetz, Melinda C. Shepherd, Dennis
Skord, Karen Sparks, Matt Stefon, David Stokes,
Noah Tesch, Amy Tikkanen, Sheila Vasich, Sylvia
Wallace, Jeffrey Wallenfeldt, Bruce Walters, Joshua
Werth Barbara Whitney, Mark Wiechec, Grace Young.

24. Hodge, David R. "Implicit Spiritual Assessment: An
    Alternative Approach for Assessing Client
    Spirituality." *Social Work* 58.3. 2013.

25. McGee, Melissa Nagel, Liza Moore, Meighan K "Although
    commonly asserted to be the core of health, spirituality
    is a relatively unexplored area". "A Study of University
    Classroom Strategies Aimed At Increasing Spiritual
    Health." *College Student Journal* Dec2003, Vol. 37
    Issue 4, p583-594.

26. McGee, Melissa Nagel, Liza Moore, Meighan K. "A Study
    of University Classroom Strategies Aimed at
    Increasing Spiritual Health." *College Student
    Journal* 37.4 2003.

27. Atwood, Joan D. Maltin, Lawrence. "Putting Eastern
    Philosophies into Western Psychotherapies." *American
    Journal of Psychotherapy* 45.3. 1991.

28. Ecklund, Elaine Howard. *Social Science Research
    Council.* No date given.

29. Atwood, Joan D. Maltin, Lawrence. "Putting Eastern Philosophies into Western Psychotherapies." *American Journal of Psychotherapy* 45.3. 1991.

30. Wangu, Madhu Bazaz. *World Religions Hinduism Revised Edition.* Pp 21. 1991. Facts on File Inc.

31. Narayanan, Vasudha. *Hinduism: Origins, Beliefs, Practices, Holy Texts, Sacred Places.* "The sacrificed based worldview of the early Vedic age gave way to philosophical inquiry and discussion in the later texts known as Aranyakas and Upanishads". Pp 14 Oxford University Press.

32. Morgan, Diane. *The Best Guide to Eastern Philosophy and Religion.* "While Westerners seek to fulfill their personalities, Hindus look to escape them to be free by removing the veil of ignorance that produces karma." pp36. 2014. St. Martin's Griffin.

33. Morgan, Diane. *The Best Guide to Eastern Philosophy and Religion.* pp 26. 2014. St. Martin's Griffin.

34. Emerson, Ralph Waldo. 1838 Harvard Divinity School graduating address to seniors in Massachusetts.

35. Adler, Jerry Scelfo, Julie Philips, Matthew. "Finding & Seeking." *Newsweek* 148.12 2006. "1960's America saw a turning point in mainstream consciousness as they were the first generation born into mass affluence, for whom material sustenance and comfort were a given, a situation that breeds spiritual hunger."

36. Bhaktivedanta, Prabhupada. *The Science of Self Realization.* 1977 Bhaktivedanta Book Trust p 2.

37. Rosenthal, Norman (2011). *Transcendence: Healing and Transformation through Transcendental Meditation.* New York: Tarcher/Penguin. p. 14.

38. Hurley, Dan. "Can Mindfulness Meditation Make You Smarter?" *Discover* Blogs June 18, 2012. http://blogs.discovermagazine.com/crux/2012/06/18/can -mindfulness-meditation-make-you- smarter/#.WGsXM4WcHIU

39. Tang, Yi-Yuan. Ma, Yinghua. Wang, Junhong. Fan, Yaxin. Feng, Shigang. Lu, Qilin Lu. Yu, Qingbao. Sui, Danny. Rothbart, Mary K. Fan, Ming. Posner, Michael I. "Short-Term Meditation Training Improves Attention and Self-Regulation." *Proceedings of the National Academy of Sciences of the United States of America.* Oct 23, 2007; 104(43): 17152–17156. Published online Oct 11, 2007. doi: http://www.ncbi.nlm.nih.gov/pmc/articles/PMC2040428 /?tool=pubmed

40. Rosenthal, Norman (2011). *Transcendence: Healing and Transformation through Transcendental Meditation.* New York: Tarcher/Penguin. p. 14.

41. Tartakovsky, Margaritea. "7 Easy Ways to be Mindful Every Day." *Psych Central* http://psychcentral.com/blog/archives/2012/06/09/7- easy-ways-to-be-mindful-every- day/?utm_source=feedburner&utm_medium=feed&ut m_campaign=Feed%3A+WorldOfPsychology+%28Worl d+of+Psychology%29.

42. Hurley, Dan. "Can Mindfulness Meditation Make You Smarter?" *Discover* Blogs June 18, 2012 http://blogs.discovermagazine.com/crux/2012/06/18/can

-mindfulness-meditation-make-you-
smarter/#.WGsXM4WcHIU

43. Seaman, Andrew M. "Mindfulness therapy helps prevent
drug and alcohol relapse". *Reuters*. Mar 21, 2014.
http://mobile.reuters.com/article/idUSBREA2J2AV201
40320?feedType=RSS&irpc=932

44. Fox, Maggie. "Empathy Workout: Brain Training May
Boost Altruism" Maggie Fox. *NBCNews.com*. First
published December 2nd, 2014.
http://www.nbcnews.com/health/mental-
health/empathy-workout-brain-training-may-boost-
altruism-n113471

45. Tartakovsky, Margarita. "7 Easy Ways to be Mindful
Every Day." *Psych Central*. Associate editor.
http://psychcentral.com/blog/archives/2012/06/09/7-
easy-ways-to-be-mindful-every-
day/?utm_source=feedburner&utm_medium=feed&ut
m_campaign=Feed%3A+WorldOfPsychology+%28Worl
d+of+Psychology%29

46. Rossano, Matt J. *Cambridge Archeological Journal*.
Volume 17, Issue 1. Feb 2007, pp 47-58.

47. Pelikan, Jaroslav. *Whose Bible Is It?* Pp 248. 2006.
Penguin Books.

48. O'hair, Madaly, Murray. *All the Questions You Ever
Wanted to Ask American Atheists.*1982 vol. ii., p. 2.

49. Senzaki, Nyogen. McCandless, Ruth Strout. *Buddhism
and Zen*. Pp 9. 1988 North Point Press.

50. Garfinkel, Perry. Buddha Rising. *National Geographic.* Dec 2005. Volume 208 Issue 6 pp 88-109.

51. Rhys Davids Caroline A. F. *Buddhist Psychology: An Inquiry into the Analysis and Theory of Mind in Pali Literature.* 2004. Forgotten Books.

52. Spzir, Michael. "An interview with Daniel Goleman". *American Scientist.* No date given. http://www.americanscientist.org/bookshelf/pub/daniel -goleman

53. Garfinkel, Perry. Paraphrased. "Buddha Rising." *National Geographic* Dec2005, Vol. 206 Issue 6, p88-109.

54. Spzir, Michael. "An interview with Daniel Goleman". *American Scientist.* No date given. http://www.americanscientist.org/bookshelf/pub/daniel -goleman

55. Morgan, Diane. *The Best Guide to Eastern Philosophy and Religion.* Diane Morgan. Pp 115. 2014. St. Martin's Griffin.

56. Shaw, Julia. Paraphrased "lay at the heart of Buddhism". "Archaeologies of Buddhist Propagation in Ancient India: 'Ritual' And 'Practical' Models Of Religious Change." *World Archaeology* 45.1 (2013): 83.

57. Brazier, David. *The New Buddhism.* Pp 82. 2002. Palgrave.

58. Larken, Geri. *Stumbling Toward Enlightenment.* Pp 159. 1997 Celestial Arts Publishing.

59. Brown, Justh S. *Dakini's Warm Breath*. Pp 215. 2001. Shambhala.

60. Wood, Graeme. "The Fortunate Ones." *Atlantic Monthly* (10727825), 10727825, Apr2011, Vol. 307, Issue 3.

61. Wood, Graeme. "The Fortunate Ones." *Atlantic Monthly* (10727825), 10727825, Apr2011, Vol. 307, Issue 3.

62. Stoeffel, Kat. Q&A: Arianna Huffington's 'Third Women's Revolution'. *New York Magazine*. March 18, 2014. Bhttp://nymag.com/thecut/2014/03/arianna-huffingtons-third-womens-revolution.html

63. "Wang, Shirley. "Is Happiness Overrated?" *Wsj.com*. March 15, 2011. http://online.wsj.com/news/articles/SB10001424052748 70489360457620047154537 9388

64. Fredrickson, B. L.: Grewen, K. M.;Coffey, K. A.; Algoe, S. B.; Firestine, A. M.;Arevalo, J. M. G.; Ma, J.; Cole, S. W. Proceedings of the Nstional Academy of Sciences, vol 110, issue 33, pp. 13684-13689. 08/2013. Harvard.edu site taking from PNAS the publishings of the hedonic study adsabs.harvard.edu/abs/2013PNAS.11013684F

65. McCormick, Charles. "Health: Happiness vs Meaning". *OaklandJournal.com*. 8/2/2013 http://theoaklandjournal.com/oaklandnj/health-happiness-vs-meaning/

66. Thurmond, Robert. *Infinite Life*. Pp 140. 2004. Riverhead Books.

67. Tsu, Lao. *Tao Te Ching: A New English Version*. Pp 9. Harper and Row Publishers. Mitchell, Stephen 1988. New York.

68. Morgan, Diane. *The Best Guide to Eastern Philosophy and Religion*. pp 127. 2014. St. Martin's Griffin.

69. Dellios, Rosita. "Mandala-Building in International Relations as A Paradigm For Peace." *Social Alternatives* 15.3. 1996.

70. Brazier, David. *The New Buddhism*. Pp82-83. 2002 Palgrave.

71. Buddhadasa, Bhikkhu. Paraphrased. Extracted from *Handbook for Mankind*. Buddhanet. No date given. http://www.buddhanet.net/e-learning/buddhism/bs-s07a.htm

72. Leming, David. *The Oxford Companion to World Mythology*. Oxford University Press. 2005

73. Clark, Carol. "Compassion meditation may boost neural basis of empathy, study finds" *Science Daily*. October 4, 2012. http://www.sciencedaily.com/releases/2012/10/1210040 93504.htm

74. Dingfelder, Sadie. "Tibetan Buddhism and research psychology: a match made in Nirvana? Collaborations between monks and psychologists yield new directions in psychological research." *American Psychological Association*. December 2003, Vol 34, No. 11. http://www.apa.org/monitor/dec03/tibetan.aspx

75. Dellios, Rosita. "Mandala-Building in International Relations as A Paradigm for Peace." *Social Alternatives* 15.3 1996. "Confucianism tends to the ethical."

76. Dellios, Rosita. "Mandala-Building in International Relations as A Paradigm for Peace." *Social Alternatives* 15.3 1996.

77. MacHovec, Frank J. "Current Therapies and The Ancient East." *American Journal of Psychotherapy* 38.1. 1984.

78. Coward, Harold. "Taoism And Jung: Synchronicity and The Self." *Philosophy East & West* 46.4. 1996.

79. Garfinkel, Perry. "Buddha Rising." *National Geographic* Dec2005, Vol. 206 Issue 6, p88-109.

80. No author given. "A Thai Perspective on Socially Engaged Buddhism: Selections from The Speeches & Writings of Sulak Sivaraksa." *Social Policy* 33.1. 2002.

81. Santangelo, Paolo. "Italian Studies on Eastern Thought in Comparative Philosophy." *Philosophy East & West* 43.3. 1993.

Service

1. Atwood, Joan D.Maltin, Lawrence. "Putting Eastern Philosophies into Western Psychotherapies." *American Journal of Psychotherapy* 45.3. 1991.

2. McKenzie, Deborah. "Are We Doomed?" *New Scientist* 197.2650 2008. Noted in New Scientist of researchers claims of the inevitability of a collapsed society. "A few researchers have been making such claims for years. Disturbingly, recent insights from fields such as complexity theory suggest that they are right. It appears that once a society develops beyond a certain level of complexity it becomes increasingly fragile. Eventually, it reaches a point at which even a relatively minor disturbance can bring everything crashing down."

3. No author given. No date given. A study conducted by researchers from University of Maryland and University of Minnesota and published in *Ecological Economics* revealed the end of civilization is within decades. Economic instability and the loss of precious planetary resources are the citing factors contributing to such a catastrophic fall.

4. Holley, Peter. "Bill Gates on dangers of artificial intelligence: 'I don't understand why some people are not concerned.'" *Washington Post.* 1/29/2015 https://www.washingtonpost.com/news/the-switch/wp/2015/01/28/bill-gates-on-dangers-of-artificial-intelligence-dont-understand-why-some-people-are-not-concerned/?utm_term=.080a9491eb65

5. Rieger, Joerg. Kwok, Pui-lan. *Occupy Religion. Theology of The Multitude*. 2012. Rowman and Littlefield Publishers.

6. Rieger, Joerg. Kwok, Pui-lan. *Occupy Religion. Theology of The Multitude*. 2012. Rowman and Littlefield Publishers.

7. Swanson, David. "Why We Allow the Destruction of Our Planet." *Humanist* 73.4 2013.

8. Moore, Stephen. "The Weekend Interview with Charles Koch: Private Enterprise". *The Wall Street Journal*. (May 6, 2006).

9. Moore, Stephen. "The Weekend Interview with Charles Koch: Private Enterprise". *The Wall Street Journal*. (May 6, 2006).

10. Borg, Marcus. *The Heart of Christianity: Rediscovering A Life of Faith*. Pp 136. Harper Collins. 2003.

11. No author given. "Holy Relevance." *The Economist*. Oct 29, 2011. http://www.economist.com/node/21534762 Print edition International.

12. Bowyer, Jerry. "Is Religion an Essential Driver of Economic Growth?" *Forbes*. May 2013 http://www.forbes.com/sites/jerrybowyer/2013/05/29/is-religion-an-essential-driver-of-economic-growth/#2087823c4b5d

13. Fitzgerald, Michael. "Satan, The Great Motivator." *Boston.com* November 2009. http://archive.boston.com/bostonglobe/ideas/articles/2009/11/15/the_curious_economic_effects_of_religion/

14. Barro, Robert. McCleary, Rachel. "Religion and Economic Growth." NBER Working Paper No. 9682. Issued in May 2003 http://www.nber.org/papers/w9682

15. Guiso, Luigi, Sapienza, Paola. Zingales, Luigi. "People's Opium? Religion and Economic Attitudes. NBER Working Paper No. 9237. Issued in September 2002 http://www.nber.org/papers/w9237

16. Schmitt, Carl. 1985. *Political Theology.* Chicago: Chicago University Press.

17. McEwan, Ian. "The Day of Judgement Part 2" *The Guardian.* May, 2008. https://www.theguardian.com/books/2008/may/31/fiction.philosophy1

18. Hodge, David R. Roby, Jini L. "Sub-Saharan African Women Living With HIV/AIDS: An Exploration of General and Spiritual Coping Strategies." *Social Work* 55.1. 2010.

19. Rainie, Harrison, Loftus, Margaret. "The state of greed." *U.S. News & World Report*, 00415537, 6/17/96, Vol. 120, Issue 24.

20. Zakaria, Fareed. "Greed Is Good (To A Point). (Cover Story)." *Newsweek* 153.25 2009.

21. Ariely, Dangruneisen, Alineritter, John. "The Price of Greed." *Scientific American Mind* 24.5. 2013.

22. Ariely, Dangruneisen, Alineritter, John. "The Price of Greed." *Scientific American Mind* 24.5. 2013.

23. Morris, Desmond. *The Human Zoo*: 1963. Pp 72.

24. Lewis, C.S. *Mere Christianity*. 1952 Harper Collins. Macmillan.

25. Raymo, Chet. Science vs. religion (I). *Commonweal* [serial online]. September 23, 1994.

26. Stanglin, Doug. "Intel Report Sees U.S. Losing Super Power Status" *USA Today*. December 10, 2012.

27. Atwood, Joan D. Maltin, Lawrence. "Putting Eastern Philosophies into Western Psychotherapies." *American Journal of Psychotherapy* 45.3 1991.

28. Zakaria, Fareed. " Greed Is Good (To A Point). (Cover Story)." *Newsweek* 153.25 2009.

29. McLaren, Brian D. *Naked Spirituality: A Life with God in 12 Simple Words*. Pp 89. Harper Collins. 2011.

Conclusion

1. Fecht, Sarah. "Science Guy Bill Nye Explains Why Evolution Belongs in Science Education." *Popularmechanics.com.* Feb 4th, 2011. 2/4/2011.http://www.popularmechanics.com/science/animals/a6455/evolution-classroom-bill-nye-science-education/

2. Krauss, Lawrence. "Teaching Doubt." *Newyorker.com.* March 15th, 2015. http://www.newyorker.com/news/news-desk/teaching-doubt

Made in the USA
Middletown, DE
28 February 2021